SALTPETER

SALTPETER
The Mother of Gunpowder

DAVID CRESSY

OXFORD
UNIVERSITY PRESS

OXFORD

UNIVERSITY PRESS

Great Clarendon Street, Oxford, OX2 6DP,
United Kingdom

Oxford University Press is a department of the University of Oxford.
It furthers the University's objective of excellence in research, scholarship,
and education by publishing worldwide. Oxford is a registered trade mark of
Oxford University Press in the UK and in certain other countries

First Edition published in 2013

Impression: 1

British Library Cataloguing in Publication Data
Data available

Library of Congress Cataloging in Publication Data
Data available

ISBN 978-0-19-969575-1

Printed in Great Britain by
Clays Ltd, St Ives plc

PREFACE

Writing this book, more any other, has been a journey of discovery. It has taken me into territories and topics that I had not previously explored. It began, modestly enough, with curiosity about the 'vexation and oppression' of the saltpetermen, cited in the Grand Remonstrance of grievances presented to Charles I in 1641. I thought to examine complaints about their activities on the eve of the English civil war, but my enquiries rapidly expanded to embrace the chemistry, industry, and politics of the English saltpeter enterprise, and the military purposes it served, over half a millennium. I have ventured beyond the early modern era, where I am most at home, to range chronologically from the fifteenth century to the twentieth. My work, as always, is centred on England, but in this case it stretches further afield, to the rest of the British Isles, northern Europe, and North Africa, and to British colonies and outposts in Asia and America.

I am beholden to those historians of science, warfare, empire, technology, and law who have introduced me to their specialities. I am grateful to colleagues and students who have helped me unravel the mysteries of saltpeter, and who have stretched my understanding of its social and political context. I have tried the patience of academic chemists who attempted to explain how saltpeter formed and how potassium nitrate worked. I have benefitted from discussion in the graduate seminar in early modern studies at the Ohio State University, the Yale University British Historical Studies Colloquium, and the Ben Franklin Forum at the Massachusetts Institute of Technology. I particularly wish to thank the following for their insights, suggestions, and corrections: T. H. Breen, John Brooke, Patricia Cleary, Robert Davis, Lisa Ford, James Frey, Matt Goldish, John Guilmartin, Bert Hall,

Derek Horton, Margaret Hunt, Michael Hunter, Scott Levi, Christopher Otter, Geoffrey Parker, Kevin Sharpe, Rudi Volti, and Keith Wrightson. Any remaining errors are mine alone.

As a working historian, rooted in the humanities, I find inspiration in the line of Gerard Manley Hopkins: 'shéer plód makes plough down sillion shine.' The work gets done, and the results sometimes sparkle. I have always embraced serendipity amid the delights of writing and research, in this case more than usual. Librarians and archivists in Britain and the United States have been generous and professional, as always, but only a chance conversation over lunch at the Huntington in California alerted me to the presence of saltpetermen in Thomas Middleton's Jacobean play *A Faire Quarrell*. I am grateful to the editors of *Past & Present* for permission to incorporate material from my essay, 'Saltpetre, State Security, and Vexation in Early Modern England', published in *Past & Present*, no. 212, August 2011.

CONTENTS

LIST OF FIGURES

A NOTE ON MEASUREMENT AND SPELLING

English weights made sixteen ounces a pound, fourteen pounds a stone, two stones a quarter, eight stones a hundredweight, and twenty hundredweight a 2,240 pound ton (1,016 kilograms). A thousandweight (abbreviated mwt) was ten times a hundredweight (cwt). Saltpeter and gunpowder were measured by hundredweights, thousandweights, and tons, and by barrels and lasts, a last comprising twenty-four barrels. Charcoal and coal were measured by the chalder (or cauldron) as well as by weight, a chalder of coal being 2,000 pounds before 1676 but 2,240 pounds (one ton) after revision.

Many of these measures varied by region, and different commodities had varying properties of weight and volume. Neither consistency nor precision should be expected. International merchants had to know that a Hamburg last was bigger than a last at Amsterdam, but smaller than a last in Prussia. A French *livre* was slightly heavier than an English pound. In England a hundredweight of saltpeter weighed 112 pounds, and a last of saltpeter 2,688 pounds (1.2 tons or 1,219 kilograms). Gunpowder, however, was measured differently. A hundredweight barrel of gunpowder weighed 100 pounds, and a twenty-four barrel last of gunpowder weighed 2,400 pounds (1.07 tons or 1,089 kilograms). The Dutch sold gunpowder and saltpeter by the quintal, which could vary from 100 to 120 pounds.[1]

Potential computational discrepancies arise with the variable formulae for gunpowder, and different ratings by hundredweights, barrels, and lasts for its constituent materials and final product. Unless otherwise indicated, I employ the standard mixture of 6:1:1, in which saltpeter is seventy-five per cent by weight of gunpowder, the rest being charcoal and sulphur. One pound of saltpeter therefore suffices to make 1.33 pounds of powder. Taking account of the differences in barrel-weight, one last of saltpeter would furnish 1.49 lasts of gunpowder. This calculation fits well with the estimate by Ordnance officials in 1588 that '112 thousandweight of saltpeter [i.e. 1,000 barrels or 41.66 lasts] will make sixty lasts of fine corn powder', whereby one last of saltpeter yields 1.44 lasts of gunpowder.[2] Allowing for spoilage and spillage, waste, and further refinement, a working multiplier of 1.45 seems appropriate for gauging how many barrels or lasts of gunpowder can be supplied from given amounts of saltpeter.

The East India Company bought saltpeter in Asia by the maund and candy (twenty maunds), and had to know that a maund in Bengal weighed seventy-five pounds, whereas a Surat maund weighed twenty-eight pounds. The Company shipped saltpeter to London by the bag, each bag weighing on average about 1.2 hundredweight. Deliveries to the Ordnance Office were by numbered bags, converted by weight into tons, hundredweights, quarters, and pounds. Saltpeter contractors also took account of the 'refraction rate', around five or six pounds per hundredweight, lost in the conversion of gross or rough saltpeter to fine.

In this work I use imperial or avoirdupois measurements, unless otherwise indicated. I follow the dating system used in early modern England, except that the year is taken to start on 1 January. I use the American and international spelling of 'saltpeter' rather than standard modern English 'saltpetre'. Sixteenth- and seventeenth-century spelling was unstable, but early modern authors commonly wrote of 'salt-peeter', 'saltpeter', or simply 'peter', as well as 'saltpetre'; etymologists thought the word referred to the rock (Latin *petra*) on which nitrous crystal salts were sometimes found. With this exception, I follow standard British English style, with modernized spelling and punctuation. All printed works cited were published in London unless otherwise noted. I use the conventional abbreviations TNA (The National Archives, Kew), BL (British Library, London), APC (*Acts of the Privy Council*), CSPD (*Calendar of State Papers, Domestic*), and HMC (Historical Manuscripts Commission).

INTRODUCTION

This book explores the lost history of saltpeter, 'the mother of gunpowder', and the efforts of early modern governments to acquire it. Neither monarchies nor armies could operate without this special commodity, yet its history has been overshadowed by more glamorous topics of politics and war. Saltpeter (potassium nitrate) was the heart and soul of gunpowder, which gave shape to a half millennium of English and European history. Its acquisition involved alchemical knowledge, exotic technology, intrusions into people's lives, and eventual dominance of the world's oceans. The quest for saltpeter in Tudor and Stuart England pitted the power of the state against the rights and liberties of the subject. In later centuries it furnished the forces of a global empire. Governments were hungry for saltpeter, and tried every means to secure it for their stores. Without saltpeter to make gunpowder they could have no national security and no firepower munitions. Only with the development of chemical explosives in the later nineteenth century did dependency on saltpeter decline.

Charcoal and sulphur, the minority ingredients of gunpowder, were easily and cheaply found, but saltpeter proved scarce and expensive. It was either imported from distant lands or extracted at high cost from soil rich in dung and urine. As one seventeenth-century gunpowder enthusiast explained, 'the saltpeter is the soul, the sulphur the life, and the coals the body of it'.[1] Others called saltpeter 'the foundation of powder' or 'the mother of gunpowder', and recognized that the explosive product was only as good as the 'master' or 'peter' from which it was made. The proportions varied with use and changed over time, but by the late sixteenth century most English cannon powder mixed six parts saltpeter to one part each of sulphur (known as brimstone) and charcoal. This combination, claimed the seventeenth-century gunner Nathaniel Nye, produced 'the strongest powder that can be made'.[2]

English governments regarded saltpeter as an 'inestimable treasure' and sought it for their 'infinite security'.[3] No regime could do without it, and none could get enough. It was the crucial link in the chain of chemistry and power, comparable in strategic importance to modern oil or uranium. Monarchs claimed the prerogative right to extract saltpeter from private property, while landowners complained of the 'vexation and oppression' this entailed.[4] Across the Tudor and Stuart reigns a succession of projectors tendered 'new' or 'secret' processes that would improve supplies of saltpeter while alleviating the pressure on English subjects. Scientists and philosophers meanwhile pondered the mysteries of saltpeter and wondered how 'this darling of nature' gave rise to 'the most fatal instrument of death that ever mankind was trusted withal'.[5] In Shakespeare's synecdoche, it was 'villainous saltpeter...digged out of the bowels of the harmless earth' that made lethal the 'vile guns' of the battlefield.[6] Successive regimes praised God for seeding the land with 'mines of saltpeter', and gave thanks for 'the great blessing of God, that this land hath means to furnish itself of this provision'.[7]

The quest for saltpeter illuminates interactions between science and technology, society and war, in the formative era of the early modern state. It is an important matter for historical investigation, not only because saltpeter equipped the state with explosive power, but also because of the social, financial, and political complications of its furnishing. The procurement of weapons-grade saltpeter involved statesmen and speculators, military planners, chemical philosophers, commercial magnates, lawyers, labourers, technicians, and owners of nitrous-rich grounds. Their dealings and conflicts generated the documentation on which the current study is based. Governors and counsellors specified their military needs, while contractors and investors sought to supply them. Their projects for the procurement, processing, refinement, and furnishing of saltpeter created a paper trail through which the social, political, and technological history of their enterprise can be traced. Written agreements, accounts, reports, inventories, petitions, and proclamations reveal the practicalities and complexities of saltpeter production. Local opposition to intrusions by the saltpetermen brought discussion of their 'vexation and oppression' to the attention of councils and courts.

The English crown's appetite for saltpeter grew with the expanding scale of warfare and the increasing heft of weapons. One simple indicator is the number of naval cannon. Henry VIII's great navy had close to 200 heavy guns. By the time of the Armada, Elizabeth I's battle fleet commanded almost 700. By 1640, the number of heavy pieces on Charles I's Ship Money fleet approached 1,200. Oliver Cromwell's navy by the end of the Interregnum sported over 4,000 guns. The royal navy grew from 35 ships in 1640 to 195 a century later, and by 1760 it was 375 vessels strong. The number of men in arms grew from peaks of 40,000 in the seventeenth century to over 100,000 in the 1760s, over 250,000 in the early 1800s. War grew more frequent and longer-lasting, from twenty-six years of the sixteenth century to forty-two years of the seventeenth century and fifty-five years of the eighteenth. Every ship and every regiment relied on gunpowder.

At the height of its war with Spain, Elizabethan England consumed close to a hundred tons of gunpowder a year. Charles I's peacetime forces in the 1630s needed more than 250 tons. By the time of Charles II's Dutch Wars, twice that amount was barely sufficient. Gunpowder consumption increased with each conflict, from 647 tons a year in the Seven Years War (1756–1763) to over 1,600 tons a year in the War of American Independence (1776–1783). By 1828 the British Government assumed that a new major war would consume 9,000 tons of gunpowder. Not even the introduction of chemical explosives such as trinitrotoluene (TNT) at the end of the Victorian era made gunpowder insignificant. As a War Cabinet report observed in 1917, 'not a single round of cordite can be fired without the use of black powder'.[8]

Though documentation is abundant, 'the somewhat unsavoury business of collecting and processing saltpeter' (as one historian described it) is almost invisible.[9] A few specialists have studied the technology of gunpowder manufacture, with reference to its constituent ingredients. Historians of science, particularly chemistry, have touched on saltpeter, but they rarely pursue the subject unless a celebrity scientist, a Boyle or a Lavoisier, became involved. Military historians, of course, deal with gunpowder, but few more than nod at saltpeter. Their arguments about the timing, content, and consequences of the 'military revolution' address the cost and performance of cannonry, siegecraft, and gun-equipped armies, but tend to take the logistics of firepower for granted. Students of international commerce, particularly the East India Company, have traced traffic in saltpeter from the seventeenth to the nineteenth century, but they too pay scant regard to its earlier history or larger context. Social, legal, and political historians have paused only briefly to examine cases that pitted the rights of the subject against the prerogatives of the crown, and have rarely placed saltpeter in that story. It remains true that 'no comprehensive study of late medieval and early modern saltpeter production has been written'.[10]

The chapters that follow explore the science and technology of saltpeter, and its social, military, and administrative history from the sixteenth to the nineteenth century. They tell a tale of need and greed, of national security, and the pursuit of profit, as planners and projectors developed the English saltpeter enterprise. They trace the cost and consequences of changing endeavours, and explain why saltpetermen were so unpopular and how that burden lifted. While centred on England, a society on its way to global dominance, this work also connects the worlds of Renaissance Europe, *ancien régime* France, and revolutionary America. It explores connections between the 'scientific revolution', the 'military revolution', and the political revolutions of the early modern era, and shows why saltpeter mattered so much to contemporaries.

Saltpeter: The Mother of Gunpowder begins with the mystery of a puzzling substance. Natural philosophers and ordnance experts from the Renaissance to the Enlightenment knew what saltpeter did, but they were at a loss to explain what it was. The substance seemed to defy categorization, at once mineral, vegetable, and animal, with elements of earth, air, fire, and water. Was it naturally occurring, or did it need nurture? Was it a substance to be cultivated or mined? What procedures, what technologies, were necessary to derive saltpeter from nitrous earth, and then to process it into gunpowder? The opening chapter follows understandings of saltpeter from the sixteenth through the eighteenth century, and shows the dependence of English governments on expertise from abroad. This chapter engages with the histories of science and technology, and lays the groundwork for the strategic, commercial, military, and social discussions that follow.

Chapter two explores 'The Gunpowder Kingship of Henry VIII'. It presents Henry VIII as a warrior monarch with a personal interest in gunnery and ballistics. Henry's wars with France and Scotland depended on gunpowder and saltpeter from continental Europe, though the king had powder-makers and a primitive saltpeter project at home. The German Hans Wolf was authorized in 1515 'to go from shire to shire to find a place where there is stuff to make saltpeter of', and his successors met local resistance when 'making of saltpeter...for the king's affairs'.[11] Flemish, Bohemian, and Italian knowledge filtered into Tudor England, while English agents scoured Europe in search of saltpeter. Thus began the enterprise that led to so much 'vexation'.

Chapter three follows 'The Elizabethan Quest for Infinite Security'. A vulnerable regime in a dangerous world needed to be able to defend itself, and William Cecil, Elizabeth's chief minister, knew that England's survival depended on munitions. 'Stout provision of saltpeter', he assured the Council, would serve the queen better than gold and treasure.[12] The quest for saltpeter, at home and abroad, paid handsomely when England was at war with Spain, especially in 1588, the year of the Armada. Stocks of saltpeter and gunpowder ran low but never ran out. This was due to energetic international procurement, including new supplies from North Africa, where English merchants acquired saltpeter in exchange for cannon balls. Elizabethan England saw repeated attempts to harness domestic reserves, and eventually a network of saltpetermen was authorized to search and dig wherever the substance could be found. The intrusions of the saltpetermen sparked local resentment, but grievances were submerged amid the quest for national security. Among foreign experts who offered secrets of saltpeter processing was the Bohemian Jew Joachim Gaunz, who had served as mineralogist on Sir Walter Raleigh's expedition to Roanoke in America. Saltpeter made England safe, but the cost was yet to be paid.

Chapter four, 'Saltpeter for a Peaceable Kingdom', looks at the changed circumstances of James I's reign, when England mostly avoided war. The crown's need for munitions diminished, and some military supplies were sold abroad, but saltpetermen continued to exploit their contracts and maximize their profits. A political backlash against the saltpetermen exposed their corruption, and lawyers challenged their right to dig on private land. The influential common lawyer Sir Edward Coke allowed that the royal prerogative permitted procurement of saltpeter for national security, but denied that the saltpetermen could dig in anyone's residence. The Jacobean playwright Thomas Middleton depicted saltpetermen as 'knaves' who could be bribed to dig someone else's ground. The legal and political consequences of their actions would resonate for the rest of the Stuart era.

Chapter five, 'The Inestimable Treasure of Charles I', examines the aggressive expansion of England's domestic saltpeter enterprise, as Charles I built up his forces while trying to escape dependence on imported supplies. The government put pressure on the saltpetermen to deliver greater quotas, and generally supported them in clashes with landowners. This chapter reviews dozens of complaints against the predations of the saltpetermen, and shows the development of informal local resistance. Saltpetermen would find gates barred, water sources unavailable, obstructions to their work. Some cases involved sabotage to their boiling pans, tubs, and carts. The government railed against disobedient, refractory, and seditious subjects, while opponents spoke against injustice and unlimited power. The saltpeter struggle mirrored better-known clashes over Ship Money and religion, but property owners across the political spectrum could unite against digging in their own houses, grounds, or barns. The problem cut to the heart of the conflict between royal authority and the liberty of the common-wealth that tore seventeenth-century England apart.

Chapter six explores the 'Saltpeter Revolution' of the mid-seventeenth century. The revolutionary parliament ended the royal monopoly on gunpowder manufacture, and set itself against the 'vexation and oppression' of the saltpetermen. But then it discovered its own need for munitions, in a civil war with the king, and attempted to establish its own saltpeter enterprise with suitable safeguards for 'liberty'. Parliamentary forces were more successful than the wartime king in securing saltpeter and manufacturing gunpowder, but both sides depended heavily on imports. Philosophical projectors in the 1640s planned to industrialize saltpeter production while putting the poor to work, but their schemes contributed more to science than munitions. An unexpected revolution in supply occurred within a year of the Regicide, when abundant supplies from India reduced the need for domestic saltpetermen. The restored monarchy in 1660 inherited enhanced military capacity, and a flow of East Indian saltpeter that no longer required digging.

Chapter seven, 'Saltpeter for a Global Power', takes the story from the Restoration to the Victorian era, from the wars of the seventeenth century to the struggles of a global empire. British forces remained gunpowder-dependent, and consumed vast amounts in both peace and war. The consumption of gunpowder in the 1780s was six times that of the 1630s, and sixteen times as great as in the Elizabethan era. The Victorian demand for material for munitions was even greater. Most of the saltpeter that furnished this appetite for gunpowder came from India. After the battle of Plassey in 1757, Britain controlled 70 per cent or more of the world's saltpeter production. This chapter traces dealings between the East India Company and the British state, and explores the expansion of military, commercial, and industrial scale. It also examines the last guttering of the domestic saltpeter enterprise, as investors tried and failed to compete with the Asian juggernaut.

Chapter eight follows the saltpeter trail to eighteenth-century America and France, where radically different enterprises were pursued. The munitions economies of Britain's neighbours and enemies illustrate alternatives to the home-based system. Facing war with Great Britain in 1775, the American Continental Congress turned to the almost forgotten art of backyard saltpeter production. Denied access to major military reserves, the rebels would have to make gunpowder for themselves. American yeomen would enrich their ground with urine and dung, and tobacco colonists would make saltpeter from waste trimmings. This patriotic activity, said Congress, would secure 'the salvation and prosperity of America' and the 'lives, liberties, and estates' of its citizens.[13] In the event the local volunteer effort proved unnecessary, because the French were happy to supply the American rebels with all the gunpowder they needed.

Like their English cousins, French kings insisted on their saltpeter monopoly, but under Louis XV they too grew dependent on imports from India. When Britain expelled the French from Bengal after 1757 they were forced to reorganize as domestic producers, improving their technology and science. Guided by Europe's preeminent chemist, Antoine Lavoisier, they developed a centralized, science-based, saltpeter industry that could produce more than a thousand tons a year. Lavoisier's *Instruction sur l'établissement de nitières et sur la fabrication du salpêtre* and *Recueil de mémoires sur la formation et sur le fabrication du salpêtre* had no English counterpart, which perhaps explains why France, not England, launched the modern 'chemical revolution'. French science and French military capability were both set back when Lavoisier was guillotined in 1794. American gunpowder independence was enhanced, however, when Lavoisier's disciple Eleuthère Irénée du Pont, the founder of DuPont Industries, fled to the fledgling United States.

A brief conclusion reconnects the histories of science, military procurement, statecraft, politics, commerce, and law, and shows how the saltpeter enterprise of the Tudors, Stuarts, and Hanoverians gave shape to the early modern state.

1

Mysterious Saltpeter

*I*N November 1646, *as parliamentary forces savoured victory in the English civil war, nineteen-year-old Robert Boyle, ensconced in his family estate at Stalbridge, Dorset, turned his mind to saltpeter. Younger brother to the royalist Earl of Cork, Boyle had been educated at Eton and had studied in France, Italy, and Switzerland. He had been introduced to the 'Invisible College' of utopian scientific enthusiasts, and his correspondence connected him to many of the men who would become founders of the Royal Society. His interest in 'that adored muck' of 'dung-coloured earth' was triggered by the attentions of 'those undermining two-legged moles we call saltpetermen', who attempted to excavate his grounds. 'My pigeon-house they are already digging up (an emblem of the practice of the times, of the ruin of unarmed innocence), and would have done the like to my cellar and stables, if I had not ransomed them with a richer mineral than that they contain', so he wrote, rather stiltedly, to the projector Benjamin Worsley. The saltpetermen, whom Boyle called 'the allowed incendiaries' of early modern England, roamed the country in search of earth impregnated with dung and urine, and were licensed to take it from private property. As Boyle and other rich landlords discovered, the depredations of the saltpetermen could sometimes be offset by bribes, but the material they delivered was indispensable for furnishing the state with munitions.*

Boyle congratulated Worsley on his 'gallant projects' to transform and centralize the processing of saltpeter. 'The welcome news that your propositions had already passed the House of Lords' had just reached Dorset,

*and Boyle conveyed his best wishes 'for the prosperity of your pious pow-
der plot'. If time permitted, amid the post-war cares and pressures of
soldiers, sequestrators, and committee-men, he promised Worsley 'to
transmit to you any thoughts or experiments of mine, that I shall judge
conducible to the furtherance of your great design'. A few years later
Boyle turned his scientific attention to the topic in 'A Physico-Chymical
Essay, Containing an Experiment, with some Considerations Touching
the Differing Parts and Redintegration of Salt-Petre', a subject, he said,
that 'may well deserve our serious enquiries'.[1]*

* * *

Like the 'gunpowder empires' of Islamic Asia (the Ottoman
Empire based in Constantinople, the Safavid Empire based in
Persia, and the Mughal Empire based in India), the Western
European 'gunpowder states' of the early modern 'military revolution' made ceaseless efforts to secure the raw materials for explosive munitions. Their siege trains, battleships, fortresses, and
musketry consumed vast amounts of powder as they vied for
dominance and projected their force beyond their frontiers. From
the fifteenth century to the nineteenth the Spanish, Portuguese,
French, Dutch, Swedes, and English built their strength on gunpowder. Neither monarchies nor armies could operate without
this special commodity. Without gunpowder weaponry they could
have no national security, and without its principal ingredient,
saltpeter, there could be no firepower munitions.[2] Only with the
development of chemical explosives in the later nineteenth century did dependence on gunpowder decline.

Familiar in Europe by the thirteenth century, gunpowder was
composed of saltpeter (potassium nitrate), sulphur (known as
brimstone), and carbon (from charcoal). Reliant on milling and
mixing, the product was only as good as the material from which
it was made. The charcoal provided solid substance for combustion, the sulphur allowed immediate ignition, while saltpeter provided oxygen for the explosion (strictly speaking, a deflagration
rather than a highly exothermic combustion). The proportions
varied with use and changed over time, but by the late sixteenth

century most English cannon powder mixed six parts saltpeter to one part each of brimstone and charcoal.[3]

Technology and knowledge

Generations of experimenters and natural philosophers sought to understand how gunpowder burned with 'a noise exceeding the roar of strong thunder, and a flash brighter than the most brilliant lightning', and could shoot a projectile the length of a battlefield.[4] Even modern chemists regard gunpowder as 'a very complex and subtle substance', leading one expert to acknowledge that its 'principles of action are not even fully understood today'.[5] This chapter examines the science and technology of munitions procurement in the age of the gunpowder state.

The ideal gunpowder burned quickly with maximum force, without damaging the 'engine' in which it was fired. 'Serpentine' powder (named for a fifteenth-century gun) was 'as fine as sand and as soft as flour', but the newer grained or 'corned' gunpowder had more explosive force with 'vacuities or airy places for the fire to be carried'.[6] Sixteenth-century gunners well knew that 'if serpentine powder should be occupied in hand guns or arquebuses, it would scant be able to drive their pellets', but 'if hand gun powder should be used in pieces of ordnance, without great discretion, it would quickly break or mar them'.[7] A Tudor gunner needed to be 'skilful in the receipt of his powder' and to 'know the authority of the same'. It was 'the real practick part of a gunner to know his powder', observed Charles I's gunner Robert Norton, and to learn all he could about the 'body', 'life', and 'soul' of its ingredients.[8] At the opening of the eighteenth century a gunner was similarly expected 'to know the nature and sympathy' of the three ingredients of gunpowder.[9] The skill or 'mystery' of the artilleryman combined alchemy, military science, and mathematical ballistics.

Primitive gunpowder in the late fourteenth century used equal amounts of saltpeter, brimstone, and charcoal. By the early fifteenth century the proportion of saltpeter had tripled, and gunners experimented with increasing amounts. Recipes varied, but a common sixteenth-century formula specified three parts of salt-peter, two of charcoal, and one of brimstone for large artillery cannon; five saltpeter, one and a half coals, and one of brimstone for smaller pieces; and ten parts of saltpeter, and one each of char-coal and sulphur for arquebuses and hand guns.[10] The product varied somewhat in grain size or dustiness, in 'earthy grossness' or impurities, in stability, and in its firepower or 'force'. Even well-made gunpowder had a tendency to decay and to absorb moisture, which could be remedied by remixing with saltpeter. 'The best powder' of the 1520s used four parts saltpeter to one each of char-coal and brimstone, and by the later sixteenth century English powder had standard proportions of 6:1:1. This combination, claimed the seventeenth-century gunner Nathaniel Nye, produced 'the strongest powder that can be made'. It was all to do with the burning qualities of the ingredients and the 'fortification' of 'the cylinder of the piece'. Cannons, muskets, and pistols each had different requirements, and older, more fragile weaponry needed more cautious loading than new. Nye recommended 4:1:1 for heavy cannon, 5:1:1 for muskets, and 6:1:1 for pistols. Other recipes included as much as 80 per cent saltpeter.[11] Discussing these for-mulae in the 1660s, the Royal Society scientist Thomas Henshaw observed that 'our English workmen are generally so curious of their secret, that I could not obtain the proportion of them with-out a promise of secrecy. But when all is done their secret is not so much the way to make the best powder, as the way to get most money by it.'[12]

The manufacturers of gunpowder needed reliable supplies of raw materials. Charcoal came easily from English woodlands, ideally from alder, lime, willow, hazel, or beech.[13] Sulphur was imported from the volcanic regions of southern Italy, but could also be obtained from domestic mineral springs. According to the contemporary observer William Harrison, there was 'great plenty of sulphur' in Elizabethan England.[14] The problem mate-rial was saltpeter, whose properties, provenance, and potency were topics for learned discussion. Lacking understanding of the nitrification associated with bacterial action on decaying organic matter, experts wondered whether saltpeter was a substance to be mined or grown. Did it occur naturally, or was saltpeter something to be nourished or cultivated by human endeavour? What impurities had to be removed, through what methods, before serviceable crystals could be obtained? Did one source or process yield better saltpeter than another, and how could supplies be guaranteed? These were serious questions, rooted in the different technologies, customs, and prerogatives pertaining to agriculture and minerals.[15] The most advanced knowledge lay in Italy and Bohemia, though it spread across Christendom in the sixteenth and seventeenth centuries.[16]

Though they knew how to harness saltpeter for explosive weaponry, theorists were hard pressed to explain its nature and properties. Alchemists, natural philosophers, military technicians, and minerals experts of the early modern era speculated on the chemistry of saltpeter as well as technologies for its extraction. None could fathom the way it was formed, nor could anyone fully explain its formidable effects. Who could tell whence came its vitalizing vigour, in applications as diverse as fertilizers, preservatives, medicine, and munitions? Was saltpeter, some wondered, identical to the 'nitre' known to the Bible and classical antiquity? The usual references are to Proverbs 25:20, Jeremiah 2:22, and the works of Pliny, Strabo, and Herodotus. If the Greeks or Romans had saltpeter, then why not gunpowder?, went one line of enquiry. Perhaps, some writers suggested, the ancients kept their art secret and the skill died with them. The general view, however, marked gunpowder as 'wholly unknown to the ancient Greeks and Arabians', and only recently Latinized as *sal bombardicum*.[17] A powerful stream of speculation wondered whether saltpeter contained the *sal nitrum* or *spiritus mundi*, the 'nitrous universal spirit', that would unlock the secrets of nature. If so, as Robert Boyle observed, the subject 'may well deserve our serious enquiries'.[18]

Understanding of the 'virtues' of saltpeter remained controversial and opaque, and changed slowly across time. The drama of scientific discovery developed falteringly alongside the bloodier drama of war. Renaissance authors commonly analysed saltpeter in terms of its humoral and elemental properties, as hot, cold, wet, or dry, or partaking of earth, air, fire, and water. They puzzled over the ambiguities of this substance which apparently shared attributes of the animal, vegetable, and mineral kingdoms. 'I cannot tell how to be resolved, to say what thing properly it is,' observed the Elizabethan theorist Peter Whitehorne, except 'it seemeth it hath the sovereignty and quality of every element'.[19] Followers of Paracelsus treated nitre as a mystical as well as a chemical substance, with occult as well as material connotations. They perceived a vital generative principle in saltpeter, 'a notable mystery the which, albeit it be taken from out of the earth, yet it may lift up our eyes to heaven'. Saltpeter encompassed the '*miraculum mundi*', the '*materia universalis*', through which 'our very lives and spirits were preserved'. Its threefold nature evoked 'that incomprehensible mystery of…the divine Trinity', marvelled the minister Thomas Timme in 1605 in his translation of the Paracelsian Joseph Duchesne.[20]

Philosophers taught Charles I's gunner Robert Norton that the saltpeter in gunpowder possessed 'a quintessence of qualities…convertible to all the elements'. Though his primary business was with weaponry, this Baconian artilleryman knew that 'the knowledge of nature's works may guide us to admirable inventions'.[21] Francis Bacon himself, Lord Chancellor and Privy Councillor under James I, dismissed 'crude and ignorant speculations' about gunpowder and its 'spirit', yet continued to identify saltpeter as the energizing 'spirit of the earth'.[22] Robert Boyle's experiments a generation later found saltpeter, 'the most catholic of salts', a most puzzling concrete, 'vegetable, animal, and even mineral', both acid and alkaline, and 'partly fixed and partly volatile'. 'The knowledge of it', Boyle opined, 'may be very conducive to the discovery of the nature of several other bodies, and to the improvement of divers parts of natural philosophy.'[23]

The Restoration virtuoso Henry Stubbe called saltpeter 'one of the most odd concretes in the world'. Though veiled by 'many noble secrets', saltpeter, 'this darling of nature', was 'universally diffused through all the elements' and was essential to their nutriment and generation, thought the Royal Society lecturer Thomas Henshaw. Saltpeter was indeed 'ubiquitarian', declared the physician William Clarke, who also named nitre as 'the hermaphroditical salt'. The Dutch medical philosopher Herman Boerhaave agreed that saltpeter had 'hermaphrodite' qualities, 'of a middle kind, between fossil and animal'.[24] The protean elusiveness of the substance made it a puzzle worth pursuing. The problem of classification in this regard exposed the weakness of classical theories of humours and elements, and eventually led to their displacement.

The practical harnessing of saltpeter was more firmly grounded than theoretical understanding of its complexities. As late as the 1770s a popular chemistry instructor allowed that 'we are much in the dark as to the origin and generation' of saltpeter, though he knew it to be found among 'earth and stones that have been impregnated with animal or vegetable juices susceptible of putrefaction, and have long been exposed to the air...It is the product of the elements, deposited in the bosom of the earth...and may not improperly be called the universal and unspecific mercury.'[25] Even Great Britain's Imperial Agricultural Chemist in the early twentieth century, J. W. Leather, could puzzle over the mysteries of saltpeter nitrification in the earth, because 'the matter has never really been examined by the chemist and bacteriologist'.[26] Modern organic chemists explain the nitrification of soil by reference to bacteria which initiate or catalyse the oxidation of ammonia in decomposing organic matter, but the process is still problematic. Much depends upon the strains of micro-organisms and the kinetics of soil metabolism, though nitrification is known to be quickened by urea (the chemical compound found in urine). Researchers have learned that the bacterial reactions vary with temperature and humidity, and with the mix of materials and composition of the soil.[27]

Written knowledge of the properties of saltpeter filtered into England following the publication of Vannoccio Biringuccio's *De la pirotechnia* at Venice in 1540. This work, which was eventually translated into English, included seminal accounts of the preparation and making of explosives. Generations of authors plagiarized this text without acknowledging their source.[28] Among them was Georgius Agricola, whose brief account of saltpeter in his work on minerals and mining, *De re metallica*, published at Basel in 1556, also had some followers.[29] The German Gerard Hoenrich set forth plans for a saltpeter system early in Queen Elizabeth's reign, but his manuscript was never published.[30] The transfer of skill and understanding accelerated when Peter Whitehorne included chapters from Biringuccio in his treatises on warfare of 1562, 1574, and 1588. Drawing on the best wisdom of the Italian Renaissance, Whitehorne did his best to explain 'the nature of saltpeter, and the manner how to make and refine it', and 'the manner how to make all sorts of gunpowder'.[31] Just as a writer needed to know how to make ink and how to prepare a pen, a gunner or bombardier needed practical knowledge of the materials on which his trade depended.

Saltpeter, Whitehorne reported, 'is a mixture of many substances, gotten out with fire and water of dry and dirty ground'. It could sometimes be found as an efflorescence or 'flower that groweth out of new walls, in cellars, or of that ground which is found loose within tombs or desolate caves where rain cannot come in'. But saltpeter could also be nourished or encouraged to grow by adding 'the dung of beasts' to the earth. A distinction was made between 'natural saltpeter' which only needed to be scraped from walls, and 'artificial saltpeter' which required digging and refinement. The two kinds partook of 'the very same virtue' (according to Whitehorne, relaying Biringuccio) except that some thought 'artificial' saltpeter to be stronger. 'The most excellent' saltpeter, he continued, 'is made of the dung of beasts, converted into earth, in stables or in dunghills of long time not used.' Dovecotes or pigeon houses were also favoured sites because of their concentration of sheltered droppings. 'Whatsoever dung it be, it is requisite that by continuance of time it be well resolved into the earth, and the humidity thereof dried.' Ideally the earth should be dry as dust, for exposure to rain could ruin it for saltpeter extraction. A skilled prospector would know how to locate soil rich in

FIG 1 Making saltpeter

Georgius Agricola, *De re metallica* (Basel, 1556), p. 456 (Huntington Library, rare book 296000, reproduced by permission of the Huntington).

saltpeter, for 'by the taste of the tongue it may be felt if it be biting, and how much'.[32]

When it came to the properties of this substance, the author admitted uncertainty. Saltpeter appeared to be 'engendered of an airy moistness drunk up and gotten of the earthy dryness, whose nature (by the effects thereof) considering, I cannot tell how to be resolved'. Guided by 'the well learned and most wise physicians', who found its taste 'salt and with exceeding subtle sharpness' and a 'great biting', one might suppose that saltpeter 'is of nature hot and dry'. But 'seeing it to be a thing engendered of air, and touched by fire to fall in a flame and vapour, and rise with a terrible violence', it would seem to be 'of an airy nature, hot and moist'. But that too was insufficient, for 'seeing it with shining and glittering whiteness, as a thing to the nature of water conformable, it seemeth that it may be said, that it is of a watery nature'. Other attributes, however, including heaviness and brittleness, suggested saltpeter 'to be of the nature of earth'.[33]

Whitehorne's treatise listed the equipment and explained the procedures for making 'a great quantity' of saltpeter for munitions. Similar accounts would occur in treatises and proposals for the next hundred years. The operatives would need 'many cauldrons, furnaces, barrels or tubs, and likewise wood, white lime, and ashes of old oak', as well as wagons for transport and fuel for fires. They would need 'a great barn' or walled workshop close to an abundant supply of water for boiling and leaching. Barrels filled with dung-rich earth would be set on a framework of joists or forms, so that water introduced at the top would trickle down to a catchment tub at the bottom. Holes drilled in the base of each barrel would allow the liquid to escape, but a cloth or straw in each hole would regulate the flow. The soluble salts would be separated through percolation or 'lixiviation', though Whitehorne does not use these terms.[34]

The next stage required further drainage of the saltpeter liquor through alternate layers of earth and ash mixed with lime. This was to precipitate out the calcium and manganese salts that otherwise made saltpeter weak and hygroscopic (prone to absorbing moisture from the atmosphere). The action might be repeated several times until the water 'bring with it all the substance and virtue of the saltpeter that was in the said earth'. A taste test would prove whether this liquor was 'biting' enough. Now it was time for boiling, in brass-walled cauldrons 'such as dyers use'. The saltpeter liquor would be heated over a wood or charcoal fire until approximately half was boiled away. It would be allowed to settle and clarify, with obvious impurities skimmed or 'purged', then more boiling would follow, with additions of ash, lime, and alum, until 'all the wateriness be vapoured away, and the substance of the saltpeter thickened'. It was then cooled until it was 'ready to congeal', to form crystals of serviceable potassium nitrate.[35]

The whole process could take a week or more, with judicious applications of water, heat, additives, and skill. The result was a crude saltpeter that needed further refinement before it could be used for gunpowder. The preferred method involved further sequences of watering and dissolving, boiling and straining, to 'make the saltpeter most white and fair, and much better than at the first seething'. An alternative but more dangerous method required melting the congealed saltpeter in a covered metal pot, then dosing it with a flaming mixture of straw and brimstone, whereby the 'gross unctuousness of the saltpeter' might be consumed. This procedure promised a product 'all in one piece white like unto a piece of marble', which was 'good saltpeter to make powder withal'. In either case, the aim was to secure 'the chief thing that is in powder' on which 'dependeth all the force'. Waste earths and liquids from the process would be returned to the ground, so that more 'saltpeter will be engendered' for the future. The miracle was that the earth 'will multiply wonderfully', and 'within the space of five or six years may again be laboured', yielding more saltpeter than ever before.[36]

Whitehorne's treatise, derived from Biringuccio, set forth procedures for the making of saltpeter that would prevail for several centuries. All that would alter would be the scale of the operation, the source of materials, and the balance of public and private involvement. Whether state-sponsored or independent, centralized or localized, working on a large scale or small, the saltpeter workers of the sixteenth, seventeenth, and eighteenth centuries were heirs to this Renaissance technological tradition.[37]

Competing with Whitehorne, and to some extent augmenting him, was Cyprian Lucar's compendium on saltpeter, attached to his *Colloquies Concerning the Arte of Shooting in Great and Small Peeces of Artillerie* (1588). This was taken 'out of divers authors in divers languages', and was heavily indebted to the Italians Biringuccio, Niccolò Tartaglia, and Girolamo Cataneo.

Lucar recommended the dung of goats and hogs to enrich the earth, and described the same method of preparing and processing saltpeter liquor. His account of the boiling, skimming, congealing, and purifying of saltpeter is almost word-for-word identical to Whitehorne's, and derived from a common source.

New to print, however, was Lucar's account of the digging of earth 'out of floors in cellars, vaults, stables, ox-stalls, goat or sheep cotes, pigeon houses, or out of the lowermost rooms in other houses'. This reflected more the practice of Tudor England's roving saltpetermen than the continentals, who worked on enriched nitre beds (managed heaps of vegetable matter mixed with excreta and ordure). One test to determine a good spot for digging involved thrusting a red-hot iron nail into a hole prepared by hammering in a wooden pin; if the nail, when removed, turned a pale yellow, 'you ought to think that the earth in that place will yield plenty of saltpeter'. Other tests deployed the saltpeterman's knowledgeable nose and tongue. There was practical advice for the workmen to 'dig not for any such earth more than the length of three inches under the face and uppermost part of the floor or ground', unless they see white veins in black soil.[38]

Lucar also described a simpler process of percolation, boiling, and congealment, more suited to a mobile operation. The earth in various barrels would be saturated, and water allowed to stand on top 'for the space of a day and a night'. The water would then be allowed to trickle through to a collection basin, and the process repeated until 'the same water tasted in your mouth will bite your tongue', and an egg 'will swim upon the top'. This 'strong water' would be boiled in a cauldron, for as long as necessary, and the scum lifted as it rose. When drops of this liquor would 'congeal' on a piece of iron, the 'master water' was ready, and it would be drained 'to congeal in a dankish, close and dark place'. The emphasis throughout was on useful knowledge that would furnish artillerymen with 'good gunpowder'. Knowing 'how to make and refine artificial saltpeter' was an essential part of the Tudor gunners' craft, for who knew when they might have to improvise supplies?[39]

A successful military manual from the time of Queen Elizabeth's Spanish war was William Bourne, *The Arte of Shooting in Great Ordnaunce*, published in 1587. By this time, in Bourne's view, 'the making of saltpeter is become…a common thing amongst a number of people', especially among men and women in Germany, and he saw no need to go into it in detail. The procurement and manufacture of saltpeter could be taken for granted, at least for current purposes, but men who dealt in ballistics still needed to understand 'the goodness or badness of powder' and the saltpeter that gave it its 'force'. Gunpowder varied in quality and was prone to decay, but 'the tasting of the tongue' would tell if 'there be sufficient of the master or peter or not'. Putting a sample to the flame would prove that the powder was 'well wrought' and the peter 'well refined'. Slow burning with a grainy residue would indicate that the saltpeter was insufficient or impure, which could make the difference between a soldier's life and death.[40]

The Tudor and Stuart eras abounded with projects for scraping saltpeter from mineral efflorescences; for extracting saltpeter from nitrous earth; for enriching the earth with dung, urine, and household debris; and for processes of percolation, boiling, and refining to produce crystallized potassium nitrate for the ever voracious Ordnance Office. A succession of foreign experts claimed knowledge of the 'secret and hidden mystery' of 'the whole work of saltpeter making', and offered to teach 'many things worthy the learning'.[41] Most of the technical and scientific knowledge that underlay these projects came from Italian treatises, augmented by German, Flemish, and Bohemian expertise. Well into the seventeenth century, English observations on the making of saltpeter recycled foreign texts without attribution.[42]

The most comprehensive account of saltpeter manufacture was by Lazarus Ercker (1530–1594), chief master of the mines of Emperor Rudolf II in Bohemia. German editions of Ercker's treatise appeared at Prague in 1574 and at Frankfurt in 1580, but there was no English publication before the 1680s.[43] Ercker described an industrial process for preparing and purifying saltpeter that was larger and more ambitious than anything attempted in England. His illustrations depicted saltpeter beds, draining tubs, and the art of crystallizing potassium nitrate. The general principles of lixiviation, percolation, boiling, and refining would have been familiar, as would the idea of recycling leftover substances to generate more saltpeter, but the scale and complexity of the operation was dazzling. Queen Elizabeth's government acquired a partial translation in manuscript in 1589, which offered to put the English saltpeter enterprise onto a more profitable centralized footing. Following Ercker, the cosmopolitan Jewish metallurgist Joachim Gaunz set down 'the right and most perfect way of the whole work of saltpeter making', from 'what sort of earth will serve', to its boiling, congealing, and further refining. Gaunz, like Ercker, insisted on careful measurement, weighing, and assaying, but his forty-page manuscript was never published and his tips remained largely unknown.[44]

In practice, most English saltpetermen plied their trade without recourse to technical manuals. They learned by doing, or by following directions from more experienced operatives. It was enough to know what worked, how to dig and boil, and how to furnish sufficient supplies to the ordnance contractors. From time to time, however, as later chapters will show, entrepreneurs or investors came forward with schemes to reveal new secrets of saltpeter production, or to implement processes that would yield better quality, quantity, and profits. These were commonly the fruit of foreign travel or study of imported texts, and governments were often receptive to them. The 'secret' behind many of these schemes was the vitalizing power of urine, which chemical philosophers had pondered for decades. As will be seen, however, the most ambitious projects fell short of their promise, and English saltpetermen continued with proven piecemeal methods until East India imports curtailed the need for their activity.

Among the last to navigate this 'sea of ingenuities' were savants in Samuel Hartlib's circle in the mid-seventeenth century, whose musings on 'philosophical saltpeter' and 'philosophical dung' served as guides to wisdom and experimentation. Hartlib (1600–1662) was a polymathic scientific enthusiast whose

FIG 2 Saltpeter beds

Lazarus Ercker, *Beschreibung allerfürnemisten mineralischen Ertzt unnd Bergkwercks Arten* (Frankfurt, 1580), facing f. 134 (Huntington Library, rare book 752815, reproduced by permission of the Huntington).

correspondence connected many of the most enquiring minds of his age. One of them, the physician Benjamin Worsley (1618– 1677), conceived of a philosophically driven, science-based, altruistic enterprise that would put the poor to work, achieve saltpeter independence, and advance man's mastery over nature. His junior associate Robert Boyle (1627–1691) shared the belief that 'the seminal principle of nitre, latent in the earth,' would make

FIG 3 Saltpeter percolation

Lazarus Ercker, *Beschreibung allerfürnemisten mineralischen Ertzt unnd Bergkwercks Arten* (Frankfurt, 1580), facing f. 129 (Huntington Library, rare book 752815, reproduced by permission of the Huntington).

possible 'a perpetual mine of saltpeter'. Like other alchemical experimenters, Boyle hoped that the study of saltpeter would stimulate natural philosophy, but government funding never materialized and the virtuosi of the Interregnum moved on to other projects.[45]

FIG 4 Saltpeter crystallizing

Lazarus Ercker, *Beschreibung allerfürnemisten mineralischen Ertzt unnd Bergkwercks Arten* (Frankfurt, 1580), f. 130 (Huntington Library, rare book 752815, reproduced by permission of the Huntington).

Philosophical saltpeter

As imported Indian saltpeter supplanted home-sourced supplies in the second half of the seventeenth century, English scientists became more interested in the chemical properties of the substance than in projects for its production. Saltpeter remained a subject for intellectual speculation, even though the East India Company had solved the problem of supply. Among leading chemical philosophers of the Restoration era, Thomas Henshaw of London and Henry Stubbe of Warwick disputed in print about the origins and nature of saltpeter. Thomas Henshaw, a founding member of the Royal Society, lectured on saltpeter in 1662 and his words were published in the 1667 history of the society's proceedings.[46] A first order of business was to determine 'whether the nitre of the ancients be of the same species with the salt which is commonly known by the name of saltpeter'. This led to disquisitions historical, philological, and mineralogical, augmented by 'private experiments' and review of 'the practice of saltpetermen', which convinced Henshaw that the saltpeter now in use 'was a modern invention'. In the course of this study he discussed the properties and composition of saltpeter, and the processes employed for its extraction, though those processes were receding into history. Henshaw's approach was empirical and Baconian, and seemingly owed little to sixteenth-century Italians.

Like Biringuccio, a century and a quarter earlier, Henshaw distinguished between natural and artificial saltpeter. In certain barren landscapes and climates, he believed, the start of the rainy season forced saltpeter to 'shoot out of the ground, as thick and white as a hoar frost'. The natives of North Africa and East India would gather this substance to sell to refiners. Closer to home could be found 'rock peter', which hung 'like icicles in arched cellars and vaults', or grew like flowers on plastered and mortared brick walls 'where the wall is defended from the rain'. This was, indeed, natural saltpeter, *sal petrae*, the 'salt stone' that provided its name, 'yet it is not there to be had in any proportion answerable to the charge in getting it'. 'In these northern countries', Henshaw noted, the only place to find saltpeter was 'in stables, pigeon houses, cellars, barns, warehouses, or indeed any place which is covered from the rain which would dissolve it, and...make it vegetate, as also from the sun which doth rarify it and cause it to be exhaled into the air'. Saltpeter was evidently an elusive and unstable substance that required skilful exploitation. One experienced workman told Henshaw that, 'no place yields peter so plentifully as the earth in churches, were it not an impiety to disturb the ashes of our ancestors in that sacred depository'. A generation earlier, in the reign of Charles I, the digging for saltpeter in churches was a major source of scandal.[47]

English saltpetermen knew by experience that saltpeter grew more readily in black earth or 'mould' than in clay or sandy soil. The taste test would tell if it had 'good store of mineral'. They knew too that 'if they mingle with the dried earth store of pigeons' dung, and mellow horse dung, and then temper it with urine...it will be fit to dig again in five or six years'. Practical knowledge of this sort accrued over a hundred years, 'before we were supplied with peter from India'. Henshaw described in detail the running of water through tubs of earth until 'it come clear, and of the colour of urine', and the boiling of this liquor in copper pots until 'it hang like oil on the sides of the brazen skimmer'. He followed the straining of this liquor through tubs of ash 'till your liquor grow clear and lose the thick colour it had when it went on', and the second boiling 'till the liquor in the copper be ready to shoot or crystallize...When the liquor is brought to this pass, every hundredweight of it containeth about threescore and ten pound weight of peter.' This enriched liquid, sometimes called the 'mother of saltpeter', would be drawn into trays or pans to 'shoot' or crystallize, leaving impurities like common salt on the sides of the tub. But the process was not yet complete, for 'it will be no good colour till it be refined'.

To refine saltpeter, Henshaw observed, you dissolved your crystals in boiling water, skimmed the froth to remove impure salts, added wine vinegar or powdered alum, and again removed the resultant scum. Some practitioners added quick lime, 'and say it makes peter the whiter, and rock the better', but there was a risk of the liquid boiling over. Eventually the liquid would be cooled in a settling tub, then drawn off into shooting trays or pans. The reward, after two more days, would be fairer crystals, 'sexangular and...fistulous and hollow like a pipe', ready for mixing into gunpowder.

The primary purpose of the saltpeter enterprise was to produce material for munitions. But Henshaw took samples for the advancement of science. He offered the Royal Society 'a few speculations I have of this salt, which if I could clearly make out, would lead us into the knowledge of many noble secrets in nature; as also to a great improvement in the art of making saltpeter'. Here were mysteries to uncover as well as rewards to be won. Observation and experiment led Henshaw, he said, to 'a theory that I am much delighted with', that nitre was 'diffused through all the elements, and must therefore make a chief ingredient in their nutriment, and by consequence of their generation'.[48] Saltpeter, it seemed, was a universal salt, at once animal, vegetable, and mineral. Not simply the primary ingredient in gunpowder but a potent and mysterious substance in its own right, saltpeter held the key to a new chemical philosophy of nature.

Henry Stubbe, a relentless critic of the Royal Society, spent over a hundred pages refuting Henshaw and charging him with plagiarism and error: 'how vain are his pretensions! how superficial his enquiries and observations!' Crediting the ancient world with knowledge of saltpeter, Stubbe rebuked the 'anti-Aristotleians' who misrepresented both present and past.[49] The advancement of the domestic saltpeter industry was no longer at issue, since England now had abundant supplies from the Indies. Rather, the debate partook of the larger intellectual struggle between ancients and moderns, between upholders of classical and Renaissance wisdom and practitioners of the new experimental science.[50]

Not only did Henshaw have 'a pique against antiquity', claimed Stubbe, he also falsified his observations and his theory. His account of the processing of saltpeter owed more to the work of the sixteenth-century German Lazarus Ercker than to any watching of saltpetermen or work in the laboratory. The addition of alum and lime for refinement, for example, which Henshaw describes, was not an English practice but came out of Ercker. Henshaw's description of 'sexangular fistulous crystals' also seemed to come from books. The main source, it appeared, was the Latin work of Johann Rudolf Glauber, printed in Amsterdam in 1659, which included transcriptions of Ercker on saltpeter. As to the novel 'theory' that gave Henshaw so much 'delight', it too came from Glauber, without attribution, and also drew on experiments by Robert Boyle. But Stubbe was less indignant that these ideas were stolen than that they were wrong. By way of recompense he cited work by Samuel Hartlib on agriculture and Casimir Simioenowicz on gunpowder, and translated two more discourses on saltpeter from *L'artigleria* of Pietro Sardi (Venice, 1629), and the venerable *Quesiti et inventioni diverse* of Niccolò Tartaglia (Venice 1546). English knowledge of the chemistry of saltpeter remained controversial, and its principal authority still derived from continental experts.[51]

Benefits to mankind

Saltpeter, by this time, furnished fruitful speculation to philosophers as well as boundless benefits to mankind. While ordnance officers pursued saltpeter as 'the mother of gunpowder', and philosophers sought in it the *spiritus mundi*, physicians prescribed nitre in curative cordials and compounds. Detached from its military use, the substance appeared more versatile than villainous, a 'darling of nature' indeed.

The Elizabethan courtier Thomas Chaloner first praised 'the most rare and excellent virtue of nitre', in a publication dedicated to his cousin, a London apothecary. This was primarily a medical tract in the Paracelsian mode, promoting the use of minerals to cure skin blemishes and illnesses. It recommended saltpeter for lesions and itches, and as a laxative and scouring agent, rather than an instrument of war. Chaloner's nitre was evidently more highly refined, less flammable, and less salt than the powder-maker's raw material. It tasted 'sour sharp, then moderately bitter, and lastly a little rank in the swallowing'. The medical use of saltpeter expanded as 'learned physicians and experimenters' developed their arsenal of cures. Most valuable among its 'manifold and sundry' applications was its contribution to beauty, in a culture that valued a pale and clear complexion. Mixed with honey, herbs, or chicken fat, nitre served to 'scour and cleanse the hair, the face, the skin, and the rest of the body, from rankness of smell and from fumosities, sweat, soil, staining and duskiness of the skin, and to fordo freckles, spotting, tawniness, sunburning, morphews, jaundices, discolourings, scurf, dandruff, scales, scabs, mange, pushes, pimples, ringworms, tetters, roughness, and all such deformities and affects of the skin'. Applied as a plaster, it softened knobs and corns. Bathed in 'young boys' urine', it served as a salve against the itch. Tinctures taken internally were said to unblock encumbrances of 'the liver, spleen, kidneys, matrice, and genitories', as well as the stomach, lungs, bladder, and bowels. Householders could similarly use solutions of nitre to remove 'filthy spots or soil' from silk or leather, and 'for scouring and whiting of linen cloth'.[52] Sir Francis Bacon was said to have dosed himself 'for many years' with small amounts of refined saltpeter, to calm 'the blood and...to condense the spirits'.[53] Cattlemen experimented with saltpeter as a remedy for bovine distemper.[54]

In 1661 the Oxford naturalist Robert Lovell anthologized 'the sum of all authors, both ancient and modern, Galenical and chemical', on this useful subject. Various compounds and tinctures of nitre, he reported, 'may be used both inwardly and outwardly' to 'make women fruitful and assuage tumours', to relieve men's 'inflammations of the testicles', and to cure 'the biting of dogs'.[55] The Restoration chemical physician William Thraster likewise celebrated saltpeter as 'a special key to the alchemist...of a most wonderful nature'. It promised a cure for 'almost uncurable diseases', including cholic, gout, scabs, fistulas, and 'all tumours and inflammations'.[56]

More ambitiously, the Restoration physician William Clarke published *The Natural History of Nitre: or, a Philosophical Discourse of the Nature, Generation, Place, and Artificial Extraction of Nitre, with its Vertues and Uses* (1670), commending its 'excellent' applications. Clarke was convinced that the ancients knew saltpeter, although they remained ignorant of its use in gunpowder. His analysis followed alchemical principles, considering such properties as figure, taste, and flammability, the effects of calcination, sublimation, and distillation, and the mysteries of saltpeter's place in nature. It seemed likely, he believed, to be the 'chief agent' in 'the great elixir' that generations of alchemists had pursued. Aerial nitre, he thought, was responsible for lightning and meteors, just as terrestrial saltpeter caused the 'vehemency' of gunpowder explosions.[57]

Like his fellow 'pyrotechnical speculators', Clarke was fascinated by the mystery of saltpeter as well as its mechanical and medicinal applications. Everyone knew that saltpeter could be found in England 'in our houses on walls, and in the earthen floors of halls, cellars, butteries, etc. and other out-houses, as barns, stables, pigeon houses, etc. which are capable of breeding and retaining it... and whence it is vulgarly known to be extracted'. Its primary application, of course, was the manufacture of gunpowder, where saltpeter was 'the soul of this fiery powder'. But saltpeter had myriad uses, both practical and speculative. Physicians could employ its humoral properties in the treatment of fevers, while more modern chemical practitioners could produce from saltpeter 'a pleasant and cooling acid, or a hot and burning corrosive', with vomitive, purgative, or diuretic effects. Cooks used saltpeter 'to pleasure our English ladies' by giving meat a red colour and 'a more savoury taste'. Not least was its use in industry to make *aqua fortis* (nitric acid) or *aqua regis* (nitro-hydrochloric acid) 'by which are dissolved all metals'. Gold-refiners under Charles I regularly requested a ton or more of saltpeter 'for the drawing of strong water for the fining of gold and the parting of gold from silver for his majesty's service'. Glass-makers under Charles II likewise drew three tons at a time from the ordnance stores. Dyers and engravers also used saltpeter products in their processes.[58]

Further popularizing this tradition, after a century of experiment and speculation, the later Stuart physician William Salmon reviewed both medical and military applications of saltpeter. Among extraordinary alleged benefits to mankind, 'it brings forth tumours... expels winds... resolves coagulated blood, and eases pain'. Mixed with wine or sugar, saltpeter helped against jaundice and was 'good against the asthma'. 'It removes all obstructions of the urine, loosens the belly, provokes stools, and... removes melancholy.' Saltpeter, in sum, had 'more wonderful virtues than other ordinary salts, being one of the most admirable and powerful agents among all natural things'. It was not only admirable 'against the gout and all arthritic pains', but 'held in the mouth it immediately helps the toothache. If burnt and used in a dentifrice, it cleans and whitens the teeth.' Salmon even found saltpeter serviceable against the plague, recalling that in London in 1665, 'not one that I gave it to... died, and such who beforehand constantly used it as a preventative never had the sickness at all'. Its use in gunpowder, *sal bombardicum*, was just as remarkable, though generally taken for granted.[59]

Chemical mysteries

The educated public of the post-Restoration era could learn about the science of saltpeter in such works as Sir John Pettus, *Fleta Minor. The Laws of Art and Nature* (1683, reprinted 1685 and 1686) and *The Works of the Highly Experienced and Famous Chymist John Rudolph Glauber* (1689). Pettus and Glauber both included translations of Lazarus Ercker on 'the manner of boiling saltpeter', finally making this century-old work available in English. Gentlemen who were 'curious in natural philosophy' could also consult George Wilson, *A Compleat Course of Chemistry*, in various editions from 1699, and Nicolas Lémery's *Course of Chymistry*, first translated from the French in 1677.[60] These publications testify to an expansion of popular chemical literacy, and mounting interest in volatile salts, but they continued to recycle older continental knowledge.

Eighteenth-century readers who wished to learn more about saltpeter had few modern texts to turn to, and none (besides Boyle) based on domestic studies. If they picked up *A New Method of Chemistry, Including the Theory and Practice of that Art* (1727) they would find that it was translated from the work of Herman Boerhaave of Leyden. Godfrey Smith's compendium, *The Laboratory, or School of Arts* (1738), advertised 'A dissertation on the nature and growth of saltpeter', but this was based on an older German text. *A Course of Practical Chemistry* (1746) added 'French memoirs' to George Wilson's seventeenth-century text. Discussion of the extraction of nitre and the purification of saltpeter in *Elements of the Theory and Practice of Chemistry* (Edinburgh, 1777) was translated from the French of Pierre-Joseph Macquer from the 1740s. Peter Shaw's *Chemical Lectures* (1734) and Richard Watson's *Chemical Essays* (1781) popularized scientific knowledge but added nothing new.[61] Derived from Glauber, the most advanced science available in revolutionary America understood saltpeter 'to be composed of three different materials: a nitrous acid, a volatile animal salt, and these two … blended together and petrified by a vegetable or mineral alkaline salt'.[62]

George Napier, the controller of George III's Royal Laboratory at Woolwich, knew that saltpeter emerged from the putrification of animal and vegetable substances. His 'Remarks on Nitre' of 1782, comparing the qualities of human and animal urine, pigeon dung, and sawdust, could have been written two hundred years earlier.[63] A treatise published in London in 1783 avowed that the making or refining of saltpeter 'doth not require a knowledge of chemistry, there being no chemical preparation to be performed'. A simple arrangement of pits filled with 'stone lime, wood ashes, wood soot, weeds or sour herbs, urine, brine', and excrement, the author suggested, would guard the English 'against future depredation on their fortunes, from the ruinous system and artful insinuation of foreigners'.[64] Continental chemists, if they read this, could only have laughed.

Despite advances in laboratory science, English understanding of the chemistry of explosives remained backward and derivative. The British scientific tradition from Robert Boyle (1627–1691) to Joseph Priestley (1733–1804) was by no means negligible, but work on gases and combustion contributed little to military technology. The Ordnance Office made vast amounts of gunpowder, almost entirely from imported saltpeter and traditional methods, while scientists focused on other problems.

The most important advances occurred in *ancien régime* France, which lacked England's access to saltpeter from India. Forced after 1757 to rely on domestic resources, the French created a centralized, science-driven saltpeter enterprise for their formidable military forces. It was French gunpowder that made possible the formation of the United States by supplying the American rebels. As the English themselves recognized in 1790, on the eve of yet another European war, 'France produces much more saltpeter than is necessary for its own consumption,' and had reserves enough for four or five years, though it cost slightly more than 'the saltpeter that comes from the East Indies'.[65]

Crucial to French success were the Régie des Poudres and the Académie Royale des Sciences, both headed by Europe's pre-eminent chemist, Antoine Lavoisier (1743–1794). Lavoisier's *Instruction sur l'établissement de nitières et sur la fabrication du salpêtre* (1777) and *Recueil de mémoires sur la formation et sur le fabrication du salpêtre* (1786) had no English equivalent. His experiments on saltpeter refinement and gunpowder detonation led directly to the 'chemical revolution', which English scientists were slow to embrace.[66] By 1830 William IV's Board of Ordnance had learned that 'saltpeter, or nitre, is a combination of nitric acid with vegetable alkali, but is never found pure, being contaminated with other salts and earthy matter, and is totally unfit for gunpowder until it has been refined'.[67] By this time, however, the initiative had shifted to Germany and America, where explosives technology was revolutionized. New sources of nitrates and new technologies of warfare based on high explosives eventually made saltpeter and gunpowder obsolete. Nitroglycerine, dynamite, and trinitrotoluene changed the world, though the interests of science, state policy, and national security remained as entwined and embedded as ever.[68]

Modern chemistry still finds commercial, agricultural, industrial, and pharmacological uses for potassium nitrate, though it is no longer sourced from dung-rich earth. The mysteries that puzzled Bacon and Boyle have mostly been solved. Saltpeter still forms the heart of 'black powder', which has limited applications in mining and weaponry. It is a major component of fertilizers, though not much use for fertilizer bombs, which mostly rely on ammonium nitrate. Saltpeter has been employed to cure meat, to make acids, to manufacture cigarettes, to desensitize toothpaste, and to promote diuresis (increased urination), though excess amounts are known to be toxic. Material safety data sheets warn that potassium nitrate may be hazardous in case of skin contact, ingestion, or inhalation, and may harm the blood, kidneys, and nervous system of those with prolonged exposure. Workers are recommended to wear rubber footwear and aprons, to use safety respirators and gloves, and to take all reasonable precautions. Early modern saltpetermen knew none of this, and it remains unknown what price they paid for close handling of materials and testing them by taste. One hopes that few people followed the advice to use saltpeter in cosmetics.[69]

Saltpeter today is more a source of amusement than the basis of military muscle or medical innovation. Folklore, erroneously, presents saltpeter as a sexual suppressant, said to reduce libido or induce impotence when slipped into a young man's food.[70] Another chain of connection links saltpeter with nitrates and nitric oxide, to experiments with blood pressure and thence to penile erection and Viagra.[71] From the battlefield to the bedroom, from alchemical explorations to the druggist's counter, saltpeter has had multiple, stimulating, and mysterious applications. As Robert Boyle said so persuasively, it warrants our serious enquiries.

2

The Gunpowder Kingship of Henry VIII

SOME time in the 1540s, most likely in the course of Henry VIII's third war with France, David Fynche of London, working in Shropshire to furnish saltpeter for the king's munitions, found himself attacked by angry residents. The townsmen of Shrewsbury railed against him as 'a false knave' and a thief for taking things without paying, and for damaging private property. Fynche insisted he was on the king's business, and cited his commission under the Great Seal 'for taking of wood and breaking of ground at times convenient for making of saltpeter'. Indeed, early Tudor gunners typically had authority to search and dig for saltpeter, and to requisition whatever supplies or equipment they needed to make gunpowder, provided they made good any injuries. David Fynche was a deputy to Anthony of Naples, Henry VIII's Italian master gunner, but this did not shield him from prosecution when a barge he was using for transport spun out of control and destroyed a mooring post in the River Severn. The owner of the mooring sued Fynche for trespass, and the case led to actions at common law and appearances in the equity court of Chancery. Fynche complained to the Lord Chancellor, Sir Thomas Wriothesley, that the post in question was very rotten and not worth twopence, and that the prosecution was driven by malice and hatred of the saltpetermen. Customary processes and legal procedures had to be observed, but the urgency of war made paramount the need for *material for munitions. This case, like many others, pitted the needs of the crown for national security against the common law rights of owners of property. Its outcome in law is unknown, but the king did not lack for munitions.*[1]

* * *

The recent recovery of cannon balls and bullet fragments from the battlefield of Bosworth, Leicestershire, reminds us that both sides in the encounter that took place there in August 1485 had gunpowder weapons. Both Richard III, who died on the battlefield, and Henry VII, who replaced him, understood the importance of firepower. They had learned from the French and Burgundians, northern Europe's leaders in military technology, that no modern state could thrive without handguns and artillery. The first Tudor monarch invested in ordnance and in the foreign specialists who could operate it. His armoury at the Tower grew from thirty heavy guns in 1489 to almost fifty by 1497, and by the end of the fifteenth century Henry VII had 200 gunners on his payroll, many of them Dutch or Flemish.[2]

Early Tudor England shared in the gunpowder economy of Renaissance warfare. Though technically not so advanced as its continental neighbours, the English state marshalled a formidable firepower. Henry VII commanded a variety of explosive resources and military expertise. His son Henry VIII spent extravagantly on garrisons, fortresses, ships, and stores, all furnished with the latest gunpowder weapons. Henry VIII himself took an interest in ordnance, and promoted advances in gunnery and ballistics. Though some historians have associated the weakness of central government in the course of the Wars of the Roses with 'a virtual "dark ages" of military technology which would last for more than a century', the Tudor state that emerged from the wreckage proved capable of complex aggressive campaigns. The most recent scholarship concludes that 'English military theory and practice was broadly in-line with that of its continental neighbours from the outset of the reign of Henry VIII', and perhaps even earlier.[3] The ordnance capacity of the English crown made it a major power in north-west Europe.

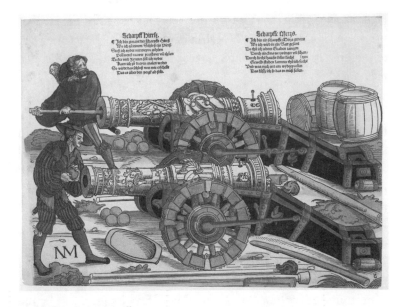

FIG 5 Renaissance artillery

Woodcut (men with cannons) by Erhard Schoen, *c.1535*. © Stiftung Schloss Friedenstein Gotha.

Though overshadowed by the Reformation and the politics of matrimony and religion, Henry VIII's reign (1509–1547) was also a history of battles, sieges, and campaigns. Conceiving himself as a warrior monarch, King Henry fought three wars against France and Scotland from 1512 to 1514, 1522 to 1525, and 1542 to 1546. In addition he supervised the hardening of coastal defences, furnished a gun-equipped navy, crushed a major revolt (the Pilgrimage of Grace), and campaigned repeatedly in Ireland. Henry's state-of-the-art Deal Castle of 1540 was designed to mount 200 cannons. English bastions at Berwick and Calais further projected royal power to the north and south with appropriate firepower. The continental triumphs of Tournai (1513) and Boulogne (1544), and the victories against the Scots at Flodden (1513) and Solway Moss (1542), were rewards for determined preparation. Alongside archers and billmen, Tudor artillery proved decisive. (Billmen wielded long-handled, edged weapons, derived from an agricultural bill-hook.)

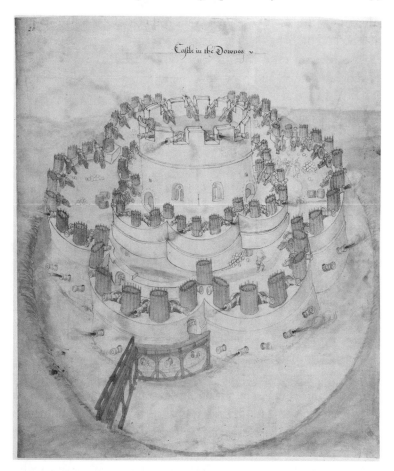

Castle in the Downes

FIG 6 Deal Castle, *c*.1540, 'Castle in the Downes'
British Library, Cotton Ms. Augustus I. i. 20. © The British Library Board (I. i. 20).

Though English longbows shared the field with English cannon, it was modern weaponry that carried the day.[4] The force that invaded France in 1513 carried 510 tons of gunpowder, and its siege guns consumed up to 32 tons a day. The assault on Boulogne in 1544 featured a siege train of 250 guns which hammered the town with 100,000 rounds of heavy shot. Such an intensity of bombardment would not be seen in England until the civil war. Henry VIII's armies were as bloated as the monarch, easily 30,000 strong.

The troops he assembled to invade France in 1544 had at least 38,000 and perhaps as many as 50,000 men, a scale of deployment not seen again until the reign of William III. A survey in 1547 found 415 cannon and over 6,700 handguns in the royal armouries. Tudor field armies carried saltpeter as well as gunpowder, and could be expected to prepare their own munitions.[5]

By forcibly enlisting merchant ships, Henry VIII could put 200 vessels to sea, including his own floating gun platforms. By the end of the reign, Henry's Royal Navy included fifteen 'great ships' and sixteen galleasses, with almost 200 heavy guns of nine pounds or greater calibre between them. Their itemized 'ordnance, artillery, munitions [and] habiliments for the war' included forty-five lasts of gunpowder. The monstrous 1,000-ton *Great Harry* or *Henri Grace à Dieu*, for example, carried two lasts of serpentine powder for its heavy weapons and six barrels of corn powder for its lighter guns. The more modest 140-ton *Dragon* had twenty-six demi-barrels of serpentine and twenty pounds of fine corn powder. All would be expended in a few hours of heavy action.[6]

An urgent matter for contemporaries, though almost unnoticed by most historians, was the procurement of gunpowder and its principal ingredient, saltpeter. Gunpowder monarchs were ciphers unless they could fire their weapons, so they wisely attended to logistics and procurement as well as strategy and diplomacy. Competitive Renaissance kingship involved arsenals and powder magazines as much as courtliness and castles. Traditionalists were grieved to learn that firepower mattered more than chivalry.

Much of Henry VIII's gunpowder, and most of the sulphur and saltpeter it was made from, was imported from continental Europe. Italian merchants, factors, and middlemen helped furnish the royal armouries. German and Flemish specialists supplied materials and skill. The Cavalcanti merchants of Florence were leading financiers and facilitators of this Renaissance international weapons trade. So too were the Steelyard merchants of the Hanseatic League, who delivered 'habiliments of war' from northern Europe. Glimpses of this traffic appear in law suits in Chancery, which document the importation of saltpeter from Palermo

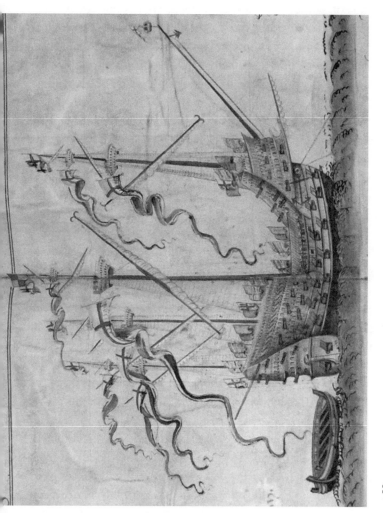

FIG 7 *Great Harry, c.*1545

Pepys Ms. 2991, Anthony Roll, fos. 2–3. © The Pepys Library, Magdalene College, Cambridge.

in the reign of Henry VII, and from the Baltic in the reign of Henry VIII.[7] Warrants for payment also detail imports from southern Europe. In November 1512, for example, the Spaniard Francis de Errona delivered 707 pounds of gunpowder and 2,906 pounds of 'saltpeter in rock' at fourpence per pound. In April 1514 Leonardo Friscobaldi provided the king's powder manufacturers with 46,218 pounds of saltpeter (just over seventeen lasts or twenty tons) at a price of sixpence per pound. The principal suppliers and processers of these materials were all foreign.[8]

To fight the French in 1513, Henry VIII's government contracted with a dozen or more gunfounders, gunmakers, and suppliers of gunpowder and its raw ingredients. The treasury accounts for 1514 include payments for saltpeter, brimstone, and powder to Thomas and John Cavalcanti, who also supplied the king with morris pikes (thrusting weapons), hagbushes (mounted arquebuses), and demi-culverins (in this case, copper cannons from Flanders). Other saltpeter suppliers at this time included Edmond Frende of the Steelyard, Hans Wolf alias Hans van Colen (who was also employed in making gunpowder), and the Lucca merchants Benedict Morovelli and Frances de Bara. English entrepreneurs also profited from the saltpeter trade, including Hugh Clopton, Humphrey Lightfoot, and the haberdasher William Marler. The king's need for weaponry brings these otherwise unknown individuals into history. The mercer William Browne served as factor for the German Hans Wolf on at least one occasion receiving payment 'for making saltpeter within England'.[9]

The English made some saltpeter at home, but never enough for modern warfare. Henry VII authorized James Hede in 1492 to take houses, land, vessels, wood, coals, and other fuel, as well as artificers, labourers, and workmen, to make saltpeter for the king's ordnance. Another patent in 1501 identified Wyvard Godfrey as one of the king's saltpeter-makers and gunners, who received sixpence a day. Officers of the Royal Ordnance knew the rudiments of saltpeter and gunpowder manufacture, but domestic production was too slender for a militarily ambitious monarchy.[10]

A case in Star Chamber sheds more light on the manufacture of gunpowder at the time of Henry VIII's first French war. At issue were accounts of the late master gunner Richard Fawkener 'for workmanship of serpentine powder-making, and for fining of saltpeter in meal', and for making 'saltpeter out of rock into meal' for Sir Sampson Norton, the Master of the Ordnance. Fawkener had established a workshop near London Wall in the parish of St Olave, 'towards the making of serpentine gunpowder and for fining and refining of saltpeter and brimstone out of rock into meal, and for coal powder and other stuff appertaining to the making of gunpowder for the use of the king'. After his death (most likely in 1521) Fawkener's creditors pursued his executor for disputed debts, and the suit reveals something of his manner of work. Fawkener's saltpeter was apparently rock saltpeter, scraped from natural efflorescences, rather than artificial saltpeter manufactured from dung-enriched earth. Sourced from various merchants, it was ground into 'meal' or fine powder, before being mixed to make gunpowder.[11] Other accounts from this period include payment to John Stanget of Ipswich for making saltpeter, though whether from local or imported material is uncertain.[12]

Though the crown operated several mills for making gunpowder, the principal raw materials were still exotic. So too were the leading technicians. The German Hans Wolf made gunpowder at the Tower for Henry VIII, supervised by the king's master gunner, Thomas Hart. His successors included a certain Luke de la Arche and Anthony of Naples. It was the foreigner Wolf who received the first commission to gather saltpeter in England. In 1515, he was authorized 'to go from shire to shire to find a place where there is stuff to make saltpeter of'. A crucial provision stipulated that 'where he and his labourers shall labour, dig, or break in any ground', they were to make compensation to its owner.[13] The stage was set for the establishment of a domestic saltpeter enterprise, and with it a collision of state and popular interests. If crown agents could take military supplies from the private property of the king's subjects, there would be no end of resentment and litigation. The royal quest for saltpeter would test the notion that an Englishman's home was his castle.

A new commission in 1531 empowered Thomas Lee, one of the king's gunners, to be principal searcher and maker of saltpeter in England. He too was authorized to search and dig for saltpeter in the king's lands and elsewhere, to hire workers in the king's name, and to take what wood carriage or houses he needed for the task, provided he paid reasonable compensation. Like Wolf before him and others after, Lee was required to 'replenish and make up plain' all ground that he had dug or broken, so that the owner be not injured.[14]

Records of this early Tudor procurement activity are almost non-existent, but a Chancery suit from the 1540s sheds oblique light on the domestic saltpeter enterprise. David Fynche of London, saltpeterman, was deputy to Anthony of Naples who held the king's commission 'for taking of wood and breaking of ground at times convenient for making of saltpeter'. Exercising this privilege at Shrewsbury, Fynche ran into difficulties when a barge he had engaged accidentally destroyed a mooring post in the River Severn. William Langley, a tailor of Shrewsbury, sued him for trespass, despite Fynche's claim that he was performing the king's business. Other townsmen charged Fynche as 'a false knave, and that he will not be able to pay for such things as he doth take'. A minor incident in a routine excursion revealed local hostility to the king's saltpeterman, and generated actions at common law and before the Lord Chancellor. There would be many more such incidents. The documents indicate that Fynche had excavated lands lately belonging to Shrewsbury abbey, and had set up a system of leaching and boiling to extract saltpeter.[15]

Another Chancery suit a few years later referred to the furnaces involved in saltpeter manufacture. Richard Browne, mercer, of Poole, Dorset, sought recovery of a furnace 'for making of saltpeter in the town of Wimborne Minster...for the king's affairs'. Exercising a superior commission, perhaps at the time of the Boulogne expedition of 1544, the mayor of Poole requisitioned Browne's furnace, promising to return it in good order with five shillings for his pains. But the mayor found Browne's furnace to be insufficient, and combined its parts with another furnace 'for the making of saltpeter'. After the military emergency was over and 'the making of saltpeter was ended', Browne sought the return of his furnace, first at common law and then in Chancery. The dispute turned on the terms of the arrangement and the condition of the furnace, but it also revealed an active programme of boiling in southern England.[16] No longer reliant on rock saltpeter, the Ordnance Office by now had thirty years' experience of extracting saltpeter from suitable domestic earths.

Knowledge of European processes for the manufacture of gunpowder and saltpeter seeped into England during Henry VIII's reign. Some came with specialist technicians, such as Hans Wolf and Anthony of Naples. More came from publications, not yet translated, such as Vannoccio Biringuccio's *De la pirotechnia* (Venice, 1540). Another Italian treatise on gunpowder, *Quesiti et inventioni diverse* (Venice, 1546) by the mathematician Niccolò Tartaglia, carried a dedication to Henry VIII, with expectations that it would be well received. An English diplomat in Venice sent a copy to London in the hope that the king 'of his noble and bountiful nature' would accept it.[17] It was well known that Henry VIII would patronize foreign talent, and his military ambitions opened doors to experts from overseas.

More transfers of technology accompanied the German military engineer Stefan von Haschenperg, who was employed to modernize Henry VIII's fortresses. In 1545 von Haschenperg offered Henry 'a way of making saltpeter, otherwise called black vitriol, in one place without going about the realm searching for it'.[18] Concentrated saltpeter farms or nitre beds had been established in Germany but remained untried in England. If experiments began under von Haschenperg's guidance they were tentative and small in scale, and left no record.

Henry VIII's wars dipped deep into his gunpowder reserves, and every crisis required merchants and manufacturers to furnish more munitions. A survey in September 1523 found just thirteen lasts of powder in the Tower, after eight lasts had been committed to the Scottish campaign. In February 1536 the Tower held thirty-nine lasts and eleven barrels of gunpowder, with only four lasts of saltpeter on hand to make more.[19] A powerful state could not afford such poverty of supply. The fleet alone required forty-five lasts per campaign, the army even more. The renewed wars of the 1540s required substantial purchases of gunpowder and saltpeter from northern Europe, at the very time when other combatants were shopping in the same market.[20]

On Henry's behalf his agent William Damesell spent thousands of pounds securing gunpowder at Antwerp, warning in August 1544 that the price would soon rise 'because of the scarcity of saltpeter'. Scouring Flanders for materials for war, the English learned by early autumn that 'there is no gunpowder to be had in all these quarters'. Damesell looked further afield, towards Bremen, Hamburg, and Lubeck, because that was where saltpeter was said to be sourced.[21] Thomas Asheley, one of the grooms of the Chamber, was also commissioned to go abroad to buy saltpeter for the king.[22] All of Europe demanded weaponry, and many of its states were enmeshed in war. Among the final warrants of Henry VIII's reign were payments of £100 to Francis Fleming (Francis the Fleming?) for making an Ordnance House at the Tower of London, and reimbursement of £400 'to be repaid to Bartholomew Fortune for saltpeter' and other warlike materials.[23]

The mid-Tudor regimes of Edward VI (1547–1553) and Mary I (1553–1558) lacked Henry VIII's martial ambition, but they too looked to Europe for habiliments of war. King Edward's Council was able to buy saltpeter from Flanders at forty-six shillings Flemish the hundredweight (approximately £3 in a volatile currency exchange).[24] A continental intelligencer told William Cecil in 1551 that there was 'great plenty of saltpeter' in Germany, 'which the English lack, and need not if they take pains'.[25] It was tempting to imagine that German techniques as well as German products (perhaps gunpowder with a Lutheran flavour) would augment Protestant England's security.

Mary Tudor and her husband, Philip, relied primarily on Spanish Flanders for munitions, especially powder, saltpeter, and armaments from Antwerp. But this supply was too often interrupted when the continental Hapsburg powers pre-empted material for themselves.[26] Frailties in the chain of supply led to arguments in favour of domestic provision, but there is little evidence of excavation and boiling in England in the 1550s. Responsible planners understood that without saltpeter the state was in peril, but mid-Tudor governments preferred not to trouble their subjects for it, but to import saltpeter from abroad.

3

The Elizabethan Quest for Infinite Security

IN the autumn of 1577 the Flemish merchant Cornelius Stephinson offered Lord Burleigh ambitious plans for a major saltpeter plant on royal forest land in Hampshire. He promised 'the furniture of her majesty with a great quantity of saltpeter, so her majesty would make him a lease of four hundred acres of ground in the New Forest'. The land was mostly heath and furze, with stands of beech, oak, thorn, and holly, which could provide the necessary charcoal for fuel and ash for refining. In exchange for a fifty-year monopoly, the projector offered to supply twenty tons of saltpeter a year, 'good perfect and well-refined', as much as twenty per cent of the nation's peacetime requirements. This arrangement, Stephinson's supporters avowed, would not only save the crown money, but would 'avoid the wonderful vexation of her majesty's people, so miserably plagued in their houses, in their carriage, in their wood and timber, in their exactions of money', by conventional saltpeter gathering.[1]

Stephinson's plan was for an artificial nitre bed of the kind that was known in Germany but had never successfully operated in England. It envisaged control of the nitrification process as well as industrial-scale processing of its product. But every stage of the project proved difficult. Problems with equipment, labour, and funding proved as burdensome as objections from holders of traditional forest rights. The project succumbed to delays and deficiencies, and although some usable saltpeter resulted it *never came close to the amount that was promised. Nor did any other scheme for the centralized manufacture of saltpeter prove more successful. The abandoned remains of Stephinson's facility are still discernible near Ashurst Lodge in the New Forest in southern England, a faint reminder of another failed project.*[2]

* * *

Enmeshed in struggles with France and Scotland, and with menaces looming at home and abroad, the government that came to power in November 1558 was painfully aware of its weaknesses. Facing a confessionally divided continent, dangerous shifts in European power balances, the flames of the Dutch insurgency, and worsening relationships with Spain, the Elizabethan state confronted conspiracy and rebellion at home, and fell into a generation of debilitating foreign war. Whether supporting Dutch rebels, confronting Spanish ships, probing distant oceans, or campaigning to quell Ireland, the crown needed effective procurement of weaponry and supplies. As Thomas Gresham and William Cecil recognized at the outset of Elizabeth's reign, the demand for gunpowder would be enormous if a 'breach of amity should chance betwixt her majesty and King Philip'.[3] Even before that breach opened, Elizabethan England was drawn deeper into the 'military revolution' that transformed the killing power of forces and stretched the finances of the early modern state.[4] Like its European neighbours and rivals, the Elizabethan regime hungered for gunpowder for its troops and warships, fortresses, and stores.

The Elizabethan treasury spent heavily on warships, to build (in Geoffrey Parker's words) 'the most powerful battle fleet afloat anywhere in the world'. Ordnance accounts of 1578 listed 504 naval 'pieces' aboard twenty-three royal ships, a force that was rapidly expanded. Packed with powder, the thirty-four royal ships that fought the Armada in 1588 carried 678 bronze or brass guns, more than triple the cannonry of Henry VIII's navy. These were supplemented by close to a 150 armed merchantmen. By 1595 the queen commanded thirty-eight fighting ships, with even more firepower. A survey in 1603 listed 1,170 pieces of naval ordnance, including 625 heavy guns rated demi-culverin or above.[5]

The naval demand for gunpowder was insatiable. A twenty-gun ship, of the kind that fought the Armada, could fire each of its cannon fifteen to eighteen times before having to be resupplied. Full cannon consumed as much as forty-six pounds of gunpowder a shot; culverins and demi-culverins, the backbone of naval ordnance, used eighteen and eleven pounds of powder respectively each time they were fired. On the Cadiz expedition in 1596 the queen's ships were issued an average of two and half lasts (sixty barrels), and the monstrous thirty-eight-gun *Ark Royal* set out with four lasts (ninety-six barrels, weighing roughly four and a quarter tons).[6] Land forces, militia training, coastal defences, and celebratory salutes added to the account. 'For powder for small shot, it is necessary there be always in store twenty lasts', insisted planners for the garrison at Brill in 1587.[7] At the height of its war with Spain the Elizabethan state consumed close to a hundred lasts of gunpowder a year.

Where did all this powder come from? Large amounts arrived from abroad. More was manufactured from imported raw materials. To shake off its reliance on foreign saltpeter, Queen Elizabeth's Council encouraged schemes for domestic production. The saltpeter project they established faced endless difficulties, both social and technological, but eventually put the country on the path to 'infinite security'.[8] This chapter tells part of that story.

Foreign dependency

In the very first month of Queen Elizabeth's reign, her ministers took stock of the nation's supplies of saltpeter and gunpowder, observing ruefully, 'better it is to have than wanting to wish'.[9] Under the direction of Sir William Cecil (ennobled 1571 as Lord Burleigh) Elizabeth's Council embarked on an urgent programme to obtain 'munitions for the wars' from continental suppliers. This was 'a dangerous merchandize', vulnerable to fire and shipwreck as well as interception and embargo. The Council was willing to pay premium prices for imported saltpeter and gunpowder, and would sometimes wink at smuggling to avoid hostile Hapsburg eyes.[10]

The international arms trade offered rich rewards, as ever, and English, Flemish, and Italian merchants lined up to meet the queen's needs.[11] In December 1558 the Italian Marco Antonio Erizzo offered to supply saltpeter at £4 13s. 4d. a hundredweight, which an English assessor judged, 'exceedeth our price in every hundredweight by ten shillings'. In 1561 the price came down to £3 10s. a hundredweight but was still considered excessive. At twenty shillings a hundredweight, however, Italian sulphur from Naples was better priced than 'brimstone of Osterland', and might even be obtained cheaper. The deal was sealed in March 1561 when the Italian promised sixty-five tons of 'saltpeter of Naples' at £3 5s. a hundredweight, and brimstone at eighteen shillings. Recognizing that the gunpowder revolution was far from complete, the Council also ordered 20,000 wooden bow staves with this consignment, at a total outlay of £6,050.[12]

Elizabeth's agent in Flanders, Sir Thomas Gresham (who in 1565 would establish the Royal Exchange), spent close to £10,000 in January 1559 for the royal armoury, and more in the months that followed. By the summer of 1560, on behalf of an impoverished crown whose funds seemed nevertheless unlimited, he had cornered the market in Germany and the Netherlands, importing over 200 tons of saltpeter. This gave England a safety margin of more than two years' supply.[13] Some of Gresham's 'Osterland' saltpeter cost £4 a hundredweight ('more by 3s. 4d. in the hundred than his commission allows') and needed further refinement before it could be used to make gunpowder.[14] But money was not the only measure of its value. Writing to Cecil in March 1563, Gresham extolled the advantages of stockpiling saltpeter, 'for there is no weapon esteemed as the gun is'. He urged the queen 'to make stout provision of saltpeter', assuring the Council that '£20,000 of it would stand her in better stead than in laying up £100,000 in gold and treasure'. It became almost proverbial, though hyperbolic, that saltpeter was worth its weight in gold.

Cecil agreed that munitions were a measure of a regime's stand-
ing, since bow staves no longer commanded the field.[15] Like many
other governments before and since, the crown was willing to
take on debt rather than deprive itself of essential military
provisions.

Elizabethan ordnance procurers were always alert for alternative sources and better bargains. While relying principally on the
markets of Hamburg, Antwerp, and Amsterdam, they cast further
afield for saltpeter from 'parts beyond the seas'. Gresham's agents
scoured Hungary and Bohemia in the spring of 1560 but found
'nothing good to be had'. In 1561 they obtained saltpeter from
Denmark. Baltic ports appeared promising, and in 1569 the Arctic
trader Stephen Borough brought home cargoes of saltpeter and
brimstone from the far north.[16]

The Elizabethan quest for saltpeter extended to North Africa.
As early as 1573 English imports from Europe were being supplemented by occasional shipments of saltpeter from the Barbary
coast of Morocco. English merchants offered cannon balls in
exchange for sugar and saltpeter, and tried to keep their dealings
secret from the Portuguese.[17] In June 1581, 'for maintenance of her
majesty's munitions', the queen herself signed the warrant for her
merchant John Symcot to export 600 tons of timber to Morocco
and 'to bring back into England as much saltpeter as he could get
in exchange for the said wood'.[18] In later years the Council considered trade with Russia and Persia, and proposed to send experienced men to learn the manufacture of saltpeter in those
places.[19]

War with Spain increased England's need for munitions while
restricting foreign sources of supply. The Ordnance Office
imported whatever it could buy, imposing exceptional demands
on its Dutch and German suppliers. In 1590, for example, saltpeter reached England from Emden, Stade, Hamburg, and
Lübeck. The Dutch arms dealer Giles de Vischer complained in
1591 of his loss delivering forty lasts of saltpeter to the Tower.[20]
Saltpeter as well as sulphur also arrived from Venice, incurring
the displeasure of the King of Spain.[21]

Patents and projects

Why could saltpeter not be made in England? A fledgling salt-peter enterprise existed under the earlier Tudors, but by the mid-sixteenth century it had all but vanished. Elizabethan councillors turned afresh to the 'benefits to her majesty and her highness's subjects, by the making saltpeter and gunpowder within this realm', and entertained proposals for domestic production. To furnish saltpeter, said Lord Treasurer Burleigh, was 'the greatest service that could be done for the security of the kingdom, especially the strength of wars being altered from bows and arrows to ordnance'.[22] All that was needed to secure this strategic material was organization, skill and money, the backing of the state, and cooperation from local landowners and officials. Foreign expertise would prove indispensable, as it had in the days of Henry VIII.

The principal justification for an English saltpeter programme, often repeated by Privy Councillors, was that it offered 'infinite security to her majesty and the state, that the land hath means in itself to defend itself, and offend the common enemies thereof'. Domestic provision would reduce reliance on international merchants, and avoid situations when foreign powers restricted the trade in munitions. The Duke of Alva's closure of the Hapsburg ports in the 1560s and the Duke of Pomerland's embargo on salt-peter at the time of the Cadiz expedition in 1595 drew particular attention to England's dependency. A domestic supply of salt-peter would be cheaper, experts reasoned, with less risk of loss, delay, or interception. Home-produced saltpeter, some claimed, was better subject to quality control. The foreign product, asserted the powder-maker Francis Lee, was overpriced and unreliable; it was sometimes excessively moist, and the gunpowder it yielded was prone to decay. An English enterprise promised the likelihood of financial profits, with the additional benefit of creating jobs and setting the poor to work. (See the appendix to this chapter for Robert Cecil's comprehensive 'remembrance of certain benefits to her majesty and her subjects, by making saltpeter and gunpowder within this realm', dated September 1600.)[23]

The government's need for saltpeter created opportunities for projectors and entrepreneurs and brought forth foreign experts who were willing to transfer their skills. In March 1561, in the same week when Marco Antonio was tendering to sell saltpeter from Naples, a German engineer, Gerard Hoenrich, offered to reveal 'the true and perfect art of making saltpeter to grow in cellars, barns, or in lime or stone quarries' in England. He explained to the Council how the mixing of earth with urine, horse dung, and lime could produce 'the mother of saltpeter' which could then be refined and crystallized. The plan called for a network of nitre beds, in which saltpeter would be nourished, and central plants for its boiling and extraction. Envisioning an industrial system of vats, chambers, brickwork, and furnaces, Hoenrich convinced the Council that he knew his business. He advised, for example, that black earth worked best, from cold and dry places; the best urine came 'of those persons which drink either wine or strong beer', the best dung 'of those horses which be fed with oats, and be afterwards kept in the stable', and the most serviceable lime from oyster shells or plaster of Paris. Sea coal, he suggested, would serve as well as charcoal for fuel for boiling, and might even be cheaper.[24] Backed by Cecil, Hoenrich entered into the first agreement to make industrial saltpeter for the English crown. His transfer of technology would earn him £300. But two months later the German complained that he had not been paid properly for revealing his secrets, and the enterprise as he envisaged it was abandoned.

Instead the government awarded an exclusive licence to the mercer Philip Cockeram and the haberdasher John Barnes to supply saltpeter from within the queen's dominions. Their monopoly would last ten years provided the 'new invention' (not specified, but perhaps derived from Hoenrich) proved 'to be of such utility and profit as is pretended'. The grant to Cockeram and Barnes empowered them to search and dig any suitable ground so long as they did not cause 'undue vexation' to the queen's subjects. The partners, in effect, were Elizabeth's first saltpetermen, with more of a foraging project than a programme of biochemical engineering. If their work took them into people's houses, barns, or stables, they were supposed to offer 'satisfaction' to the owners for any damage they caused.[25] Here again, as in Hans Wolf's project of 1515, was the problem that would bedevil saltpeter procurement for a hundred years: how to meet the security needs of the crown without trampling too heavily on the rights of the subject.

The early Elizabethan operation was experimental, small in scale, and not highly successful. But other projectors soon sought patents to find or manufacture saltpeter in England. The ingredients, as the German had listed them, were not hard to find. The trick was to locate suitable nitrate-rich soil, to extract the chemical from the earth, and to set up a process to leach out, crystallize, and refine the native saltpeter. A textbook published in April 1562 explained how it should be done. Derived from the Italian Biringuccio's *De la pirotechnia,* published in Venice in 1540, Peter Whitehorne's *Certain Waies for the orderyng of Souldiers in battelray* outlined the basic process of lixiviation, straining, and boiling, to make 'saltpeter most white and fair'. The work was attached to Whitehorne's translation of Machiavelli's *Art of War* (1562), and was reprinted in 1574 and 1588.[26] Other knowledge circulated in manuscript or by trial and error.

Over the next decade a procurement system developed that would serve until the 1640s. Answerable to the Privy Council and the Lords of the Admiralty, the Commissioners for Gunpowder and Saltpeter supervised the Ordnance Office, who engaged with regional saltpetermen to supply raw materials.[27] The crown saltpetermen, a dozen or so somewhat shady men of business, accepted commissions to deliver set amounts from designated territories or groups of counties. They in turn employed deputies and agents, down to the workmen who did the actual digging and boiling, who were the immediate cause of the subjects' 'vexation'. The crown claimed the prerogative right to sole control of this business, comparable to its command of the mines of precious metals, and often spoke of 'the mines of saltpeter'. Although there were periodic attempts to cultivate saltpeter and force its nourishment through biochemical means, the main domestic enterprise involved

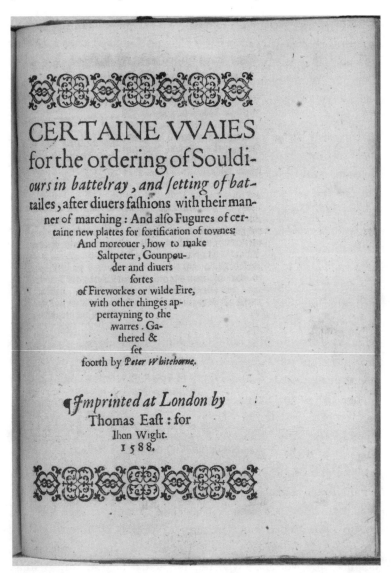

FIG 8 How to make saltpeter

Peter Whitehorne, *Certaine Waies for the ordering of Souldiours in battelray…And moreover, how to make Saltpeter, Gounpouder, and divers sortes of Fireworkes* (1588), title page (Huntington Library, rare book 62010, reproduced by permission of the Huntington).

prospecting for suitable earth, and digging wherever it was found.

The saltpetermen were roving entrepreneurs who contributed increasing amounts to England's military posture. Their names appear from time to time in government records, usually when making deliveries to the Tower or struggling to thwart their rivals. Year by year their reach expanded and their technological acumen improved. The gunpowder patentees of 1562—Brian Hogge, Robert Thomas, and Francis Lee—contracted to use both domestic and imported saltpeter in making a hundred lasts of corn powder and a hundred lasts of serpentine powder each year. Such targets would require 150 lasts of saltpeter (180 tons), and it is unlikely that more than a small fraction came from English earth.[28] By the late 1560s the brothers Thomas and Robert Robinson were established as saltpetermen, though their early efforts met less than a tenth of the crown's needs. In 1589 they claimed to have been making saltpeter for twenty-seven or twenty-eight years, from the first introduction of that art into England.[29] In 1569, when the rebellion of the northern earls exposed England's dependency on foreign supplies and 'no provision was to be had', the powderman Francis Lee proudly remembered, 'they found means in that extremity to make saltpeter within this realm and did convert the same into powder'.[30]

A fresh commission in 1569, renewed in 1573, empowered the Earl of Warwick, Master of the Ordnance, and his lieutenant William Pelham, 'to dig and break ground in...stables and other places convenient for saltpeter' and to supply the same to the queen's stores. Their warrant extended to castles and former monasteries as well as agricultural lands. Warwick and Pelham were not about to get their hands dirty, but delegated the task to agents and assigns. Their commission allowed them to buy wood, faggots, turf, peat, coal, barrels, and casks, and to take up such labourers and carriage as they needed.[31]

All the queen's saltpeter, whether domestic or exotic, went to the royal gunpowder mills. There would be no unlicensed manufacture of such a dangerous and vital material. The main facilities were along the Thames, from Kingston upriver to Rotherhithe downstream, and by the Tower. Exchequer receipts occasionally shed light on this traffic. In 1574, for example, the *John* of Maldon delivered one hogshead and two small barrels of saltpeter, the *Jonas* delivered one hogshead, and the *Edward* one heavy barrel. These sailing barges from the Essex marshes delivered small loads to Robert Hogge at the Minories, 'to the queen's majesty's use in saltpeter'.[32] Adjacent to the Tower of London, these munitions works at the Minories used facilities from a dissolved convent of Minoresses, and would flourish for more than 200 years. The area around Dock Street, to the east of the Tower, was known until the nineteenth century as Saltpetre Bank.

Faced with pressing needs and an uncertain supply, Elizabeth's government made generous bestowal of 'exclusive' privileges to suppliers of weapons-grade material. But patents could be called in as easily as they were extended, and saltpetermen who thought they had monopolies discovered that in fact they had competition. In 1575 the London gentleman John Bovyat obtained an exclusive patent to manufacture saltpeter and gunpowder from stone mineral. Having travelled abroad, at great cost and risk, to find out 'the secret and hidden mystery' of this mode of extraction, Bovyat secured a monopoly privilege for twenty-one years. The grant entitled him to prospect on any subject's land within the queen's dominions, and promised him assistance from all mayors, justices, constables, bailiffs, and local officers. However, it left intact the rights of other projectors 'that have heretofore usually made their saltpeter and gunpowder of mud walls or earth', by more conventional methods.[33] Bovyat immediately sought parliamentary protection and endorsement of his patent, and periodically petitioned (in 1581 and 1595) that his grant be continued. On one occasion he asked Lord Burleigh 'whether he shall go forward with the same, or whether so great a treasure shall be smothered and lost', but there is little evidence to show that his efforts were productive.[34]

Despite these grants and patents, the queen received precious little powder from domestic sources before the start of the Spanish war. An Ordnance Office analysis in 1571 found less than ten per cent of the saltpeter used to make gunpowder in England to be home-produced, though twenty years later a figure approaching thirty per cent became possible.[35] The royal gunpowder-maker Francis Lee claimed in 1575 that although he had made powder from saltpeter gathered in England, the realm remained dangerously dependent on supplies from Hamburg, Antwerp, and Barbary. These imports, he warned, were of dubious quality and the supply was easily interrupted.[36]

Faced with a worsening international situation, and looming threats from the Hapsburg powers, Elizabeth's Privy Council sought new ways to secure domestic supplies of saltpeter. They turned again to foreign experts such as Leonard Engelbreght (or Engelstedt) of Aachen, who negotiated with Burleigh in 1577 for a twenty-year privilege to make saltpeter in England. The deal with the German met difficulties, however, when a more plausible and better backed project came to hand.[37] In the autumn of 1577 the Flemish merchant Cornelius Stephinson presented ambitious plans for a major saltpeter plant on royal forest land in Hampshire. He offered 'the furniture of her majesty with a great quantity of saltpeter, so her majesty would make him a lease of four hundred acres of ground in the New Forest'. This was mostly heath and furze, with stands of beech, oak, thorn, and holly, which could provide the necessary charcoal for fuel and ash for straining. The project had the support of the royal postmaster, Sir Thomas Randolph, and Sir Edward Horsey, Captain of the Isle of Wight. Randolph praised Stephinson's mastery of a near-secret art. If successful, it would 'supply such a want as this realm cannot be without'.[38] Confidence in this augmentation of supply may have shaped the decision in April 1578 to allow the export of 4,000 pounds of saltpeter and gunpowder (forty barrels) to the Dutch rebel city of Ghent.[39]

Cornelius (as most of the records refer to him) secured his grant and began to set up his furnace and tubs, but the project proved more difficult than imagined. Problems with equipment, labour and funding handicapped the operation. Holders of traditional common rights in the New Forest objected to this alien intrusion. The project was supposed to deliver twenty tons of saltpeter a year, 'good perfect and well-refined', but never came close to that amount. In July 1579 Cornelius sought pardon from Lord Burleigh for his deficiencies and requested more time to produce the saltpeter he had promised.[40] A year later, amid fears of a Spanish descent on Ireland, Sir Edward Horsey assured Burleigh that 'Cornelius is now boiling of his earth', but it had not yet 'come to perfection'. But by this time the Fleming faced ruin, with the failure of 'a thing which the multitude thought impossible to be done'.[41]

The remains of Stephinson's saltpeter facility are still discernible on the ground, just short of Ashurst Lodge, Hampshire, in the New Forest. A sketch plan of another plant near Ispwich, dated 1593, shows a similar arrangement of enclosures and embankments that may have served as beds for nourishing the production of saltpeter.[42] The technology of generating saltpeter was in fact quite widely known, but centralized operations of this sort contributed little to the Elizabethan ordnance effort. The Council was always interested in alternative means of securing or processing saltpeter, at home or abroad, but rarely offered financial support. In June 1583 they took note of Henry Pope's experiments at Fulstone, Yorkshire, where material excavated from a local cliff yielded promising results. All being well, Pope assured Secretary Walsingham, he hoped to produce a ton of saltpeter by midsummer, though there is no evidence that he was successful.[43]

The outbreak of war in 1585 heightened Burleigh's anxiety about England's vulnerability, and put all his provision for the husbanding of gunpowder to the test. More saltpeter than ever was needed for the royal stores, and every effort was made to find it abroad or at home. English and foreign merchants brought in tons of saltpeter for the Ordnance Office, and experts both native and foreign offered to augment supplies. Before 1588 'the principal provision for the kingdom was of foreign gunpowder', according to a late Elizabethan survey, but afterwards the balance shifted to domestic production. The target in 1588 was 120 lasts of gunpowder,

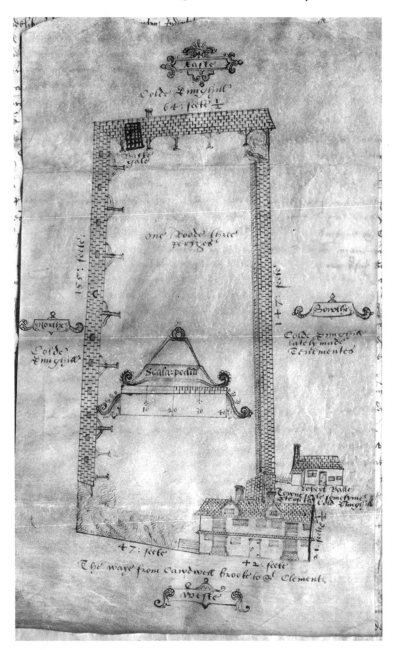

FIG 9 Saltpeter works at Ipswich, 1593

Suffolk Record Office, Ipswich, C/3/8/4/31, Ipswich Records, reproduced by permission of Ipswich Borough Council.

for which eighty-three lasts of saltpeter would be needed.[44] Fourteen named saltpetermen between them delivered 652 hundredweight (twenty-seven lasts) in the year ending October 1589, which was still less than a third of the total required. The list did not include John Grange, a veteran saltpeterman, whose ten sets of tubs in the City of London made 200 hundredweight of saltpeter a year (approximately eight lasts).[45] By 1589 George and John Evelyn held the principal contract to manufacture gunpowder, in partnership with Richard Hill, and their family would dominate the business for more than fifty years.[46]

The crisis of 1588 put English ordnance provision to the test. The queen put thirty-four ships to sea with some 678 heavy guns, or 883 total cannon.[47] More gunpowder furnished shore batteries and castles, Leicester's army at Tilbury, local trained bands, and England's allies in Holland. But despite repeated references to 'scarcity', the supply of powder never ran out. English naval gunners acquitted themselves admirably against the Spanish Armada, and their munitions outmatched those of the enemy. Burleigh's policy of saltpeter procurement enabled Elizabeth's regime to meet its most dangerous challenge, but with very little in reserve.

In March 1588 the Ordnance Office reported that 'there remaineth in her majesty's store 112 thousandweight of saltpeter [approximately forty-two lasts] which converted into powder will make sixty lasts of fine corn powder … of which provision there is great want, the present store being but fifty-eight lasts'. Three-quarters of a year later, after the most demanding expenditure of military materials in Tudor naval history, the gunpowder store had been replenished. An inventory at the Tower in December 1588 found sixty lasts of corn powder on hand, and enough saltpeter to make twenty lasts more.[48] England had weathered the storm, and still had munitions on hand. There would even be gunpowder to supply the queen's allies. Several friendly shipments crossed the Channel, including 400 barrels of powder for the French in January 1591.[49]

The Armada crisis accelerated the English saltpeter enterprise. Several projectors offered plans to boost the supply, and incidentally

FIG 10 Loading and aiming cannon

Joseph Boillot, *Artifices de Feu, & divers Instruments de Guerre* (Strasburg, 1603), p. 123 (Huntington Library, rare book 752893, reproduced by permission of the Huntington).

to make themselves wealthy. 'Knowing peter and powder to be at a very high rate and her majesty's stores not well furnished', Ralph Hockenhull and his backers came up with a scheme in 1588 to take over the saltpeter business in London. At this time, saltpeter was 'worth five or six pounds the hundredweight, by reason of the Spaniards being on the narrow seas'. But it soon emerged that Hockenhull was short-changing the crown, despite the national emergency, and selling black powder on the black market. His rival, the Londoner John Grange who made these charges, offered to supply saltpeter to the crown at the old rate of £3 6s. 8d. per hundredweight. Grange, who had been making saltpeter in London since around 1578, claimed to have learned his art 'under the Prince of Orange in the Low Countries as also in divers countries out of Christendom'.[50]

The experienced powder-maker Francis Lee, son of a munitions supplier to Henry VIII, proposed another scheme in 1588 to boil saltpeter using sea coal, 'a secret never found before' (despite Gerard Hoenrich's experiments with this fuel a quarter of a century earlier). All he needed was a thirty-year exclusive grant, and his operation at Rotherhithe would supply the queen with gunpowder at ninepence per pound, or £3 15s. a hundredweight.[51]

Yet another scheme to transform the saltpeter industry came from Christopher Coult and his associates. Coult informed Burleigh in October 1588 that his many years of foreign travel had taught him 'many things worthy the learning', including 'a perfect way to find out saltpeter and the making of powder, both good and profitable to serve any prince'. Understanding that 'in this time of trouble there hath been some want of powder', Coult offered to show the Council how 'to find out more saltpeter and deliver more powder than all England shall need'. The scheme entailed centralized direction of a national rotation of saltpeter kettles, fifteen to a region, which would deliver 5,000 hundredweight of saltpeter a year (enough for more than 300 lasts of gunpowder). It was preposterously ambitious, alien to English instincts, and seems to have come to nothing.[52]

Expertise from Bohemia arrived in 1589 in the form of a paper on 'the right and most perfect way of the whole work of saltpeter making'. The work of the metallurgist Joachim Gaunz of Prague (a true rarity, a Jew in Elizabethan England and, remarkably, a veteran of Raleigh's Roanoke venture to America), it was based on a treatise by Lazarus Ercker, chief master of Rudolf II's imperial mines, that had been published in German in 1574 and 1580. Observing that saltpetermen in England 'work blindly and without knowledge', with more loss than profit, Gaunz offered to set the enterprise on a firmer scientific basis, explaining the varying properties of earth, techniques for boiling, congealing, refining, and separating, and the disposal of the used earth 'that the same may after serve again'. Crucial to Gaunz's method was the careful measuring, weighing, and assaying of samples, to gauge 'whether it be worth the doing'. In 1589 Gaunz faced charges of blasphemy for denying the divinity of Jesus, and his forty-page manuscript, dedicated to Sir Francis Walsingham, may have been designed to secure him his liberty. Its survival among the papers of Lord Burleigh testifies to its military and economic significance, though there is no evidence that its insights were ever applied.[53]

Saltpeter projects continued to occupy the government's attention. In June 1589 the Privy Council received a petition from Thomas and Robert Robinson for the privilege of setting up saltpeter works within the City of London. The Robinsons offered to supply twenty thousandweight yearly (enough for a dozen lasts of gunpowder) 'without troubling her majesty's subjects for the same'.[54] The following year the Council awarded a twenty-one-year contract to Robert Constable, esquire, his deputies, factors, and assigns, 'to dig open and work for saltpeter' in Yorkshire, Nottinghamshire, Lancashire, Northumberland, Westmorland, and the lands of the Bishopric of Durham. Local officials were enjoined to assist them 'in all things necessary'.[55] They granted more privileges, powers, and authority to saltpetermen in 1592, and in 1595 gave countenance to a proposal to obtain saltpeter in Wales.[56]

This was the environment in which the courtier Hugh Plat, fascinated by 'profitable inventions', projected yet another 'secret' for multiplying the store of saltpeter. Plat wrote in 1594 of 'a new course in the making of saltpeter, far exceeding the common practice at this day used', promising efficiencies in labour and fuel 'without committing such offences as are daily offered, in the breaking up of stables, barns, cellars, etc.' He offered to 'discover' this 'conceit' to the saltpeter patentees, in exchange for one-third of their profit, but his scheme was never adopted.[57]

Yet another projector, John Wrenham, one of the queen's saltpeter patentees, claimed in 1602 to have 'an invention for making saltpeter without digging up any house', and offered to set it up at his own charge, 'if he may have the benefit thereof for forty years'. The plan involved some sort of spreading ground and 'the preparation of earths fit for the generation of saltpeter' that might 'grow to perfection'. Sir John Davies wrote to Sir Robert Cecil in 1602 commending this proposal 'to find a matter for saltpeter to serve perpetually within a mile of London, be the occasions never so great'. If successful, it would 'save her majesty instantly a fourth part of all the powder spent in her shipping, which amounteth commonly to fifty lasts'.[58] Similar schemes emerged from time to time for centralizing the saltpeter process but none of them came to fruition. Late Tudor England still relied on importers for the bulk of its saltpeter, and on roving saltpetermen for its home-made supplement.

Exactions

Elizabethan councillors aspired to national sufficiency in munitions, and wished to exploit the 'mines' of saltpeter more effectively, but they recognized that the collection and processing of earth caused 'vexation'. It could not be done without digging and damage, intrusion, 'discommodity', and distress. Though the security of the realm was paramount, the rights of the subject could not be ignored. The trick, wrote Lord Burleigh in 1588, was 'to provide for her majesty's stores by all means possible', while minimizing or deflecting complaints. One possible means was to direct prospectors to the property of 'inferior persons', in order that 'the grounds of the better sort not [be] meddled with', though this only displaced discontent to another social level.[59] The aim was to keep social costs to a minimum without jeopardizing supplies of materials for war.

The balance between domestic and strategic ambitions was maintained as much by rhetoric as by policy and law. Because England's foreign danger was so pressing, with Rome and Spain threatening ruin, the case for national security was made easily. Who could gainsay the queen's need for gunpowder, or the necessary work of her saltpetermen, when God's enemies were active on the narrow seas? Surely Elizabeth's loyal subjects would permit the digging of their grounds it if helped to keep Spain and the papists at bay.

The social cost of saltpeter gathering was understood to be one reason the country relied so heavily on imports. The powdermaker Francis Lee claimed in 1575 that the queen's reluctance 'to have her subjects' houses digged' encouraged dependence on foreign supplies. Lee himself offered twice to make saltpeter 'with less annoyance than heretofore'.[60] The succession of speculative schemes for intensive saltpeter production invariably promised to protect private interests. When a grand saltpeter facility was planned for the New Forest in 1577 it promised to 'avoid the wonderful vexation of her majesty's people, so miserably plagued in their houses, in their carriage, in their wood and timber, in their exactions of money, in not paying for that they take at their own will, as it is lamentable'.[61] Christopher Coult's scheme in 1588 for a national system of saltpeter kettles would likewise avoid the 'breaking up of fair halls, parlours or chambers' and the undermining of building foundations caused by the roving saltpetermen. Plans to use sea coal instead of charcoal would alleviate the 'disturbing and hurting of her majesty's loving subjects' that accrued from conventional processes, and would save the nation 3,000 loads of wood a year at a time when scarcity of timber and charcoal was beginning to pinch.[62]

Queen Elizabeth's government was well aware that saltpeter extraction generated grievances. The Master of the Ordnance acknowledged complaints in 1576 against the 'unjust exactions' of saltpetermen in Surrey.[63] In 1589 the Council heard from Nottinghamshire justices that 'the whole country' complained of saltpetermen who took carts for sixteen miles to carry charcoal, or demanded bribes of four shillings a load instead.[64] Attorney General Edward Coke complained to Burleigh in 1597 about the 'grief and discontentment' occasioned by the saltpeter deputies in Suffolk. Adding to the nation's woes in a time of hardship and scarcity, these 'very base and beggarly persons do wonderfully oppress the poorer sort' by their exactions. At Woodbridge they demanded carriage 'in the midst of winter when the ways were depressed', and threatened to return again during harvest time.[65] Aggrieved landowners, tenants, and countrymen added to the noise from the provinces.

Attentive to complaints from aggrieved subjects, the regime positioned itself as the arbiter of disputes rather than the author of oppressive policies. Indeed, recognition of the notorious 'exactions' associated with the extraction of saltpeter lent force to the arguments for new processes that were thought to be less intrusive. Successive grants, patents, judgments, and proclamations regarding saltpeter reminded subjects of the queen's concern that they not be 'greatly abused'. Because digging on private property produced problems, and the requisitioning of carts and supplies caused complaints, the commissions for saltpeter required the patentees or their deputies to ask permission and offer compensation wherever they worked. If abuses arose, as surely they would, local justices were supposed to take care of them, with the Master of the Ordnance and Privy Council as arbiters of last recourse.[66]

A royal proclamation in 1590, repeated in 1595, acknowledged the 'exactions', 'forcements', and 'misusages' of the saltpetermen, and the 'great grievance and disturbance' they caused to 'her majesty's loving subjects', as they targeted people's carriages, houses, grounds, and woods. The crown would act 'for the more ease of her highness's subjects, and repressing of such enormities', by yet another reorganization of the saltpeter commission. The power of the state was directed against 'bad and evil disposed persons' who interfered with collecting, spoiled the saltpeter grounds, or broke up the works, and against rogue saltpetermen who worked with false or expired commissions.[67]

It became a standard pledge of saltpeter projectors that they would proceed 'without troubling the subjects'. When they dug rooms at the Steelyard in London they promised 'to make up in as good sort' as before they came in. Responding to complaints that the saltpetermen caused 'great hinderance' to trade in the City, the Lord Mayor enjoined them 'to use more discretion and moderation in the execution of their warrant'.[68] Despite these niceties, the security demands of the state always outweighed the 'discommodity' of the subject. National strategic requirements overrode private rights, and justified invasive digging and vexatious hauling.

Neither lawyers nor villagers could stop the saltpeter juggernaut. While recognizing that 'the digging of houses and taking of carriages for making saltpeter are cumbersome to the subjects', Elizabeth's Council stood resolute that the work must go on. In any choice pitting local rights against national security the regime always sided with its saltpeter commissioners. It was unfortunate that their digging caused 'great grievances', but it would be much worse for the land to be 'unfurnished of this munition in these perilous seasons'. Misdemeanours and abuses were but 'petty matters ... compared to that profit and infinite security which the performance of this service bringeth to her majesty' and her subjects.[69]

As well as being notorious for their 'contentions and controversies ... corruptions and abuses', the saltpetermen themselves were often at each other's throats.[70] The London saltpeterman Ralph Hockenhull in particular stirred up a storm of enmity among his colleagues. While victims railed at his 'exactions', competitors sought his business for themselves. The rival projector John Grange petitioned Burleigh in 1589 to restore him to the monopoly of making saltpeter in London that Hockenhull had apparently usurped. Though Hockenhull had the backing of the Earl of Warwick, the Master of the Ordnance, he abused his position by skimming off material for his own 'private gain'. The crown might permit suppliers to inconvenience other subjects, but could allow no cheating of itself, especially in times of national emergency.[71] Ralph Hockenhull, of course, protested his innocence as an upstanding member of the saltpeter community, and blamed his difficulties on the 'indignation' of a 'busy...impudent fellow', John Grange. At its core this problem concerned rival contractors rather than aggrieved property-holders, but when fresh bidders sought the London saltpeter contract they offered to supply twenty thousandweight yearly 'without troubling her majesty's subjects for the same'.[72]

Further evidence of corruption emerged in 1592 when John Powell, the Surveyor of the Ordnance at the Tower, was charged with deceiving the queen. The investigation exposed scandals of short measure, illicit re-casking, shoddy materials, and deals under the counter that implicated the Evelyn brothers. Powell, who held a patent for making saltpeter, apparently diverted supplies for private sales and engaged in schemes of false weighing. Coopers who casked saltpeter brought in by 'merchant strangers' testified that on one occasion John Evelyn 'was at the weighing thereof' and went away with unspecified amounts, 'by which deceit her majesty was very much prejudiced and hindered'. The additional charge that George Evelyn had spoken seditiously in favour of the Spaniards was an especially serious crime in one responsible for the nation's gunpowder, but the crisis passed and the Evelyns were soon back at work.[73]

Grievances against saltpetermen added to the frustration with monopolists, projectors, and patentees of all sorts that erupted in the closing years of Elizabeth's reign. But when a royal proclamation in 1601 assured sufferers that they could seek remedy at law, the saltpeter project proved to be exempt. In some districts, the patentees claimed, 'divers saltpeter works are ceased and the rest much hindered by the late proclamation [against monopolies], whereby ignorant people pretend that those works should be no further proceeded in'.[74] The government moved quickly to remove misunderstanding. The saltpeter works, it insisted, were 'altogether without the compass of monopolies', and were congruent with both equity and common law. Anyone who 'shall seditiously or contemptuously call in question the power or validity of her majesty's prerogative royal' in this regard risked 'severe punishment according to their desert'. The intrusion, digging, and carting would have to go on. Given the perils of the world and the risks to the crown, went the argument, it was essential that the realm be supplied with munitions: 'There is nothing of so forcible a quality as saltpeter, the mother of gunpowder and indeed the chiefest and in effect the only substance thereof.' Fortunately, Elizabeth's subjects were told, 'it is the great blessing of God, that this land hath means to furnish itself of this provision'. Its value was incalculable. 'The benefit of making saltpeter and gunpowder within this land is so infinite that it stretcheth not only to the security of the goods, lands, and lives of all her majesty's subjects, but also to the preservation of her highness' royal person, her crown and dignity, and the maintenance of true religion.'[75]

Royal rights in this regard were beyond question because 'the sole making of saltpeter and gunpowder within her majesty's dominions pertaineth to the crown by her highness's prerogative royal'. The queen had no desire to offend her subjects, but 'saltpeter, the principal substance of gunpowder, is of such scarcity within this land, where it groweth only in houses and in places defended from much moisture, as it cannot be hereby sufficiently had in the particular possessions of the crown to defend the same'. Her majesty therefore exercised her royal prerogative by empowering patentees to dig in the land and houses of her subjects. In past years there was never 'above twenty or thirty lasts of gunpowder at most of English provision yearly delivered into the store', but now up to eighty lasts, perhaps half of the kingdom's annual needs, could be made from saltpeter from the queen's dominions. Her councillors 'accounted it the greatest service that could be done for the security of the state'. Robert Cecil's 'remembrance of certain benefits to her majesty and her subjects, by making saltpeter and gunpowder within this realm' of September 1600 (see below) rehearsed arguments similar to those made by William Cecil forty years earlier, except that now the projected domestic enterprise was up and running.[76]

By the close of the Elizabethan era a national network was in place for the extraction and processing of saltpeter. Saltpetermen operated in every county, and they furnished up to half of the kingdom's annual needs. A regime that began in scarcity ended in 1603 with gunpowder and munitions in abundance. Foreign expertise had been naturalized for local processing, though the most technologically ambitious schemes had come to nought. Based on the royal prerogative and protected by powerful officials, England's saltpeter enterprise was so vital for national security that local complaints were largely set aside. Like so many other problems of Queen Elizabeth's reign, the legal, social, and environmental consequences of saltpeter extraction remained unresolved. 'Vexations' and 'discommodities' would fester, and would cause occasional disorders, until either centralized industrial production brought an end to local impositions, or an alternative source of saltpeter came on line. The resolution of this matter, like so many others, was reserved for Elizabeth's successors.

APPENDIX TO CHAPTER THREE

'A remembrance of certain benefits to her majesty and her subjects, by making saltpeter and gunpowder within this realm' (Robert Cecil, September 1600).[77]

First, there is infinite security to her majesty and the state, that the land hath means in itself to defend itself, and offend the common enemies thereof, whereas otherwise her majesty would be enforced for matter of defence to depend upon the pleasure and displeasure of foreign princes, who have refused to suffer this provision to pass out of their dominions for any money; whereof experience was had anno 1595, at which time Mr Furner, a merchant of London, now a patentee in this behalf, being commanded to provide a hundred lasts of salt-peter, which he undertook to deliver her majesty within six months, to supply the provision that went out of her majesty's stores for the Cales [i.e. Cadiz] voyage, for performance whereof factors were employed in Germany, could not perform the same, for that the Duke of Pomerland there would not suffer his country to be weakened of a matter of such strength; so as her majesty was disappointed and could get but eleven lasts thereof, and that two months after the time appointed, whereby a supply was of necessity made within this land.

Secondly, although it were certain that this provision might be had in foreign parts (which is not known how that may be in sufficient quantity), yet not withstanding it cannot be brought to this land but with danger of being intercepted by enemies, of delays by contrary winds, and of delay and loss by shipwreck, whereupon it were not fit (without necessity) to suffer the safety of a kingdom to depend.

Thirdly, whereas her majesty hath usually paid twelvepence a pound for foreign powder, her highness hath saved by the making of saltpeter and gunpowder within the land, which hath been delivered into her highness' store at eightpence per pound, £4,000 in every hundred lasts during the last patent before this, whereby there were delivered four score lasts ordinarily, and upon especial occasions far greater quantities. As also her highness' subjects in their expense have saved well near as much, so as her majesty or her highness' subjects have saved by the last patent before this, in the making of saltpeter and gunpowder within the land eleven years, little less than a hundred thousand pounds.

Fourthly, whereas her majesty is now served an hundred lasts of powder yearly at sevenpence per pound, her highness saveth therein, under the said price of foreign powder, £5,000 per annum, and hath indented for twenty lasts more yearly to be delivered (if it be required), viz., for forty lasts yearly more than was usually delivered by the former patent; so as her majesty hath saved, and may save by this patent in ten years above £60,000 under the said price of foreign powder, and her majesty's subjects in like propor-tion as much. Viz., in the whole about an hundred thousand pounds.

Fifthly, the making of saltpeter and gunpowder within the land doth not only raise a hidden benefit (the want whereof would carry great sums of money or other commodities of like value to foreign parts, to the enriching thereof, and impoverishment of this land), but also it setteth many people to work, whereby they have their maintenance.

Sixthly, it appeareth by the accounts in the office of the ordnance, that her majesty, before the said two last letters patents in this behalf, never had above twenty or thirty lasts of gunpowder at the most of English provision yearly delivered into the store, partly for that there wanted men of skill to make the same, but chiefly for that (although there were letters patents granted for the making thereof), yet there was no certain person enjoined to bring any certain quantity into the store, but the matter was left at large, until the want of powder anno 1588 (notwithstanding all the provision that then could be had amongst the merchants of foreign powder) hazarded the land; which thereupon occasioned the then lords of her majesty's most honourable Privy Council to contract that the provision for the land in this behalf might be chiefly made within itself. Of which contract the Lord Treasurer then being oftentimes took great pleasure other times to speak, as of the greatest service that could be done for the security of the kingdom, especially the strength of the wars being altered from bows and arrows to ordnance. Now by this patent for as much as a hundred and twenty lasts of powder are indented for yearly, viz., forty lasts more than at any time hitherto have usually been delivered for her majesty's provision, besides the provision for her highness' subjects, these great services (viz. that her highness and her majesty's subjects also might be wholly furnished within the land, which could not be made without dealing in some equality, for good example's sake, as well with the grounds of the better sort, not heretofore meddled with, as well as with those of inferior persons) have stirred up that discontent which has appeared in the parliament house. Howbeit, it is to be looked for that the matter of saltpeter making should be complained of (although it be used in the best manner that can be devised), for that it carryeth with it a continual offence in itself, viz. for breaking of earths and taking of carriages. Which business when it cometh to be performed (as needs it must) by many hands, and those of the ruder sort (albeit there have been all possible care taken for good order in this behalf), it is like that oftentimes there fall out great discontentment upon small occasions.

Seventhly, whereas there are said to be great grievances in the digging of houses, what just cause of grief, or rather what punishment had been sufficient for the leaving of houses undigged, and so the land unfurnished of this munition in these perilous seasons? If it be an offence to secure their land it seemeth to be very venial. If there be any just cause of offence, it is fit that it be punished accordingly. But if all these petty matters were compared to that profit and infinite security which the performance of this service brings to her majesty and those her highness' subjects which are most grieved, they have so little cause of offence, as they may think it their great happiness that they may be sufficiently furnished for their defence, and that thereby their houses, goods, lands, and lives are protected.

4

Saltpeter for a Peaceable Kingdom

THE saltpetermen appear on stage in Thomas Middleton's tragicomedy 'A Faire Quarrell' (co-written with William Rowley) which was acted before the king and performed in public theatres before it was printed in 1617. In the opening scene a servant tells Citizen Russell that two strangers seek access to his house: 'They come with commission, they say, sir, to taste of your earth; if they like it, they'll turn it into gunpowder.' The audience would have recognized these characters as saltpetermen, who exercised rights of entry into private property, and used the taste test to gauge the suitability of the soil. Russell immediately understands their purpose: 'Oh, they are saltpetermen, before me, and they bring commission: the king's power indeed! They must have entrance, but the knaves will be bribed, there's all the hope we have in officers, they were too dangerous in a commonwealth but that they will be very well corrupted. Necessary varlets.' The authority and corruptibility of these 'necessary varlets' is invoked to comic effect, and Russell instructs his servant to permit their entry, but also to 'give 'em very good words to save my ground unravished, unbroken up'. We are now thick with double entendres, since Russell's daughter is the object of several suitors' attentions. The householder continues, telling a visiting Colonel: 'Mine's yet a virgin earth: the worm hath not been seen to wriggle in her chaste bowels, and I'd be loath a gunpowder fellow should deflower her now.' The saltpetermen announce themselves: 'We come to take a view and taste of your ground, sir,' but then they reveal that they are not saltpetermen at all, but sergeants come to arrest one of

Mistress Russell's suitors, using the ruse to penetrate the house. The Colonel upbraids them, with a contemporary allusion that none could miss: 'A plague upon your gunpowder treason, ye quick-damned varlets, is this your saltpeter proving, your tasting earth? Would you might never feed better, nor none of your catchpole tribe.' The play alludes comedically to the arrogance and venality of the saltpetermen, whose unpopularity intensified in the reign of James I.[1]

* * *

In the spring of 1603 a naval salute of 355 pieces to celebrate the accession of James I rocked ships in the Thames by the Tower. More guns roared in welcome throughout England. A Dutch print of the occasion shows ships and shore-men firing their guns, alongside joyful bonfires, trumpets, and drums. When the new king reached Berwick in April, he was met by 'a better peal of ordinance' than 'in any soldier's memory', and the next day King James himself fired a cannon, 'with such sign of experience that the most expert gunners there beheld it not without admiration'. Fortunately the piece behaved better than the one that exploded and killed his ancestor James II of Scotland at the siege of Roxburgh in 1460. The new monarch avowed 'how much he loved and respected the art military'.[2]

But as a king who made and maintained peace, James needed less gunpowder, and therefore less saltpeter, than his predecessor. The new regime had no use for half the gunpowder furnished by the royal mills, and began to dispose of the surplus on the international market. Some of it may have found its way to the Catesby–Guy Fawkes plotters of 1605. An inventory of royal ordnance at the beginning of James I's reign found 240 lasts of gunpowder in the Tower of London.[3] Considering that reserves had shrunk to sixty lasts at the height of Elizabeth's war with Spain, the kingdom was remarkably well supplied. The Venetians were quick to come shopping for this surplus, being informed 'that now is the moment to buy saltpeter, of which there is great abundance in England'.[4] In 1610 the Council permitted the sale of gunpowder 'to such parts beyond seas as are in amity with us'. The King of Denmark became a major purchaser in 1612. In some

FIG 11 Celebration for King James, 1603

Yale Center for British Art, Paul Mellon Collection, B.1997.14.17888, detail, reproduced by permission.

years as many as fifty lasts of powder were available for export to countries that were formerly sources of England's supply.[5] Festive firing on state occasions helped to consume the surplus. The investiture of the Prince of Wales in 1610 and the marriage of his sister Elizabeth in 1613 occasioned lavish festive expenditure on 'fire and powder', with cannonades at the Tower, mock-battles on the Thames, and thundering peals across Lambeth marsh.[6]

Aggrieved subjects

James's reign opened with a minor revolt against the domestic saltpetermen and saw challenges to their constitutional legitimacy. Claiming that the Elizabethan saltpeter warrants had expired, landowners refused to allow prospectors to enter their grounds. The patentees for saltpeter and gunpowder had to seek urgent confirmation of their authority, the validity of which had been questioned since the late queen's death. They artfully reminded the king that their grant was 'no monopoly, but a matter by royal prerogative inseparably belonging to the imperial crown', and invited his majesty to side with them against 'ignorant people and such as are obstinately minded'.[7] There followed a flurry of legal and political manoeuvring, in which Sir Edward Coke (1552–1634) stood up for the propertied class, while the gunpowder interests sought to maintain their privileges. The patentees offered to supply the king with sixty, 100, or 120 lasts of powder per annum, in exchange for the assurance that they would mitigate the impact of their digging. John and Robert Evelyn and their partner Richard Harding promised in October 1604 that they would dig no place more than once in six years, 'except when extraordinary service is required for the safety and defence of the state', and they promised more care when excavating pigeon houses. A revised contract awarded the Evelyns a twenty-one-year privilege to furnish the king with 120 lasts a year 'of good and serviceable corn powder', and re-empowered them to 'make and work for saltpeter in all convenient places in England and Wales'.[8] Surviving accounts from the first half of 1605 show payments to seventeen saltpetermen of around £3 7s. per hundredweight. The champion producer, Francis Stretton, brought in 119½ hundredweight, for which he was paid £401 12s. 2d. Most of the saltpetermen signed for their cash, but Thomas Hilliard, Francis Maxon, Edward Spenser, and Robert York made marks, suggesting that they were not fully literate. Unfortunately the manuscript is damaged, but surviving entries register 82,791 pounds of saltpeter (almost 31 lasts), and an outlay of £2,469 13s. 8d.[9]

The saltpeter enterprise continued to provoke grumbling, and aggrieved subjects occasionally sought redress from the crown and the courts. Sporadic complaints claimed the Council's attention, though most were of the kind that Elizabethans had called 'petty'. Members of parliament complained in 1606 of 'unseasonal' digging of dovecotes and taking up carriages 'against their owners' wills', although they conceded that the work was 'necessary' for the nation. Their greatest grievance was that saltpetermen behaved 'in more violent and unlawful sort now than in time of war', and diverted some of their product to private uses. One member observed that 'since the king's coming, neither peter nor powder hath come into' the ordnance store, but was transported to foreign nations. Another urged Secretary Cecil 'to endeavour reformation of things that be out of square'.[10] Sir Edward Coke warned magistrates at Norwich about saltpetermen who abused their authority, and 'made plain and simple people believe that [they] will without their leave break up the floor of their dwelling house, unless they will compound with them to the contrary'.[11] As the crown recognized in its 1606 proclamation on purveyances, 'wheresoever there must be a trust in vulgar persons, it is not possible to keep their actions from errors and abuses'.[12]

With national security less threatened by foreign foes, the Jacobean armaments industry turned sluggish and its corruptions became more exposed. The saltpetermen continued to dig and to boil, but if they produced more than the king needed they were permitted to sell their surplus at profit on the open market. The incentive to overproduce was irresistible. These activities were not only 'very offensive and troublesome to the subjects', causing them to complain to parliament, but also wasted resources and weakened the kingdom. A report on saltpeter in 1606 observed that 'neither his majesty nor his Council do know what is yearly made nor to whom it is sold'. One danger was that 'men of bad disposition' could acquire weapons-grade material, and assist the enemies of Christendom. Anxieties on this score sharpened in the shadow of the Gunpowder Plot. Another concern was that overproduction was unsustainable, and 'wasteth much fuel, above cause or the kingdom's necessity'. The report concluded that 'if the patentees continue this course of excessive making, they will in five years utterly waste the mines of saltpeter', and a note in the margin affirmed, 'this divers petermen do avouch'. Corrective action might involve revoking the saltpeter patent, or at least making sure that the crown shared in the profits.[13]

The saltpetermen were still on the defensive in 1606 when the legality of their enterprise exercised senior justices at Serjeants' Inn. Sir Edward Coke, recently appointed Chief Justice of the Common Pleas, summarized the judgment in his famous *Reports*. The justices agreed that 'digging and taking of saltpeter to make gunpowder' was among the king's prerogative rights. It was understood as a purveyance, a necessary provisioning for the crown, for 'the defence of the whole realm, in which every subject hath benefit'. But it was not to be done without 'limitations'. To avoid wronging the king's subjects, his agents were obliged to leave the land they worked 'in so good plight as they found it'. They could dig in 'outhouses or barns, stables, dove-houses, mills, or any other buildings', provided they did not 'undermine, weaken, or impair' the walls or foundations. But they could not dig in private dwellings. The judges were adamant that 'the habitation of subjects be preserved and maintained'. In Coke's view, though not necessarily the crown's, 'the house of every one is to him as his castle and fortress, as well for his defense against injury and violence as for his repose'. There should be no disturbance of an Englishman's corn or hay, no dislodging of horses or cattle. Saltpeter work should be conducted only at convenient times, between sunrise and sunset, and the saltpetermen should erect no furnaces or kettles without the landowner's consent. Requisitioning of carts should be limited to nine miles, with payment of compensation of fourpence a mile 'laden and empty'.[14]

In response the gunpowder interests protested that it might prove 'impossible...to furnish the kingdom thereof by home store...if the digging of houses, barns and stables be left out'. Sir Robert Johnson warned the Council against 'a popular applause that carries with it a dangerous inconvenience', and claimed that 'the safety of the kingdom' mattered more than mere 'annoys'. He also advised the Council 'in no wise to divulge these judgements in point of law, which were more fit for the secrecy of a Council of State', lest homeowners discover that their dwellings were as sacrosanct as Coke said they were. Contentious legal maxims were *arcana imperii*, secrets of state, and not for general parlance. To secure their contract, however, and to gain good will, the saltpetermen agreed to other conditions. Concerning 'pigeon houses, which are the chiefest nurses of saltpeter of this kingdom', they promised to dig for no more than half an hour in any day, and only between the hours of nine and three; and if any birds or eggs 'be lost by that occasion, they will satisfy the party the full value thereof'. They would not only repair any damage, but leave the grounds 'in much better state than they are now'.[15] Each of these provisions would be tested and violated in years to come.

Politics and profit

The politics of the Jacobean saltpeter patent were tortuous and confusing. Any privilege yielding profit was worth having, and courtiers manoeuvred to maximize their financial rewards. Between the Lords of the Admiralty, the Ordnance Office, the Privy Council, and their many clients and dependants, the opportunities for venality were abundant. Critics remarked on the 'self-enrichment' and 'corruption' of the gunpowder patentees, and the 'danger' this posed to national security. The Evelyns had been making gunpowder since the 1570s, not without some stain, and now Jacobean aristocrats claimed 'that the service had not sufficient countenance because it was not in the government of some person of honour'. By way of remedy the Earl of Worcester obtained licence in May 1607 for the sole making of saltpeter and gunpowder in England and Ireland for twenty-one years, revocable at the king's pleasure.[16] Worcester relinquished his monopoly in January 1620, and four months later it was given to the royal favourite the Lord Admiral (the Marquess of Buckingham), the Master of the Ordnance (Lord Carew), and the Master of the Court of Wards (Sir Lionel Cranfield, soon to be Earl of Middlesex). Buckingham and Carew renewed the patent in June 1624 after Cranfield fell from grace.[17] These aristocrats, of course, delegated the work to professionals, so the Evelyns and their deputies continued the actual business of grinding and refining. By December 1620 they had already made thirty-nine lasts of powder that year, and had enough saltpeter on hand to make sixty more.[18]

New projectors periodically entered the fray with promises to transform the process. Continental books and methods provided recurrent inspiration. Early in James's reign (most likely in 1607) Simon Read and Robert Jackson claimed knowledge of a new way to 'rear saltpeter out of earth and grounds which in appearance and judgement of men of that faculty have in them no saltpeter or substance of that nature'. They claimed competence 'to deal with the reparation and restoration of abandoned and derelict saltpeter mines', and asked for a monopoly so long as they would not have to reveal their 'secrets'.[19] In 1620 the patentees were restricted from 'making saltpeter by mixing and blending of earth, chalk, etc., according to the new invention', and in 1623 a fresh grant was awarded 'to make saltpeter in a new manner within England and Ireland, with provision of not interfering with the present commission'. The entire business was supposed to be conducted in ways that 'may best stand with the furtherance of his majesty's service and the ease of the country', an almost impossible contradiction of principles.[20] The projectors typically claimed to possess new knowledge, and demanded safeguards for secrecy, but none of them actually expanded production or dislodged the established saltpeter interests.

Periodically, in response to complaints, the government reviewed safeguards against abuses, but just as often the saltpetermen went unpunished. In 1618, 'for the avoiding of such inconveniences as have formerly fallen upon his majesty's subjects by cart-taking', the government reaffirmed the distance that 'wains, carts, and teams' could be pressed to carry saltpeter at nine miles, the carters to be paid eightpence a mile 'in ready money'. But these regulations, as usual, were observed more in the breach than to the letter.[21]

Parishioners of Croydon, Surrey, complained in 1619 about the exactions of the saltpetermen, who exceeded their privilege by forcing the carriage of materials over excessive distances. The principal regional saltpeter house was at Kingston upon Thames, and when churchwardens measured the road there from Croydon they found it more than ten miles. The saltpetermen also threatened the weaver Richard Gilbert with ruin by proposing to dig in his workshop. Gilbert offered to allow them to dig elsewhere in his house, but pleaded that they spare the shop on which his livelihood depended.[22] Gilbert's problem puts a human face on the saltpeter programme, and also illuminates interaction between the Jacobean state and its subjects.

Aggrieved complainants demanded to know what the government would do on their behalf. The answer, in effect, was nothing. Hostilities had broken out in Europe in 1618 (the start of the Thirty Years War), and councillors would privilege the procurement of munitions over the rights of the subject, unless exactions were exceptionally egregious. A rare sense of urgency developed about 'the king's resumption of saltpeter manufacture, by which he can provide his own gunpowder'. The Earl of Worcester's yielding of the gunpowder contract in 1620 left the saltpeter enterprise 'at a stand, to the disservice of the kingdom', and there was much catching up to be done.[23]

Since the richest saltpeter was found in cellars, dovecotes, and stables, and such facilities belonged primarily to gentlemen, the digging hit hardest on the landed class. Property owners found myriad ways to thwart the hated saltpetermen. Most effective was the outright bribe, a payment to go away and bother someone else. 'The knaves will be bribed; there's all the hope we have in officers,' says a character in Thomas Middleton's *A Faire Quarrell* (1617) when saltpetermen come to 'taste' his ground.[24] The furnishing of solid floors in farmyard buildings could hinder their excavation. Agriculturalists who dug their own dung-rich earth to manure their fields also inadvertently ruined that ground for saltpeter mining; the saltpetermen called it stealing from the king. Simple obstructive non-cooperation also hindered the national project. Landowners refused access or facilities, and carters, 'by way of combination', refused to provide transport at any price.

Local officials, justices, mayors, constables, and headboroughs, who were supposed to assist the saltpetermen, also proved slack or recalcitrant, and impeded the saltpeter enterprise. In 1620, while the commission was in transfer, magistrates in Dorset, Worcestershire, and Nottinghamshire had some of the saltpetermen arrested.[25] The Leicestershire baronet Sir George Shirley complained in January 1621 of 'an oppression' at Ragdale, when the saltpetermen dug up his tenants' houses at Christmas, 'not sparing the rooms wherein the poor men did live'. Since their letters of deputation came from the Earl of Worcester, whose patent for saltpeter had expired, and the commission did not extend to dwelling houses, the work was doubly illegal. Shirley sought compensation for the loss, and punishment for the offenders, but probably received neither.[26]

Warlike supplies

As the European security situation worsened in the 1620s, the crown paid more urgent attention to its store of munitions. Although King James's policy was peace, he was obliged to prepare for war. A proclamation in January 1623 addressed the problem of defective gunpowder that had rendered some of the royal ships defenceless. To avoid 'imminent and perilous enormities', there would now be tighter control of the manufacture of saltpeter and powder. The king's powder barrels would henceforth be marked with three crowns for the 'best' quality, two crowns if 'new, strong and good', and one crown for 'old powder, new wrought' though still serviceable. Anyone caught adulterating gunpowder, or dealing in it illicitly, risked the king's 'indignation and displeasure' and 'severe censure of his high court of Star Chamber'.[27]

The prospect of war caused a scramble for saltpeter, and a drive to secure foreign supplies. Merchants turned again to the Low Countries to make up the deficit. In May 1624 the government ordered 'that a great quantity of gunpowder should with all speed be made', and the saltpetermen should double their deliveries 'as the pressing occasions of these times do require'. The limit of carriage was raised from nine to twelve miles, and refusers faced citation for contempt of the king's 'so great and weighty service'. The new saltpeter contract called for delivery of 240 lasts a year, significantly more than Elizabethan wartime levels.[28]

A further proclamation in December 1624 directly concerned the gathering of saltpeter. Borrowing language from Elizabethan pronouncements of a quarter-century earlier, it rehearsed the benefits of a domestic source to make gunpowder: security for the king and kingdom, reduced dependence on foreign suppliers, less risk of loss from shipwreck or interception, saving of money, and the putting of poor people to work. Now, however, with the safety of the nation again at stake, it was time to confront the 'evil dealings of many ill-disposed persons' who interfered with the saltpeter project. The government knew their tricks, and was determined to stop them. Going into exceptional detail about subterfuges and shortcomings, the proclamation forbade anyone to 'pave or lay with brick, stone, plank boards, lime, sand, gravel, or other thing whatsoever that shall or may hurt, hinder or prejudice the growth and increase of the mine of saltpeter, any dove house or dovecote, or any warehouse or outhouse...cellar or vault...stables...or...manger', and provided for inspection to see that the grounds were kept 'fit for our service'. Landowners were not to destroy the 'mine' by spreading good earth on their own ground, but were to reserve 'the richest, mellowest, and best mould of earth or horse dung, being rotten and dry', to the king's saltpetermen. If the saltpetermen seeded ground 'for the better increase and growth of saltpeter' in the future, 'no owners of the said grounds shall interrupt or hinder them in their so doing'. Anyone who corruptly paid money 'to spare their grounds from being digged' would earn the king's anger for defrauding his service. Offenders would be referred to the Commissioners for the Navy or be prosecuted in Star Chamber. The proclamation applied to all 'persons whatsoever, of whatever degree or quality', with no privilege for rank or position. The only exemption was for 'cellars and vaults...wherein noblemen and gentlemen do lay or hold their wine, beer, or cider for the provision of their household'.

Otherwise the saltpetermen had carte blanche to enter and dig as they chose. Only in its final section, in a perfunctory afterword, was there any reference to 'abuse' by the saltpetermen, and assurance that the government would hear 'the just complaints' of any subjects.[29]

King James's peaceable foreign policy ended in 1624, as Prince Charles and the Duke of Buckingham moved England towards war. Sir Edward Coke's concern for the rights of householders was further eclipsed, in the interest of national security. The saltpeter enterprise quickened, and its local unpopularity intensified, as the second Stuart regime flexed its martial muscles. Saltpeter collectors under Charles I became more aggressive than ever, as if to make up for lost time.

5

The Inestimable Treasure of Charles I

COMPETING lines of patronage and authority clashed in Wiltshire in 1637 when the saltpeterman Thomas Thornhill made the mistake of tangling with Dr Christopher Wren, the rector of Knoyle Magna. When Thornhill's men dug out the floor of Wren's pigeon house, without his permission, they did so much damage that the north wall fell in and the birds 'forsook the house'. The rector lost 'three breeds, whereof the least never yielded fewer than thirty or forty dozen', and now he faced a suit for dilapidations. The pigeon house was a stone structure twenty feet high with walls more than three feet thick, but the saltpetermen reduced it to a ruin. Thornhill, for his part, claimed that the wall was already cracked, and that it fell down 'on the great windy night that blew down so many houses, barns and trees in all parts of the kingdom', by no means due to his digging. As a servant of the crown, engaged in work of national importance, he sought relief from the Council against the rector's 'unjust molestation'.[1]

Wren, however, commanded unusual political resources, as Dean of Windsor, Registrar of the Order of the Garter, and brother of the Bishop of Norwich. Bypassing the Council he addressed himself directly to King Charles on the occasion of the Feast of St George. As an officer of the Garter, Wren claimed royal protection, and the king took his registrar's side against his saltpeterman. A committee under Lord Treasurer Bishop Juxon concluded in

January 1638 that the pigeon house fell down in consequence of Thornhill's digging, not by casualty of wind and weather, and the rector could sue for reparations.[2] The future architect Christopher Wren junior, who was five years old at the time of the pigeon house incident, may have learned something about politics, and about the solidity of buildings.

* * *

War raged in Europe throughout Charles I's reign and periodically threatened to involve the Stuart dominions. The Council issued urgent orders in 1625 'for the better maintaining of the breed and increase of saltpeter, and the true making of gunpowder', and bustled to mobilize munitions.[3] The Dutch pyrotechnician Cornelius Drebbel was among foreign experts engaged in 1626 'to apply their skill for his majesty's service' to make explosives, fireships, and even submarines.[4] The Ordnance Office shipped ten brass siege guns and as many field pieces to Cadiz in 1625, but there is no evidence that they were ever deployed. Several of those sent to the Isle of Rhé in 1627 were defective, and one exploded on its second shot.[5] These early conflicts with Spain and France were politically and financially ruinous, and achieved neither benefit nor renown.

Charles kept England out of continental wars after 1629, but his reckless religious policies caused two unnecessary wars with Scotland. The Bishops' Wars of 1639–1640 lit fuses in all three Stuart kingdoms, and opened a decade of civil war throughout the British Isles. Even before this conflagration, the crown required more gunpowder for its forts and forces, for its reformed militia, and to furnish its expanded navy; there could be no neglect of national security in a dangerous world. Garrisons at Portsmouth, Hull, and Berwick needed munitions and training. Dunkirk raiders, Barbary corsairs, and rag-tag pirates had to be countered and pursued. Even in peacetime the annual Caroline demand for gunpowder topped 250 lasts, reaching 292 lasts in 1638, more than triple the Elizabethan level. England's saltpetermen were never so busy, with never so many opportunities for abuse.

FIG 12 Making grenades

Nathaniel, Nye, *The Art of Gunnery. Wherein is described the true way to make all sorts of gunpowder, gun-match, the art of shooting in great and small ordnance* (1670), p. 74 (Huntington Library, rare book 433841, reproduced by permission of the Huntington).

Imports

By the crown's own estimate in 1627, only a third of the saltpeter needed for state purposes came from within the king's dominions. The rest was imported 'from foreign parts', with all the 'inconveniences' of 'peril and hazard' that entailed.[6] Most of it still came from Hamburg and Amsterdam, with all the complications of overseas procurement that had troubled the Elizabethans. Charles I's emergency build-up stretched English military resources, and the government searched anxiously for additional sources of supply. In December 1625 the Council urged merchants to 'be industrious' in securing supplies from 'Germany and the east countries', and pressed the East Indies traders 'to ballast ships homeward bound with saltpeter'.[7] In January 1626 councillors again invited the Merchant Adventurers to enquire, 'what store of peter or powder might be had' beyond the seas. The Baltic area seemed particularly promising, except that the King of Denmark wanted the region's saltpeter for himself. Because the English Ordnance Office remained 'generally unfurnished', the merchants were urged to import as much saltpeter as they could 'with all possible expedition'.[8]

The international trading community responded vigorously to these invitations. At 'his majesty's request', the financier Philip Burlamachi agreed 'to provide from beyond the seas…the full quantity and proportion of one hundred lasts of gunpowder, or of one hundred lasts of saltpeter, or of one hundred lasts of gunpowder and saltpeter together'. Ready-made or ready to make, it did not matter, so long as the material was 'merchantable and well conditioned' and available in time for the war.[9] In November 1627 the Ordnance Office negotiated directly for saltpeter from Hamburg and Amsterdam. In January 1628, with war continuing, 'his majesty was forced to provide himself in the Netherlands at an excessive price and yet worse powder'.[10] Foreign imports continued throughout Charles I's reign, despite aggressive efforts to achieve saltpeter independence.

Even Ireland might yield material for munitions, some thought, so long as the authorities remained 'careful to keep the manufacture thereof from the knowledge of the Irish'.[11] Others conjectured the existence of saltpeter reserves on remote English islands. Claiming that his agents had discovered 'a true way of making saltpeter, powder and match', the Earl of Linlithgow, Charles's High Admiral of Scotland, received a patent in 1628 to manufacture saltpeter, but a report on 'the scarcity of powder' in 1634 observed that there was no saltpeter in Scotland. Colonial investors hoped that Virginia, Barbados, or Connecticut would yield a saltpeter mine, but American ventures of this time came to nothing.[12]

Following pioneering efforts by the Dutch, the East India Company began regular shipments of saltpeter in Charles I's reign, reaching 170 tons by 1629 and 200 tons a year or more in the 1630s. The crown's powder-makers were pleasantly surprised by the quality of this Indian saltpeter. Some years even saw a surplus, when the king's stores were 'sufficiently supplied', and excess saltpeter could be re-exported.[13] The future of England's munitions lay with East India supplies, though nobody could know this for a generation.

Reviving an Elizabethan connection, the Barbary merchants contributed to the king's service. In June 1627 they brought in twenty tons of saltpeter from Morocco. So successful was their trade that by 1631 they complained of having more on hand than they could sell, when peace with Spain made a dent in their profits. The Ordnance Office was pleased to find Barbary saltpeter too was 'of equal goodness with English saltpeter'.[14] In 1637 the Barbary merchant Robert Blake came up with an ingenious scheme to secure Moroccan saltpeter and to free English captives. At least 1,500 of Charles I's subjects were held in 'Turkish' or Islamic captivity, and raiders took more every year. The plan was for the Moroccans to liberate English slaves and to provide saltpeter in exchange for cloth and other commodities, especially cannon balls. Secretary of State Nicholas endorsed Blake's proposal, noting that 'the Lords will speak with the king for it, in regard the petitioner is to furnish saltpeter'. The fruits of this deal included twenty-four tons of Barbary saltpeter that reached London in April 1637, with 100 more tons arriving in December.[15] It is not known how many captives came home, but Archbishop Laud went so far as to prepare a form of service to reconcile English apostates who had accepted the 'Turkish' religion. Nor is it known how many English cannon balls were subsequently used against Christian shipping.[16]

Projects

King Charles had barely taken his throne before petitioners flooded him with schemes 'for enriching his majesty with many millions', plans 'to discover a secret means of rendering cannon useless', and projects to discover *Terra Australis Incognita*. Other projectors had dreams of increasing the speed of ships, drying

FIG 13   Making saltpeter

Francis Malthus, *Pratique de la guerre: contenant l'usage de l'artillerie, bombes et mortiers, feux artificiels & petards, sappes & mines, ponts & pontons, tranchées & travaux* (Paris, 1681), following p. 150 (Huntington Library, rare book 486839, reproduced by permission of the Huntington).

hops and malt 'without the annoyance of smoke', and of course, transforming the production of saltpeter.[17] Secretary Coke reminded colleagues that 'in Italy the mines of saltpeter are improved by art, and many such projects have been here offered and happily by encouragement from the state might have some good fruit'.[18] There was no shortage of supplicants for that 'encouragement', especially in time of war.

A quartet of Essex gentlemen (Sir William Luckin, Sir Gamaliel Capell, Francis Quarles the poet, and William Lyde) persuaded parliament in 1626 to draft a bill in their favour 'for the preservation of the mine of saltpeter, and increase of the means for making saltpeter, and for the ease of the subject from the grievance they now bear'. In support they repeated the familiar argument that saltpeter was 'necessary for the defence of the kingdom', that importation created 'hazardous dependence upon foreign princes or states', and that conventional domestic procurement caused 'great charge, trouble and vexation of the subject'. Instead of sending diggers to 'the dwelling houses, cellars, malting house, dove houses, barns, stables, and other outhouses of his majesty's loving subjects', the projectors proposed a centralized industrial process that would yield 500 tons of saltpeter yearly. Though not spelled out in detail, their plan would require all 'silversmiths, refiners, dyers, innkeepers, vintners, butchers, barbers, victuallers, alehouse keepers, tippling houses, slaughter houses, and tobacco shops' throughout the kingdom to save their 'refuse waters', slops and sweepings, to be collected 'for engendering saltpeter' through 'a new way of enriching earth'. The bill said little about the actual process, but took pains to penalize 'refractory people...enemies to the common good, and molesters and hinderers of so needful a work'. The bill had two readings in April 1626 and then was set aside.[19]

Offering a variant scheme, Thomas Russell, esquire, petitioned the king in parliament in 1626 to support plans to make saltpeter in London. The idea, which he had previously presented to King James, was to manufacture saltpeter centrally rather than forage for it throughout the kingdom. At present, Russell noted, saltpeter was either imported 'from Barbary, France, Poland, Hamburg and other places in Germany', or gathered domestically, to the great prejudice and inconvenience of his majesty's subjects. Though billed as 'a new way and means, not heretofore known', his proposal was similar to ideas for nitre beds first aired in the sixteenth century, and not unlike the bill so recently before parliament. Russell's scheme would put London beggars to work to collect the city's urine, to be spread on specially prepared grounds. Then, 'after the earth is ripened and impregnated', there would be a constant and abundant supply of high-quality saltpeter ready for processing. All that was needed was £20,000 to get the facility up and running.[20]

Russell's scheme would make him rich, and would make England safer, if only he could secure funding. It would transform a contentious and haphazard process into an orderly and predictable system, to deliver 500 tons of saltpeter yearly with both social and financial benefits to the nation. Convinced that this projector knew his stuff, the government decided to back him, to secure 'that inestimable treasure' of saltpeter 'without digging any of our subjects' houses, or outhouses of any kind, or charging them at all with carriages'. The crown granted a patent in 1626 for the making of saltpeter from urine, and a royal proclamation in January 1627 authorized the collection and storage of urine, not only in London, where Russell and his partner Sir John Brooke had made a trial, but in 'all...cities, towns and villages within this our realm of England'. The urine was to be kept in 'convenient vessels or receptacles fit for that service', along with 'all the stale of beasts which they can save and gather together', to be collected daily in summer and every other day in winter. Anyone who was 'remiss or negligent in the due observance' of this work would be esteemed 'contemptuous and ill-affected both to our person and state'. The proclamation invoked the king's 'prerogative royal', and was followed by letters asking towns and cities to contribute to the cost.[21] There was to be a command economy of urine and dung, centrally mobilized for the kingdom's protection.

Instead of multiplying the supply of saltpeter as promised, the proclamation supporting Russell's urine scheme brought conventional production to a halt. Property owners decided they were now excused, and refused to cooperate with the saltpetermen. The saltpetermen themselves feared loss of employment under the new dispensation, and in their 'distraction' refused to renew their contracts with the government. An alarmed Earl of Totnes, Master of the Ordnance, warned Secretary Coke in July 1627 that without intervention 'the works must fall, which will be a great detriment to the king's service'. According to the Commissioners for the Navy, the established saltpetermen demanded 'further power to dig all grounds and to have carriage at easier rates, and other indefinite liberties, which would prove grievous to the subject'.[22] The result was another proclamation, dated 23 July 1627, which sought 'to quicken the former orders and constitutions' and to safeguard the 'digging for saltpeter in the old and approved way'. The provisions of a proclamation of April 1625 concerning dovecotes, stables, and support of the saltpetermen were repeated almost word for word.[23]

Undeterred, the ever hopeful Thomas Russell proposed a variant scheme in December 1627 that would 'make 1000 tons of saltpeter without any charge to his majesty...or grievance to the subject, but much for their ease in time to come'. Instead of saving their urine for collection, every household was now to 'lay a load of earth in some corner of a barn, stable, outhouse or hovel, and cast the urine that is made in that house upon this earth for three months together, and then let it rest three months longer, it will be ripe for saltpeter'. Estimating 10,000 villages or parishes in England, besides cities and towns, with an average of forty houses and four persons per house, Russell calculated 'this 400,000 load of earth will make 100,000 tons of liquor, which will make 1000 tons of powder'. Even better, the crown could make a profit of £30 a ton by selling any surplus on the open market. In a revised version, Russell proposed enlisting 'the ministers, vicars or curates in every parish' to supervise the dispensing of the urine, and to keep a register of 'the names of all such as shall be refractory'. Though thoughtful and ingenious the scheme was far too ambitious, and foundered on its own impracticabilities. Russell continued to petition parliament for support in June 1628, but the steam was going out of his efforts.[24]

Other projectors sought government 'encouragement'. David Ramsey claimed to have found a new way to multiply saltpeter, and in January 1631 he was licensed to put his invention into practice.[25] Another projector named Barton obtained the 'secrets' of making 'double refined saltpeter in a new way, not yet known or practiced', and was looking for investors.[26] In May 1634 two unlikely sounding partners, Sir Philberto Vernatti, the fen drainer, and John Battalion of Yardley, Hertfordshire, claimed knowledge of 'the secret way of making excellent saltpeter'. But before it could go into operation they wanted the unfulfilled patent for using the city excrements, formerly assigned to Thomas Russell, to be granted exclusively to them.[27] In April 1638 the experienced saltpeter worker John Morton proposed a scheme to increase the yield six-fold from dove houses, 'which are the chief nurseries of saltpeter'.[28] While these and other projects sought backing and money, the routine work of prospecting, digging, and boiling went on through the saltpetermen and their local deputies. None of these schemes came to pass, but hopeful projects kept reappearing. Similar plans would emerge in the 1640s from the pens of projecting philosophers, but with no greater chance of success.[29]

Domestic saltpeter

From its inception Charles I's government encouraged the munitions industry. Within days of his accession in March 1625 King Charles's saltpetermen covenanted to double their proportion to 240 lasts.[30] A new commission in April reauthorized the gunpowder patentees under the Lords of the Admiralty, and a proclamation later that month set forth 'orders and constitutions, to be from henceforth inviolably kept and observed, for the better maintaining of the breed and increase of saltpeter, and the true making of gunpowder'. With the tone typical of the Caroline regime, the 1625 proclamation expressed the king's 'heavy displeasure' at 'contemnors of his majesty's royal commandment', and threatened the Star Chamber against any who challenged his prerogative in this regard.[31]

Though James I had insisted extravagantly on his royal prerogative powers, it was Charles who turned the saltpeter business into a test of the constitution. It was God's blessing, he said, to have seeded England with 'mines of saltpeter', and it was the monarch's task to secure that material for his own and the nation's benefit. The proclamation of April 1625 talked of 'reforming abuses', but more by facilitating the work of the saltpetermen than by addressing misdemeanours they may have committed. Owners of dovecotes and stables were forbidden to lay down flooring of stone, brick, plank, or gravel, and instead were to 'suffer the floor or ground thereof to lie open, with good and mellow earth, apt to breed increase of the said mine and saltpeter'. Any persons who 'carried out the good mould' for their own use, or installed floors in such buildings, were ordered within three months to restore the ground fit for saltpeter extraction. Constables, officers, and justices were enlisted to assist the saltpetermen in their digging and carriage, and to punish anyone who would 'hinder or deny' their work. The proclamation forbade bribes or gratuities 'for the sparing or forbearing of any ground or place', and generally sought to maximize production. As a concession to complainers, however, it limited saltpeter digging to 'convenient' times and seasons, and required workmen to leave the ground 'in such good and orderly case as they found the same'. Most of these provisions had appeared in the last proclamation on saltpeter by the dying James I (26 December 1624), but the invocation of 'his majesty's prerogative royal' gave them higher consequence. The reiteration of complaints and sanctions suggests that the saltpetermen routinely faced local obstructions.[32]

Charles I's government was well aware that some saltpetermen exceeded their commissions and burdened the king's subjects. They cut corners, threw their weight about, and caused 'trouble and grievance'. The intrusions of the saltpetermen 'occasioned many complaints', and their notorious tendency to corruption was 'very offensive to many of our good subjects'. But however distasteful the enterprise, the security of the kingdom required it to proceed. In renewing the saltpeter warrants the Council took pains to say that 'all due care hath been taken for the ease of the subject, so much as may be', but 'so much as may be' left acres of room for contention.[33]

Complaints arose wherever the saltpetermen worked, but were more likely to have effect when raised by an aristocrat. Robert Leigh (or Light), a saltpeterman in Flintshire, north Wales, made the wrong enemy when he intruded on the property of the powerful Lord Strange. He broke locks to enter his lordship's stables, tore up the planking on the floor, and dug so deep that he endangered the foundations. He followed this feat by digging in Hawarden Castle, despite being expressly forbidden to enter. Living riotously, on pretence of being the king's servants, Leigh and his men terrorized the town. At night, 'in their pots', they cried out 'the town is ours...to the great grief and amazement of the poor inhabitants', whose lodging they took without paying rent. They returned to the same ground within three years of its last digging, and left everything 'in a ruinous manner'. Lord Strange leaned on the Earl of Totnes, the Master of the Ordnance, who wrote to Secretary Coke in July 1627 to seek punishment for these 'abuses and insolences'. The Council summoned Leigh to answer charges, and eventually he acknowledged his 'miscarriage and abuses' and withdrew from the saltpeter service.[34]

The Earl of Danby brought the case of the Oxfordshire saltpeterman Nicholas Stephens to the Duke of Buckingham's attention in April 1628. Buckingham, as Lord Admiral, was joint holder of the saltpeter patent with Totnes, the Master of the Ordnance. 'Having grievously oppressed the people of these parts', Stephens had been cited at the Quarter Sessions for his 'manifold abuses', but claimed protection through the Duke of Buckingham's commission. Danby was willing to suspend proceedings against the saltpetermen, he said, if Buckingham would 'take care to reform their lewd courses'.[35]

By this time 'an act for the getting of saltpeter' was under discussion in the House of Commons. It aimed at relieving the subject as well as furnishing the realm, but it never became law. Citing abuses from several counties, members concentrated on predations in Berkshire and Oxfordshire. The showcase villain was Nicholas Stephens, a Buckingham client, who had gone so far as to dig in churches and in houses 'where women lie in childbed'. His worst outrage was at Chipping Norton, where Stephens dug twenty loads of saltpeter from the parish church. Pulling up seats to get to the earth, he left 'the ground unlevelled so as the parishioners are not able to perform their duties of divine service'. When he was finished there was 'no place to sit or kneel in the church', and parishioners 'could not conveniently bury their dead'. When the parish clerk objected that God's house was no fit place for digging, the workmen answered 'with obscene jests, that the earth in churches is best for their turns, for the women piss in their seats, which causes excellent saltpeter'. The disturbance continued outside, where Stephens pulled down part of the churchyard wall to set up his boilers, and 'his tubs stood in the churchyard so as they could scarce come into the church'. Puritans and ceremonialists could band together against these blasphemous transgressions, though the Oxfordshire incident was by no means unique. Stephens had dug other churches at Coventry, Warwick, and Oxford, believing them 'not excepted' in his saltpeter commission, and similar 'sacrilegious abuse' had occurred in Wales.[36] Even St Paul's cathedral was at risk when the 'urgent necessity' of the crown required saltpetermen to dig in its 'cellars and vaults'.[37] The fact that some churches had 'pissing places' and others suffered from incontinent sermon sitters increased their suitability for the saltpeter service. Councillors occasionally asked the saltpeter commission to exercise 'restraint of digging in churches, churchyards, and other hallowed places', but with little immediate effect.[38]

Stephens made more enemies by taking seven loads of coal from Sir Anthony Hungerford's house at Black Bourton, Oxfordshire, without the owner's consent, saying 'he must have them, and opened the gate and carried them away, and neither tendered nor left the king's price'. He forced carts to carry materials for as many as thirty miles when the customary maximum was twelve, paid for half loads instead of full ones, and reimbursed but twopence a mile instead of the established rate of eightpence. Stephens even had a tariff for bribes or compounding, taking from ten to thirty shillings in lieu of forcing carriage. In his defence, Stephens flourished his royal commission. It empowered him, he said, 'to dig in houses against consent, and to carry without setting down how far'. Armed with authority from the Duke of Buckingham, he threatened Star Chamber against his challengers, and refused to answer parliament without a better warrant.[39]

Parliament was still smarting from its failure to impeach the Duke of Buckingham, and in the spring of 1628 was proceeding with the Petition of Right (a restatement of the rights of the subject against an encroaching royal prerogative). The Commons sent for witnesses against the rogue saltpetermen on the very day that the Petition of Right was engrossed. Local grievances became framed in terms of constitutional principle, and the saltpeter squabble raised challenges to the royal prerogative. Sir John Eliot and Sir Robert Phelips, in particular, spoke out against the 'boldness' of the saltpetermen, their 'great abuses in the whole kingdom', and their contempt for the House of Commons. 'A commission to break up churches and lay illegal charges upon the country suits well with the unlimited power of some men's commands, which is most unjust,' declared an indignant Eliot. Sir Edward Coke rehearsed his Jacobean argument that the king's right to saltpeter was 'only as a purveyance', and gave no entitlement to enter private houses: 'They cannot dig any house or wall, for it is for the commonwealth to have houses of habitation. They may dig in floors, in stables, cellars and vaults or mud walls, so as they be repaired again, but not in dovecotes or barns.' The saltpeter commissioners, of course, disagreed, and parliament's bill to reform abuses never became law.[40]

Meanwhile, a flood of complaints clamoured for attention. Robert More, a former flax dresser, 'having no experience nor knowledge in saltpeter, nor in the mystery of making it', was said to have 'wasted and disabled' people's grounds in East Anglia, and 'vexed and troubled the king's subjects'. He also failed to pay his workers, and it was these men, rather than unhappy property owners, who pressed the complaint.[41] One grand jury in Essex heard of saltpetermen who broke doors and dug in houses, despite accepting bribes and promising 'not to meddle'. Another complained of the cost and inconvenience of carting saltpeter through their county from Norfolk and Suffolk to London.[42] The steward of one estate in Essex even recorded in his account book the expenditure of five shillings, 'paid in a bribe to the saltpetermen to refrain digging some cellars'. At Framlingham, Suffolk (where the earls of Suffolk owned Framlingham Castle), officials expended the hefty sum of 14s. 4d. in 1630, 'laid out to get the saltpetermen gone out of town.'[43]

Thomas Hilliard, whose territory now embraced Dorset, Somerset, Wiltshire, and Gloucestershire, joined Nicholas Stephens as the evil face of the saltpeter enterprise. Sir Francis Seymour complained to Secretary Coke about Hilliard's 'oppressions' in Wiltshire, where he and his men dug where they pleased, 'in any man's house, in any room, and at any time'. Among other 'abuses common to the saltpetermen', they spoiled malthouses, interfered with planting and harvest, and underpaid for transport.[44] Another of Hilliard's victims, Thomas Bond, told the Attorney General in March 1630 that the saltpetermen 'tyrannize over poor people', and warned that if they escaped justice, 'it would strike such an everlasting despair into the heart of the country, as they will never attempt to complain again'. Bond charged Hilliard with overdigging, undermining, misuse of horses, and intrusion into bedchambers, among a 'multiplicity of these oppressions', but the saltpeterman cast the landowner rather than himself as the delinquent.[45]

By spring 1630 the cascade of complaint was too loud to ignore. A four-page report summarized grievances against Hilliard and Stephens, and recommended that they be further examined. They had dug 'in all places without distinction, as in parlours, bed-chambers, threshing floors, malting houses and shops; yea, God's own house they have not forborne, but have digged in churches, hallowed chapels and churchyards, tearing men's bones and ashes out of their graves to make gunpowder of'. They worked without regard to time or season, upsetting dovecotes, disrupting maltings, and undermining foundations, and 'seldom or never fill up or repair the places they have digged in, but leave the houses and rooms full of great heaps of earth, rubbish, dirt, and mire'. In 'placing their tubs by bedsides of the old and impotent, sick and diseased, of women with their children sucking at their breasts, and even of women in childbed and of sick persons lying on their deathbeds', they operated beyond the bounds of common decency. Further scandal accrued from their 'profane and impious proceedings, in ringing of bells and disorderly drinking in the church'. By making demands and issuing threats in the name of the king, the saltpetermen brought royal authority into discredit. By calling people who opposed them 'rogues, rebels and traitors', they sowed the seeds of sedition. For the work to go forward, as surely it must, the saltpetermen would have to 'demean themselves soberly and modestly' under scrutiny of justices of the peace.[46]

The dispute, however, was not one-sided. While property owners catalogued local abuses, the saltpetermen themselves complained of being 'opposed and hindered by divers refractory persons, and therefore unable to perform his majesty's service'. Having 'engaged their estates and credits' for the king, they claimed that they now faced ruin. Appealing to the Privy Council, the saltpetermen represented themselves as loyal toilers on the crown's behalf against obdurate countrymen and slack local officials.[47]

Faced with Star Chamber, a court that he himself had threatened against his enemies, the saltpeterman Nicholas Stephens pleaded for proceedings to be dropped. He had worked, he said, in times of 'great necessity and danger', when the kingdom's store of powder was 'exhausted', and had done no more than discharge his duty to the king. The authorities had pressured him 'to deliver in a double weekly proportion', despite there being 'great spoil of grounds by several undue courses'. Stephens held that the church was 'not excepted' in the saltpeter commission, and if he had caused 'scandal' at Chipping Norton it was not intended, for he had dug other churches without opposition. As a sign of his contrition, he cast the workman responsible for the worst abuses into Oxford gaol, and declared himself ready to turn over a new leaf.[48]

Thomas Hilliard also pointed to the great seal on his commission, which entitled him, he said, to dig in private houses and 'all privileged places' including churches. Anyone who opposed him opposed the king, and risked 'the fearful threat of his majesty's displeasure'.[49] Other saltpetermen depicted their enemies as refractory and obstructive, and turned accusations against the accusers. The East Anglian saltpeterman Hugh Grove blamed 'the decay of the supply of saltpeter' on people who 'destroy the generation of saltpeter within their possessions', and he sought punishment for anyone who refused to transport his barrels. His colleague John Gifford complained that 'not half the persons who were warned sent carts', and local justices refused assistance. Thomas Thornhill blamed Londoners who paved cellars with stone or filled them with gravel for 'great damage and hindrance...that his majesty's mines of saltpeter may [be] utterly ruined'.[50]

Other landowners allegedly cheated the state by planking their dovecotes and flooring their stables, by making the earth inaccessible, or by taking it themselves to manure their own fields. They restricted entry to rich saltpeter grounds, and obstructed the diggers and boilers. They fanned opposition to the state saltpeter enterprise, and failed to supply its agents with the requisite shelter, transport, or fuel. At the heart of the problem, from this point of view, was not the predatory practice of a few bad apples, but a failure of subjects to give due support to the crown. Privy Councillors argued that offenders should 'answer their contempt and neglect of...this so necessary and behooveful a service for the safety of the kingdom'.[51]

As in previous reigns, the Council awarded annual contracts for supplies of saltpeter from particular territories. The South and the

Table 1: Saltpeter Assignments, 1628–1629

Name and Territory	Assignment	Brought In (to nearest hundredweight)
Nicholas Stephens (Berkshire, Oxfordshire, Warwickshire, Middlesex)	624	552
Thomas Hilliard (Hampshire, Wiltshire, Dorset)	312	347
John Gifford (Gloucestershire, Somerset, Devon, Cornwall)	364	371
William Burrowes (Nottinghamshire, Leicestershire, Staffordshire, Derbyshire)	468	254
Stephen Barratt (Lincolnshire, Rutland, Huntingdonshire, Cambridgeshire)	416	220
Hugh Grove (Essex, Norfolk, Suffolk)	502	378
John Vincent (Surrey, Sussex, Kent)	468	371
Thomas Thornhill (London and two miles compass)	416	312
Edward Thornhill (Bedfordshire, Buckinghamshire, Northamptonshire, Hertfordshire)	572	485
John Melton (Yorkshire, Durham, Northumberland)	312	154
William Richardson (Worcestershire, Shropshire, Herefordshire)	364	112
William Richardson, sr (Wales)	208	0

continued

Name and Territory	Assignment	Brought In (to nearest hundredweight)
John Cooper (Cheshire, Lancashire)	208	0
Total:	5,234	3,462 (*recte* 3,556 cwt)

Midlands, with their richer soils and larger populations, were generally more productive than the North. Table 1 shows the names of the principal saltpetermen, the counties they worked, the targets they were assigned, and the actual amounts they delivered between 1 May 1628 and 30 April 1629. The ambitious target this year was 5,234 hundredweight of saltpeter, almost 262 tons, which would have furnished 316 lasts of gunpowder. But the Ordnance Office could account for only 3,462 hundredweight, just over 173 tons, enough for 210 lasts of powder. Though still short of the nation's needs, this represents an aggressive effort by men like Grove, Hilliard, Stephens, and Thornhill to bring England closer to saltpeter independence.[52]

Abuse and complaints in the age of personal rule

By the early 1630s the political environment was changing, and the demand for saltpeter briefly slackened. The assassination of the Duke of Buckingham in 1628 removed that controversial figure from the Ordnance Commission and lowered the political temperature. The king's determination to govern without parliament after 1629 removed a forum for the airing of landowners' grievances. Most important, the ending of foreign wars seemed likely to reduce the crown's need for gunpowder. Peace with France was sealed in April 1629 by the Treaty of Susa, and hostilities with Spain ended in November 1630 with the Treaty of Madrid. After half a decade of struggle to furnish 240 lasts of saltpeter a year, the Council planned 'to reduce the proportion to the former single rate of 120 lasts per annum'. This allowed the government to review the system of procurement, to introduce reforms, and to remove saltpetermen judged abusive or insufficient.[53]

The saltpetermen again agreed to reformed practices, promising more 'sober and modest carriage' that would generate less controversy. Though still authorized to enter private houses (despite the common lawyers' objection), they promised not to dig where people lay in bed. Though still permitted to dig in dovecotes, they would now work around the breeding cycle of the birds. Still empowered to compel transportation, they grudgingly agreed to pay fourpence a mile, a rate doubled to eightpence by 1634.[54] Manoeuvring for advantage, some saltpetermen launched aggressive litigation to denounce their rivals and undercut each other's business.[55]

Rival saltpetermen circled around Thomas Hilliard when he looked likely to lose his commission. He had survived attacks in parliament in 1628, but his troubles intensified in the period of personal rule. If it was wrong for him to take bribes to spare people's carts and grounds, and scandalous that he allowed his wife to ride around 'in a cart in the nature of a carriage' that was hired for the public service, it was unforgivable that he should attempt to defraud the king. Already suspected of secret deals in London, 'to his own private profit and benefit', Hilliard was reported to have shipped 'close sacks and barrels' by night to black-market powdermen in Bristol, and to have made other arrangements 'for his own advantage'. 'Embezzling his majesty's saltpeter' was much more serious than trampling on the rights of the subject, and the case swept up not just Hilliard but his wife, his workmen, his associates, and his customers. It was this, as much as complaints from the localities, that led to Star Chamber proceedings against Thomas Hilliard in 1633.[56]

By cheating the king, Hilliard had weakened the kingdom. His private sales and diversions, prosecutors alleged, had left the king's store 'so scanted, that the Commissioners for the Navy were forced to buy [saltpeter] at a dear rate from foreign parts'. The saltpeterman's corruption 'betray[ed] the whole realm to danger'. The Star Chamber judges demanded a heavy sentence, a fine of £5,000, the pillory, and a lifetime ban from office. Hilliard's wife and partner, who had helped him tamper with witnesses, also suffered fines and sanctions. The last to be heard of him was a report in 1634 that 'Hilliard the saltpeterman' had fled.[57]

Most complaints involving saltpetermen were determined in the interest of the crown. In March 1633 the patentee John Vincent presented charges against George Mynnes of Croydon, whose servants, armed with pitchforks and bills, set chains across the highway and denied the salterpetermen access to his pigeon house. The armed standoff ended when Mynnes's bailiff displayed a privilege which, he said, freed his master's ground from such service. George Mynnes, it turned out, had court connections as a Clerk of the Hanaper (a sub-office of the court of Chancery), and was prepared to do battle with the saltpetermen. The tussle continued for several months, each side alleging obstruction or illegality by the other. On one occasion, when the saltpetermen persisted in demanding access, Mynnes told them to 'hold their peace, for one word of his mouth to the Lords would hang them all'. On another, when the saltpetermen sought water from Mynnes's well, his servants laughed at them, 'and said that they knew no service that the king had there; but if the king came that way he should have the key'. The upshot was a victory for Vincent's saltpeter operation, the Council instructing Mynnes firmly, 'he is to permit his pigeon house to be digged'.[58]

The patentees also prevailed in Essex, after the saltpeterman Hugh Grove complained in November 1633 of hindrance to his lawful activity. Property owners refused to rent him warehouses convenient for the king's service, the ash he needed for refining had all been bought for the soap works, and local justices gave him no support. When Grove demanded that Daniel Chappell turn over his barn at Matching Green, the farmer denied him, 'having in it his hay, and his corn soon after'. This defiance cost the men of Matching an appearance before authorities in London, after which, suitably chastened, they were discharged and the saltpeter work went forward.[59] Troublemakers in Berkshire were likewise discharged on bond 'not to hinder or interrupt the saltpeter works'.[60]

In London, saltpetermen complained, 'the cellars, vaults, warehouses and stables, where the mine of saltpeter used formerly to grow, are so destroyed with paving and pitching and other hurtful stuff', that without some urgent course 'those mines...will be utterly destroyed'.[61] In Somerset, they alleged, 'the mine of saltpeter is destroyed, not only to the prejudice of his majesty's saltpeter-makers, but to the great disservice of his majesty and loss of the kingdom', and this was done 'merely upon spleen'. In Dorset, opponents obstructed the carriage of liquids to the boiling house at Sherborne. The underlying problem, advised the Berkshire saltpeterman Richard Bagnall, was the 'unwillingness among most of his majesty's subjects to do anything for the advance of this service'.[62] Browbeaten by the saltpeterman, William Browne of Alveston, Gloucestershire, represented himself as 'an innocent and honest man, maliciously persecuted by such as would reign over poor men in their office'.[63]

It was little comfort, when a man's home was invaded, his barn occupied, or his livelihood threatened, to be thanked for assisting the king's service. Even more galling was to be cast as a malignant for simply protecting one's property. Ever watchful for 'refractory' persons, Charles I's government had little difficulty finding such people in the years of the personal rule (1629–1640). Ordnance officials suggested in 1634 that 'the names of such as have paved their pigeon houses' should be certified, and the saltpetermen so informed.[64]

As always, the saltpetermen blamed obstructive landlords, refractory carters, and unhelpful justices for their insufficiencies. They managed to make modern farming practices resemble sedition, and the improving of agricultural outbuildings seem like a conspiracy to defraud the king. The lofting and flooring of pigeon houses and the planking or paving of stables may have been sound infrastructure investments, but they thwarted the saltpeter enterprise. So too did the agricultural practice of digging up mould to spread on pasture land. Pigeon dung was among the best manures for grassland, and graziers valued it as highly as did the saltpetermen.[65]

Arguments about dovecotes and carts might seem like minor matters compared to the other contentious issues of the day, such as Ship Money or Habeas Corpus. But vital issues of law and custom were at stake. The king needed supplies for his ordnance, and his prerogative entitled him to obtain them. The work was supposed to be consensual, with compensation for inconvenience. But it ran across competing concerns about property and honour, including the deep-felt English claim that 'a man's home is his castle'. Though disputes turned on whether or not barns were empty, pigeons breeding, or stables fit for digging; they also involved fundamental issues of equity and governance. A ban on planking stables or paving cellars was supposed to nourish the saltpeter grounds, but it cut into the interests of the elite who thought they knew best how to manage their estates. Stables and dovecotes were seigneurial accoutrements, markers of privilege as well as wealth, so that assaults on them touched a landowner's honour as well as his purse.[66]

Saltpeter policy changed again in the mid-1630s as Charles I's government built up its forces. Though England remained aloof from European conflict, the threat of military involvement had not abated. Barbary slavers from North Africa and Dunkirk raiders from across the Channel became more audacious, and invasion by Catholic powers was not unthinkable. It was a responsible course of action for the government to fortify the coasts and revive the Elizabethan battle fleet. It was an assertion of royal honour to restore England's 'sovereignty of the seas'. With thirty-four ships, the Royal Navy of the Ship Money era was no larger than in the days of the Armada, but its tonnage and firepower was almost doubled. The *Sovereign of the Seas*, launched in 1637, was the most powerful warship afloat, with a complement of 102 guns. King Charles's fleet by 1640 bore almost 1,200 guns. By estimates of February 1638, before the start of the Scottish war, Charles I needed 292 lasts of gunpowder a year, more than three times the requirements of the Elizabethan wartime regime (and much more than English saltpetermen could supply). The trained bands alone would need ninety-four lasts a year for musters and training.[67] Celebratory shots and salutes also ate up supplies, so much so that the practice had to be curtailed. In an unfortunate accident in 1635, five members of the king's nephew's entourage were killed when 'Captain Pennington's gunner discharging a piece of ordnance by way of salute', in honour of the visiting Elector Palatine, forgot to check if it was loaded.[68]

Charles I's military build-up increased the pressure on saltpetermen to fulfil larger assignments, and officials grew testy when delivery fell short of the quotas. Gunpowder contracts from the mid-1630s specified delivery of 240 lasts of powder each year, but the king's powder-maker repeatedly complained 'that he wants saltpeter to keep his majesty's mills in work'.[69]

Intensive lobbying by the saltpeter interests led to a proclamation in March 1635 'for preservation of grounds for making of saltpeter, and to restore such grounds as are now destroyed, and to command assistance to be given to his majesty's saltpeter-makers'. The proclamation reprimanded 'disobedient subjects' who 'impaired and destroyed the growth and mines of saltpeter', and advised 'all sorts of delinquents' against paving or planking their outbuildings or raising their dovecotes off the ground. Anyone responsible for such 'impediments and mischiefs' had two months to restore their property for digging, and justices were empowered to see that they complied. 'Refractory persons' who disobeyed 'our royal commandment, in a matter of so high consequence for the public service and safety of our state and kingdom', faced 'penalties and punishments' from the highest of courts. The state supported the aggressive pursuit of saltpeter, and chose to treat opponents as malignants. The 1635 proclamation made two important exemptions, however, in line with other Caroline sensibilities. Henceforth, it declared, 'we will not have any sacred ground be stirred, digged, or opened' by authority of the saltpeter commission. Churches were at last off limits. And notwithstanding the

assertion that the proclamation applied to 'all subjects of whatsoever estate, degree, or condition', it specifically excused 'the stables
of the lords spiritual and temporal, and of gentlemen of quality',
from the rules against paving or gravelling. The same elite class
that was protected by the revived court of honour (the High
Court of Chivalry) now gained another privilege. But rank and
status did not otherwise exempt English aristocrats from the
attentions of saltpeter prospectors, as it did their contemporaries
in France. When Sir John Rayney of Wrotham, Kent, refused to
cooperate with the saltpetermen in 1637, citing his status as a
knight and baronet, local justices countered 'that he was no more
exempt than any other gentleman'.[70]

Backed by the state, the saltpetermen threw their weight around
in the months and years that followed. Wrapping themselves in
royal authority, they gained favourable hearings from the Privy
Council and officers responsible for gunpowder procurement.
They reported dozens of 'acts of ill-affectedness to his majesty's
service' that cost them 'great loss and charges'. Saltpetermen complained when a magistrate on the Isle of Wight called one of their
deputies 'vagabond and rogue' and gave him two nights in prison.
They appealed to the Council when bailiffs and officers at Lichfield
frustrated 'his majesty's service'. When a London woodmonger
balked at carrying coals for the saltpetermen, they committed him
to the Marshalsea and pursued him in the courts. On complaint
by Francis Vincent, the saltpeterman for Kent, Thomas May of
Norton went to prison in December 1635 for removing soil from
his own pigeon house. He was only released on condition of
restoring the floor 'with one foot of mellow earth fit for the
growth of the mine of saltpeter'. Another Kentish gentleman
faced costs and damages for calling men at Gravesend 'unwise' to
carry sea coals to the saltpeter house.[71]

The saltpetermen at Norwich complained about 'the slackness
and uneffectualness of the performance of his majesty's service',
and hoped that city officials would discover 'his majesty's just and
high displeasure in slighting his royal commands'. Civil relations
deteriorated when citizens used 'reproachful speeches' against the

saltpetermen, and one of their workmen threatened to throw a parish officer into a well. The mayor of Norwich claimed that the digging undermined the foundations of the town hall, 'so as the whole fabric and structure of the house is in great danger to fall'. The saltpetermen insisted on digging in the gaol, where 'dangerous' prisoners were housed, and even dug in those rooms 'where distracted mad persons are usually put'. The saltpetermen, of course, denied these outrages, and intimidated the workmen sent to assess the damage.[72] Petitioners elsewhere in Norfolk complained of the 'great abuses, oppressions and extortions' of the saltpetermen whose 'disorderly, shameless and riotous behaviour' included 'breaking up houses and barns in most unseasonable times, receiving of moneys under hand, forcing of carriages to remote places, only to weary the country thereby to gain bribes'. These saltpetermen included 'persons of low condition, assuming to themselves names as Grey Jack, Dallygood and such like conceited names, which they take in one place and lay down in another to keep themselves from being so readily discovered'.[73]

Saltpetermen in Herefordshire sought the ruin of a man whose servant sabotaged their boiling tubs, an act of 'abuse and contempt of his majesty's service'. They wanted parishioners and constables at Idleston, Berkshire, to answer for their similar 'great contempt and neglect'. Saltpetermen harassed Sir John Rayney in Kent and sided, so he said, with a neighbour 'who seeketh all occasions though never so small and frivolous to vex and trouble me'. Throughout England they insisted on their 'power, licence, liberty and authority to break open and work for saltpeter' in anyone's 'houses, lands, grounds and possessions', with complete disregard for the strictures of common law.[74]

Saltpetermen at Oxford and Cambridge protested claims by the universities to be exempt from their intrusions. Hugh Grove complained that at Cambridge he sustained 'great loss for want of assistance' when carters refused to transport his materials. Townsmen claimed privilege because of their attachment to a college, the vice-chancellor claimed exemptions for university servants, grounds, and animals, and nobody would supply the necessary carts. Grove asked the Council for remedy against this 'contempt and hinderance' of the king's service.[75] Likewise at Oxford, when Richard Bagnall needed barns and outhouses to set up his utensils, their owner Richard Napper claimed 'that all digging for saltpeter is prohibited in the colleges, and other places that belong to them or their servants', and that all carts within five miles of the city were similarly protected. Bagnall wanted the Council to override this objection, and make Napper 'answer his contempt'.[76]

When Bagnall sought to dig in the king's house at Woodstock in May 1636 his majesty temporized but could hardly refuse outright. The Council took note that 'the king likes it well, but the saltpetermen [must] first attend the Lord Chamberlain for order to the housekeeper, without whom the saltpeterman is to do nothing in it'. Half a year later Bagnall still waited for permission to dig in the king's hunting lodge. In February 1637 he entreated again to dig Woodstock House, promising to leave it in as good repair as he found it, and the request was renewed four months later. Although King Charles himself was willing for the saltpetermen to dig up his house at Woodstock, repeated applications were repeatedly blocked.[77]

In Somerset the saltpeter dispute pitted champions of liberty against guardians of authority. It was always about more than the commodity of gunpowder. Sir Robert Phelips, once prominent in parliament, faced censure in 1636 for refusing to allow his carts to carry the saltpetermen's coals. Appealing to the Clerk of the Council, Phelips claimed that rather than advancing the king's service, the saltpetermen pursued their own ends, and 'to ease themselves, endeavour to make his majesty's subjects their slaves'. They put the country to 'an immense charge', he said, and 'under pretence of his majesty's service, require unreasonable things'. Phelips himself, of course, 'yielded all obedience unto his majesty's service', but balked at being 'pressed so unreasonably' and in such a 'peremptory manner'.[78]

Denzil Holles, another parliamentary stalwart, suffered defeat in February 1637 when the Commissioners for Saltpeter and Gunpowder insisted that he allow his dovecote at Damerham,

Wiltshire, to be dug. Holles had sent the saltpetermen packing with angry words, but now he had to yield and cover their expenses. A new commission for saltpeter in June 1637 warned 'obstinate and unreasonable' property owners like Holles and Phelips that they were liable for punishment if they 'disobey our authority and royal commandment herein'.[79]

Another squabble in Wiltshire pitted Thomas Thornhill, the most energetic of saltpetermen, against Christopher Wren, the rector of Knoyle Magna (now East Knoyle), who was also Dean of Windsor, Registrar of the Order of the Garter, and brother to the Bishop of Norwich. When Thornhill's men dug Wren's pigeon house at Knoyle, by Wren's account, they did so much damage that the north wall fell in and the birds 'forsook the house'. The rector lost 'three breeds, whereof the least never yielded fewer than thirty or forty dozen', and now faced a suit for dilapidations. The pigeon house was a stone structure twenty feet high with walls more than three feet thick, that had already been weakened by previous saltpeter work. Now it was reduced to a ruin. Thornhill, for his part, claimed that the wall was already cracked, and that it fell down 'on the great windy night that blew down so many houses, barns and trees in all parts of the kingdom', by no means due to his digging. As a servant of the crown, engaged in work of national importance, he sought relief from the Council against the rector's 'unjust molestation'.[80]

Wren, however, complained not to the Council or local justices but directly to King Charles himself on the occasion of the Feast of St George. As an officer of the Order of the Garter, Wren claimed royal protection, and the king took his registrar's side against his saltpeterman. A high-level committee under Lord Treasurer Bishop Juxon concluded in January 1638 that the pigeon house fell down in consequence of Thornhill's digging, and not by casualty of wind and weather, so the rector could sue for damages. But by this time Thornhill's commission had expired, and he was replaced by his son-in-law and fellow saltpeterman Richard Bagnall. The case exposed competing lines of authority and patronage in a dispute that might not otherwise have been documented.[81]

Other well-placed complainers against the saltpetermen included Lionel Cranfield, Earl of Middlesex, and Sir John Lucas, the recently knighted former sheriff of Essex. Middlesex, himself a former commissioner for saltpeter and gunpowder, waxed indignant when 'some mean fellows under pretence of a patent for digging for saltpeter' broke into his house 'like thieves' and dug in some unfloored rooms. He wanted 'exemplary' punishment against these 'lewd people', who used 'saucy and unbecoming language' and left a trail of damage on his property.[82] Lucas too was outraged by the breaking of locks and 'unlawful' digging at his mother's house in Colchester, especially since there were 'many inns and other houses in the town fit for their purpose'. But it was less the damage than the affront that exercised him. Like Middlesex, Lucas took exception to the insolent, insulting 'incivility' of the saltpetermen as they 'violated the privileges of the house'. In April 1640 he launched a lawsuit against them, because 'necessity enforces me to vindicate my right and the privileges of my house'.[83]

Few people had the access and connections of a nobleman, an aristocrat, or an officer of the Order of the Garter. Most were reduced to private grumbling. Some property owners became bolder, or more ingenious, in foiling the saltpeter enterprise. Their gates were locked, their carts unavailable, their tenants obstreperous. Wagons developed problems with their axles, horses went lame, and barrels suffered mysterious accidents. No fuel could be found for boiling, and the ashes needed for refining had all been pre-empted for other purposes. The only charcoal available was mixed with dirt. Saltpetermen reported a 'mutiny' against them in Hertfordshire in May 1638, 'whereby his majesty's said officers were in danger of being killed'.[84] Nighttime raiders in Lincolnshire overthrew saltpeter tubs and spoiled their mixtures, and local magistrates turned blind eyes to the offenders. In Kent in December 1639 'malignants' with cudgels beat up the saltpeter operatives and locked them in the stocks, saying 'the king employed more rogues in his works than any man'.[85] Complaints came from all points of the ideological spectrum, from champions of parliament like Eliot and Phelips to arch-royalists like Lucas and Wren. Though divided on other matters, landowners agreed that the crown's quest for saltpeter was vexatious, especially when it touched their own estates.

Charles I's saltpeter enterprise became further stressed when shortages of money threatened to bring it to a halt. The crown fell behind in payments to the saltpetermen, who were accused in turn of defaulting on their workers' wages. Officers complained of 'the want of gunpowder', at the very time when war with Scotland placed new pressures on military procurement, and powder-makers blamed saltpetermen for failing to deliver their quotas.[86] Gunpowder manufacture threatened to grind to a halt in July 1640, just as the Scottish war reached its crisis. The crown owed the powder-maker Samuel Cordewell £4,000, and he was unable to pay his suppliers. The domestic saltpetermen went unpaid, and the merchant importers had £1,150 owing to them. The powder problem was just another blight in a thoroughly miserable campaign season.[87]

By its own estimate the crown needed 292 lasts of gunpowder a year for its war with Scotland.[88] But the powder manufacturers were contracted to supply only 240 lasts, and always fell short of their quota. Gunpowder reserves stood at 271 lasts in February 1640, but fell to 196 lasts by the end of June, with further depletions to follow. Domestic saltpeter supplies became erratic, and only foreign purchases could fill the gap. Saltpeter deliveries to the royal stores for the year ending November 1637 reached 243 lasts, fell to 207 lasts in 1638, then recovered to 237 lasts in 1639. It could not help that Charles chose this moment to sell £5,000 worth of gunpowder (forty lasts) as a 'favour to the Spaniards'.[89] In 1640, the crucial year of the Scottish war, only 206 lasts of saltpeter reached the royal stores, and forty-six of these came in through merchantmen. Saltpeter deliveries fell to their lowest level between November 1640 and November 1641 (the first year of the Long Parliament) when only 100 lasts reached the stores.[90]

The Council recognized the seriousness of the problem, noting in February 1639 that 'all the saltpeter made in the kingdom is not enough by above forty lasts' to meet the king's needs, and observing the following year that 'home-made saltpeter falls short about eighty lasts'.[91] By February 1639 the price of gunpowder topped £7 a barrel, more than double its peacetime level, though prices eased as stocks recovered.[92] Only imported saltpeter could keep the royal powder mills at full capacity, and only powder purchased on the international market could keep the magazines at the Tower and Portsmouth from falling dangerously short.

Rogue gunpowder

Since Tudor times the crown reserved to itself 'all saltpeter made in England', and maintained the royal monopoly on the manufacture of gunpowder. These strategic materials were too vital for national security to allow interlopers into the trade. But from time to time in the 1620s the state monopoly developed cracks. In November 1625 the Privy Council allowed the maritime city of Bristol to make powder for its own needs, but only from imported saltpeter. There was to be no diversion of 'saltpeter made within this kingdom, which is not to be meddled with by any others than such as are authorized by his majesty's commission'. To increase supplies for the impending war the Council considered 'setting free' the making of gunpowder and cancelling the contract with the Evelyns, but drew back from so radical a step. One argument in favour of the status quo was that 'subjects will not give way to have their houses and cellars broken for the service of any other but the king'. Another was that 'by the promiscuous making it will assuredly be made worse'.[93] In January 1626, at a time of intense gunpowder shortage, the Master of the Ordnance suggested 'that the shires and maritime towns should be warned to make provisions for themselves without depending on the king's stores, and that liberty should be given for home consumption from foreign saltpeter'. Within months there were reports of 'private men' making gunpowder in Dorset and the west midlands.[94] Advocates thought it 'would be a great ease to the country' to have more diversity of supply, but royal policy proved resistant.

Unauthorized powder mills in Bristol, Dorset, and Sussex were suppressed in 1627, and the following year an artisan at Chester was arrested for 'making gunpowder'.[95]

The East India Company was almost a law unto itself. Finding the king's mills 'not sufficient to furnish powder for the public service', the Company decided late in 1624 to establish gunpowder mills of its own 'and fetch saltpeter from foreign parts'. The Company's mills in Surrey operated under licence, with a permit in 1626 to make gunpowder from their own imported saltpeter. But later in 1632, when England's involvement in foreign war was ended, they were called upon 'to surrender the patent granted unto them by his majesty for the making of powder', and their manager was investigated 'to see what peter and powder he hath by him'.[96] In the long run the Company held the key to England's saltpeter problem, but under Charles I they too were subject to royal discipline.

John Evelyn's commission gave him the sole right to make gunpowder from English saltpeter. But it left open the possibility that businesses like the East India Company and cities like Bristol could work their own mills with imported materials.[97] When the Council discovered that home-bred saltpeter was going to the Bristol powder-makers, and that the saltpeterman Thomas Hilliard was selling loads privately that should have gone to the king, they reacted with indignation. Freelance enterprises in Dorset and Wiltshire were also found to be trading in unauthorized supplies. Exploiting an old pigeon house at Sherston, one local partnership produced several hundredweight of low-grade saltpeter before being stopped.[98]

John Evelyn's new contract in 1635 specifically gave him 'the sole working and converting into gunpowder' of imported saltpeter, as well as all saltpeter 'got, digged and made within this realm of England'. His successor Samuel Cordewell secured similar conditions.[99] The state monopoly was reaffirmed, but outlaw manufacturers proved hard to suppress. William Baber's mill at Bristol produced a barrel or two of gunpowder a week by December 1638, though its quality was not the best. This operation was suspended in April 1639 and its equipment confiscated, but another Bristol powder mill was soon in business. The gunpowder commissioners suppressed an illicit powder mill in Surrey in November 1639, and called for another crackdown at Bristol in the following spring.[100]

The government also pursued unauthorized powder manufacturers in the shadow of the Tower of London. One notorious freelancer, Robert Davis, was discovered when an accident at his backyard mill at Whitechapel set a neighbour's house on fire. Under examination, Davis said he learned to make gunpowder by reading about it in a book. He bought his saltpeter directly from the Barbary merchants in London, and also dealt in powder embezzled from the king's ships. Condemned to Newgate in 1639, he was freed on condition that he never make gunpowder again.[101] Only when parliament met late in 1640 was there serious consideration of ending the royal monopoly.

Overall, between 1625 and 1640, Charles I's efforts increased the amount of saltpeter extracted from English earth. His pressure on the saltpetermen, and his general support for their projects, raised the home-bred proportion of this 'inestimable treasure' from one-third to occasionally as much as two-thirds of the kingdom's needs. But the social costs of this expansion were incalculable. Resentments and frustrations accumulated as the saltpetermen filled their quotas, and grievance about their 'vexation and oppression' in the period of personal rule added fuel to the discords of the revolutionary 1640s.

6

Saltpeter Revolution

WILLIAM Baber operated an illicit gunpowder mill at Bristol in the 1630s, buying saltpeter by night and selling powder on the black market. Early in 1639 he produced a barrel or two a week, of uncertain quality, before his operation was suspended and his equipment seized. When civil war broke out in 1642 Baber tendered his talents to his sovereign, and his fortunes were transformed. As powder-maker to the king at Oxford, Baber turned out thirty-two barrels a month in good times, and in May 1643 he outdid himself with fifty-five barrels of gunpowder. This was but a fraction of the royalist gunpowder budget, but its production required ingenuity and enterprise. Baber operated a saltpeter house at Oxford, and gathered local materials for munitions, but he faced opposition from rival ordnance commissioners. When royalists regained control of Bristol in the summer of 1643 Baber returned to his home and resumed his manufactures, until the city fell finally to parliament in September 1645. At that time the city's defences included more than 150 guns. Bristol garrisons, both royalist and parliamentarian, hungered for gunpowder but depended more on imports than home-produced supplies. Like the rest of the country under Protector Cromwell they switched from domestic to East India sources of saltpeter. William Baber's post-war career is opaque, but he claimed to have been 'undone' and to have suffered losses in Charles I's service. After the Restoration he sued for payments due to him for civil-war gunpowder, and for relief from his 'merciless creditors'.

Baber's career spanned the English revolution, and saw both the rise and decline of the hated roving saltpetermen.[1]

* * *

The royal saltpeter enterprise unravelled and the crown monopoly of gunpowder collapsed in 1641 as England slid towards civil war and revolution. But saltpeter was too valuable a commodity to be neglected, as state security still depended on munitions. Royalists and parliamentarians would both soon demand huge amounts of gunpowder for their armies, and both sides sought ways to secure the vital ingredients. Projectors again promoted alternative schemes, but saltpeter self-sufficiency was only achieved in the 1650s when the East India Company effected a revolution of supply.

Revolutionary saltpeter

The members of the Long Parliament who first took their seats in November 1640 had many more claims on their attention than the social impact of ordnance procurement. Royal and ecclesiastical authority were crumbling, as the nation coped with the aftermath of the Scottish war. Amid fears of popish plotting and popular disturbances, and pressure from military, financial, and religious exigencies, the parliamentary leadership struggled to reverse the policies of the previous eleven years. Accumulated frustrations fuelled debate on the powers of the crown, and subjects who had suffered from the exactions of the saltpetermen found sympathetic hearings at Westminster.

Among them was Richard Cowdray, a husbandman from Berkshire, who petitioned parliament in February 1641 for recompense for losses he had suffered twenty months earlier when the saltpeterman Richard Bagnall requisitioned his barn. Cowdray said that he entreated Bagnall to go elsewhere, but with no 'consent or any agreement' and 'without any toleration or bargain', the saltpeterman 'violently entered upon the same barn', tending to Cowdray's 'utter undoing'.[2] This was small beer, after tales of collapsing pigeon houses and unfair dealing, and trivial compared to the wars of religion between England and Scotland (1639–1640), but it kept the matter on the political agenda. The Kentish squire Sir Anthony Weldon wrote to his members of parliament in May 1641 about 'a grievance to us far more pressing than Ship Money, or anything that I know', because of the 'insolent carriage' of the 'base' local operatives and 'the charge' involved in compliance. Since the matter had come to parliamentary attention the offenders 'have raged in much more violence, and even now are as insolent as ever in these parts'. Weldon does not explicitly identify the saltpetermen, though his observations match their profile; the letter to Sir Edward Dering and Sir John Culpeper is clearly endorsed 'gunpowder men'.[3]

Two separate issues became entwined. Political winds blew strongly against 'monopolisers and projectors' and against the royal prerogatives that had nourished them.[4] At the same time parliament took note of 'the abuses of the saltpetermen's proceedings in digging of men's houses, and all other abuse of their proceedings'. Though the Commons and country were deeply divided, the 'great grievance' of the saltpeter enterprise cut across ideological lines. Members spoke from their own experience of 'the great oppression and insolency of those who digged for saltpeter' on their properties. The grievance in parliament's Grand Remonstrance of November 1641 concerning the 'vexation and oppression' of the saltpetermen addressed widely shared concerns.[5] Sir Edward Coke's claim that an Englishman's home was his castle was about to gain legal and institutional support.

Branded in 1641 as 'most pernicious', the royal gunpowder monopoly was in trouble. Early that year a petition to the House of Commons 'that every man that will might make gunpowder' threatened ruin to the established powder-makers. Parliamentary critics attacked the old privileged practice as 'a grievance and a monopoly and against the liberty of the subject', though John Evelyn of Surrey predictably protested it was 'no grievance, nor…any inconvenience'. The lawyer Bulstrode Whitelocke argued in May 1641 'that the making of saltpeter can be no prerogative of the king's...for we know well when powder came first into England'. A medieval invention could not claim privilege from ancient rights of the crown. Other members asserted the making and marketing of gunpowder to be the right of any free Englishman.[6]

At the end of July, lawmakers passed 'An act for the free bringing in of gunpowder and saltpeter from foreign parts and for the free making of gunpowder in this realm', which effectively ended the crown monopoly.[7] In these circumstances few of the king's saltpetermen were inclined to work as usual. Saltpeter deliveries for 1641 reached barely eight lasts a month, half the level of earlier years and significantly short of the quota.[8] Rather anxiously, the House of Lords asked to confer with the Commons 'concerning the preservation of the mines of saltpeter in this kingdom'.[9] The recent political effort was designed to open the business up, not to close it down.

Three saltpetermen who offered supplies to the government in October 1641 'desired notice might be taken they did not deliver it to Mr Cordewell [the king's gunpowder-maker] as peter made by virtue of any commission or authority derived from his majesty, but as a commodity sold to him by way of merchandize'. The royal prerogative of purveyance no longer inspired awe, and the material was now no more than a commodity like any other. The national saltpeter enterprise was effectively suppressed, and the government's ability to command gunpowder supplies was severely compromised. The revolutionary wind that blew through the halls of power left state security in a compromised condition.[10] Anxious ordnance officers reported in February 1642 that 'no powder has been delivered into the magazine here these thirteen months, and when all the proportions already ordered by sea and land shall be issued, there will remain but four lasts nine hundredweight of powder'. By the time the Irish expedition was furnished, advised Sir John Byron, looking to the spring and summer, 'there will be little or none left'.[11] King Charles's 'inestimable treasure' had all but disappeared.

Saltpeter for civil war

Gunpowder was at a premium in England as civil war approached. Competition for control of local magazines fuelled minor skirmishes that preceded the actual fighting. Street battles broke out at Manchester in July 1642 as rival groups sought to secure stores of munitions.[12] A military forecast on the eve of the civil war estimated that a field army of 10,000 men would need seven and a half tons of gunpowder for its foot, and ten tons more for its artillery. Actual campaigns showed these estimates to be inadequate. Civil-war armies ranged up to 30,000 strong, and by 1643 there were said to be 100,000 men in arms. At Marston Moor, in July 1644, there were more than 46,000 men in combat and a hundred pieces of artillery on the battlefield. Commanders on both sides complained of chronic shortages of munitions as their

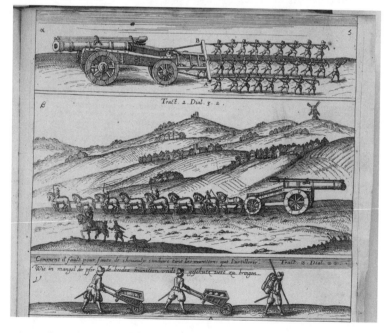

FIG 14 Siege guns

Robert Norton, *The Gunner: Shewing the Whole Practise of Artillerie* (1628), following p. 122 (Huntington Library, rare book 60110, reproduced by permission of the Huntington).

artillery consumed vast amounts of gunpowder. Parliamentary forces besieging Chester late in 1645 expended seven tons of powder in seven weeks.[13] Firepower proved decisive in scores of engagements, and quartermasters struggled to keep their powder barrels filled.

Parliament had immediate advantages in its control of government gunpowder mills and the magazines at London, Portsmouth, and Hull. Most of the king's stockpile of powder and saltpeter was turned against him. Both sides set up gunpowder works, and scavenged for saltpeter and supplies. The royal powder-maker Samuel Cordewell continued to make gunpowder for parliament, but his works at Chilworth, Surrey, were slighted twice in the early months of the war, once by parliamentarians as the king advanced on London, and then by royalists as they withdrew. Parliament also received supplies from John Beresford, who set up gunpowder mills in Essex. Domestic sources provided parliament with roughly 150 lasts of gunpowder a year at the height of the civil war, perhaps half of its total needs.[14]

Royalists operated gunpowder mills in various places, most notably Oxford, where the freelance Bristol powder-maker William Baber set up shop. He was soon producing some thirty-two barrels a month, though in May 1643 he outdid himself with fifty-five. By spring 1644, when Baber returned to Bristol, the king's ordnance commissioners took control of the Oxford powder works, and may have boosted output to eighty barrels a month or forty lasts a year. In any case, it was a fraction of their requirements, and much inferior to parliament's gunpowder production. Only imports kept royalist hopes alive, and shipments arrived at every port under the king's control.[15] One of the king's self-taught gunpowder manufacturers, Edward Morton, blew himself up while mixing a batch, in an explosion that destroyed his family and his house.[16]

All sides to the conflict sought humble saltpeter. In April 1642, 'in regard of the great expense of gunpowder in Ireland, and the necessary provision both for the occasion and defence of this kingdom', and 'seeing the magazines have been lately so exhausted',

FIG 15 Firing a mortar

Francis Malthus, *Pratique de la guerre: contenant l'usage de l'artillerie, bombes et mortiers, feux artificiels & petards, sappes & mines, ponts & pontons, tranchées & travaux* (Paris, 1681), following p. 4 (Huntington Library, rare book 486839, reproduced by permission of the Huntington).

the saltpeter interests prepared a draft Commons order to put them back in business. Describing the gathering of saltpeter as 'a service very acceptable to the commonwealth for the present safety', and warning, 'if that work should now be let fall it must needs turn to the prejudice and danger of the kingdom', they proposed that 'the saltpeter men may be permitted in all counties, at seasonable times and hours, to dig grounds apt for that purpose'. An amendment scrupulously excluded 'dwelling houses', but permitted the excavation of outhouses, dovecotes, barns, and latrines. To make their project more acceptable they specified that carts should not be laden above two hundredweight, and should not have to go more than twelve miles. 'If bribes be taken...the offenders shall be punished.'[17] With support from Westminster the rudiments of the old system, grievances and all, would be mobilized for parliament's purposes.

The civil-war demand for munitions made saltpeter all the more valuable. By the spring of 1643 'the great expense of gunpowder occasioned by the present war' had seriously weakened parliament's 'navy, forts, and land armies'. Reserves were nearly exhausted, and imports barely filled the gap. The solution was to re-establish a saltpeter programme, but with safeguards 'to prevent the reviving of those oppressions and vexations exercised upon the people' in previous years. Work began in April on 'an ordinance for furnishing the state with saltpeter', which cleared all committees by October. Like previous royal proclamations, the parliamentary ordinance empowered the state's agents 'to search and dig for saltpeter in all pigeon houses, stables, and all other outhouses, yards, and places likely to afford that earth, at fit seasons and hours, between sun rising and sun setting, except all dwelling houses, shops and milk houses'. Within these limitations, which echoed and extended the concerns of Sir Edward Coke, the state's saltpetermen could dig wherever necessary, at least in areas under parliamentary control. Anyone who refused them access risked sanction. They could requisition carts for their work, so long as 'the journey exceed not ten miles', and so long as they recompensed the owner eightpence a mile. They were, of course, as always, required to make good any damage done, and to leave the ground 'in as good order as before breaking up'. The ordinance was renewed in April 1644 for two years, and continued in February 1646 for three more.[18] Samuel Cordewell's accounts under this programme include records of three saltpetermen who furnished him with 651 hundredweight of saltpeter (roughly twenty-seven lasts) between October 1644 and June 1645.[19]

The saltpetermen inevitably sparked grievances, notwithstanding that in wartime 'the murmurings and repining of that kind have lately been repressed and hindered'.[20] From time to time parliament proceeded against delinquents who thwarted their saltpeter enterprise, just as the regime of Charles I had done several years earlier. Two men in Dorset, for example, who 'determinately endeavoured the hindrance' of the state's saltpetermen, were cited before the Committee of Both Kingdoms in 1646. They had allegedly 'incited others to threaten the demolition of the works, and invited divers soldiers to set fire on the houses'. Owners of pigeon houses in Sussex showed similar signs of resistance. The perpetrators exhibited 'contempt' for public authority, though this was not necessarily a sign of royalist allegiance. The Committee instructed that the Dorset saltpeterman 'may peaceably and safely proceed in his work', and that 'all due encouragement should be given to those employed therein' in Sussex.[21] The young Robert Boyle wrote in 1646 of being 'vexed by those undermining two-legged moles we call saltpetermen', who dug up his pigeon house at Stalbridge, Dorset, 'and would have done the like to my cellar and stables, if I had not ransomed them with a richer mineral than that they contained' (in other words, a bribe). In Boyle's case his indignation as a landowner was offset by his curiosity as a scientist, and saltpeter would occupy his studies for several years.[22]

Saltpeter, as well as gunpowder, reached England from overseas, including shipments from India and North Africa. In April 1644 parliament contracted William Courten, a Barbary merchant and India-trade interloper, for enough saltpeter to make 600 barrels of gunpowder. In partnership with another international merchant, William Toomes, Courten agreed in October 1644 to supply 'several quantities of saltpeter to the value of £12,000, payable £1,500 per month'.[23] At £4 10s. a barrel this amounted to 2,667 barrels or 111 lasts. Another ordinance in December 1644 reserved £6,000 out of the 'grand excise or new impost' towards this procurement, but within a few years the payment fell into arrears. Parliament learned in March 1648 that unpaid saltpetermen had discontinued their work, and the armed forces were once again under-supplied.[24]

The end of civil war in England by no means lessened the state's demand for gunpowder. Campaigns in Scotland and Ireland required huge amounts of firepower, and the Commonwealth's expanded navy was hungry for munitions. Oliver Cromwell's artillery train in August 1649, for example, included fifty-six 'great guns' and 600 barrels of powder.[25] England's Dutch Wars and imperial ambitions in the Caribbean further boosted military expenditure. From a thirty-five-ship navy in 1642 with 1,199 heavy guns, the Commonwealth's fleet grew to 139 vessels with 4,214 guns by 1659. Not all the ships were fit for service, and not all of the guns were heavy cannon, but the naval demand for gunpowder may well have expanded fourfold across these two decades. Cromwell's army, 54,000 strong in 1654, also stretched the nation's gunpowder reserves.[26]

Philosophical saltpeter

Only three ways were known to secure saltpeter for gunpowder. First, the material could be imported from foreign suppliers, and this practice continued and expanded. Second, a network of saltpetermen could extract the matter from nitrous earth, wherever it could be found, and process it in the localities. Finally, as had often been proposed, a centralized facility could be established to hasten the formation of saltpeter through additions of dung and urine. The Interregnum regime tried each of these approaches, though eventually imports won the day.

In 1646 an ambitious group of projectors revived the notion of centralized, industrialized saltpeter plants. The physician Benjamin

Worsley, a member of the 'invisible college' of experimental natural philosophers and an associate of Samuel Hartlib's schemes for
universal improvement, offered parliament a plan that would
secure supplies for gunpowder while simultaneously addressing
the kingdom's social and economic problems. A philosophically
driven, science-based, altruistic enterprise would put the poor to
work, achieve saltpeter independence, and advance man's mastery
over nature. These were synergistic benefits of the kind that politicians often find appealing. Underlying Worsley's projected arrangements of vats and furnaces, factories and labourers, fluids and fuel,
was confidence in human ability to 'translate corruption into policy'. Ordure would become a strategically valuable commodity
through application of the mysterious 'philosophical dung'. The
cost of establishing this 'Mystery or Corporation of Saltpeter-
makers', he suggested, could be met from the confiscation of the
lands of 'papists' and 'delinquents'.[27]

Worsley wanted the state to set up workhouses for the poor,
with separate lodgings for men and women, where all their 'eas-
ing' of excrement and urine could be collected and processed. 'The
scavengers of every city' would bring them more material to enrich
the earth and accelerate the process of nitrification. Political arithmetic taught Worsley that 150 poor people would generate 'matter
for ten ton of peter in a year', which would more than cover the
cost of keeping them. This 'new way of producing saltpeter' would
not only secure gunpowder independence and save the state
money, but would also promise 'not to entrench upon the liberty
or infringe the just privilege of any subject whatsoever'. It was a
familiar claim harking back to projectors of the late sixteenth and
early seventeenth centuries. The novelty lay in making the poor
both producers and processors in a centralized urine economy.[28]

Worsley's grand scheme came to nothing, although it gained
attention and stimulated scientific and philosophical enquiry. The
Council of State encouraged the 'breeding' of saltpeter, but made
no new investment.[29] Some kind of plan gained traction early in
the Interregnum, when the government authorized Thomas
March 'to make an experiment for generating and increasing the

growth of saltpeter, not entrenching on private property'. New legislation in 1653 restricting saltpetermen from digging in 'any house or ground employed or used for making of gunpowder, or by any special art designed and prepared for breeding or making of saltpeter', suggests that nitre beds of some sort existed. The Hartlib circle again became excited, but more in terms of theory than practice.[30] The technology of nitre beds had been canvassed for a hundred years, but large-scale undertakings had never worked successfully in England. Nor did the Interregnum effort yield the hoped for quantities or profits.

Meanwhile domestic extraction continued, as it had for more than a century. Having countered the worst abuses of the salt-petermen, the revolutionary regime determined to put the enter-prise on a firmer legal footing. A new 'Act for Making Saltpeter' took force in February 1653, which authorized state agents 'to dig for saltpeter in all stables, cellars, vaults, warehouses and other outhouses, yards, and other places not paved or planked, like to afford that earth, at fitting seasons in the day time'. There was no mention of dwelling houses or churches, so presumably those places were off limits. Anyone who hindered the state's saltpeter-men or refused them access faced committal before a justice of the peace. A new provision permitted saltpetermen to 'draw water fit for their said works out of any river, spring, pond, brook, well, pump or conduit, without let or molestation', which suggests that this activity was a common source of friction. The digging of pigeon houses, which caused so much distress to pigeon owners, was limited to the daylight hours of eleven till three. The saltpeter-men and their workers were required to repair any floors or planks that they broke, and to leave the ground 'in good and sufficient order to the content of the owner'. The forced carriage of materials was limited to seven miles (compared to ten miles in 1643), com-pensation was set at twelvepence a mile (instead of eightpence), and measures were enacted to prevent saltpetermen from taking bribes. Anyone who fell short of these standards faced proceedings at law. The intention was to secure necessary supplies without trampling too much on the privileges of property owners. Another clause in an Act of 1656 insisted that there be no digging for salt-peter or taking of carriages without the owner's 'leave first obtained and had'.[31] This was significant, for in principle the procurement henceforth would be consensual, and landowners could deny the saltpetermen access. Records of this activity are scarce, but a diminished domestic saltpeter enterprise seems to have continued without too much fuss beyond the Restoration.

Saltpeter from India

The revolutionary transformation of the English saltpeter enter-prise was achieved through imports, not technology or science. Sixteenth-century monarchs had depended on foreign saltpeter before encouraging domestic providers, and the mid-seventeenth-century state resumed that practice on a greatly expanded scale from new directions. Exotic saltpeter would empower the English arms industry, and would lead to the expansion of the military imperial state.

The revolution in supply had its origin in James I's reign, with quiet beginnings. The Jacobean East India Company furnished its ships with gunpowder from the king's store in London and from merchants in the Low Countries, but they began to cast around for alternative supplies. In 1617 they found saltpeter 'so scarce that it will be very difficult to procure sufficient for the company's use'. In 1618 they found it 'very dear', despite shipments from Ham-burg and Danzig.[32] In the early 1620s the Company decided to emulate the Dutch and secure provisions directly from India. The Dutch were already shipping saltpeter from the Coromandel coast of southern India, and large deposits were reported to be available in Bengal. In February 1624, in addition to supplies for their own use, the East India Company contracted for the first time to bring home saltpeter 'for the service of the state'. In December of that year, with war in the offing and the king's mills 'not sufficient to furnish powder for the public service', the Com-pany decided to establish gunpowder mills of its own 'and fetch saltpeter from foreign parts'.[33] This was a radical break from the royal monopoly on the manufacture of explosives, and it began a process of procurement that would eventually make the English domestic saltpeter enterprise unnecessary.

The importation of saltpeter from India began as a trickle at the outset of Charles I's reign, and rose to a flood in the later Stuart period. In April 1629 the Company brought home 170 tons of saltpeter, more than the king needed, and was allowed to ship seventy tons to Holland. By the mid-1630s the Company was importing up to 200 tons a year, mostly in ballast, and was selling it to the king for between £3 and £4 a hundredweight. Some went to the Company's own gunpowder mills, and the profitable surplus was re-exported to the continent.[34]

Indian saltpeter arrived intermittently in the 1640s, the price dipping briefly at the end of the civil wars. The East India company charged £4 10s. a hundredweight in 1645, and £4 5s. in 1646, but by September 1648 they were willing to sell saltpeter at £3 10s. a hundredweight. By August 1649, however, the East India price was again £4 5s. Price fluctuations reflected changes in military demand as well complications in the local Indian supply. The English had to deal with Dutch competitors, and with local rulers and governors whose own intrigues and wars periodically disrupted traffic.[35]

In April 1649 the Council of State established a committee 'for providing saltpeter, without making it at home'. Dutch and Barbary merchants would provide what they could, but the East India trade seemed capable of limitless expansion. Seven East India ships arrived in July 1649 with holds filled with saltpeter, which the state purchased at the reasonable rate of £4 5s. per hundredweight. In September the Council moved 'to import as much saltpeter as may be needful for the service of the Commonwealth', and agreed to buy all that the East India Company could provide. The state established itself as a regular purchaser, and the Company took steps to expand its supply. In September 1651, for example, the Ordnance Office took delivery of 4,552 hundredweight (roughly 228 tons or 190 lasts) of East India saltpeter, almost equivalent to the entire annual output of the saltpetermen of the 1630s.[36]

The East India Company provided the government with loans as well as vital commodities, and was rewarded in 1657 with a new charter of trading privileges. With supplies in abundance, and the Dutch war now concluded, the Company secured permission again in 1658 to sell surplus saltpeter on the Amsterdam market.[37]

The Ordnance Office's embrace of the East India product coincided with the Company's new focus on Bengal, where saltpeter was cheaper and more plentiful than in other Indian regions. The Company's new agency in Bengal made saltpeter a prime object of trade, consuming fifty per cent of available capital. The East India Company could buy saltpeter at less than twenty shillings a hundredweight in India, and sell it in England for four times that amount. Dutch competition threatened to raise prices, though open war with the Dutch made Bengal saltpeter an even more valuable commodity in London.[38]

By 1660 the military might of the British state was significantly greater than twenty years earlier. The restored regime of Charles II inherited a well-equipped army, a greatly expanded navy, and supplies of saltpeter that no longer required domestic digging. The revolution had opened the press, freed the spirit, expanded the public sphere, and raised unquenchable questions about the bases of authority. Almost accidentally, it also revolutionized the security foundations of the state and quelled the problem of saltpeter 'vexation and oppression'. England's subsequent imperial expansion could now proceed without this particular inconvenience at home.

7

Saltpeter for a Global Power

'MOST of the saltpeter which is sold in Guzuratta comes from Asmer, sixty leagues from Agra, and they get it out of lands that have lain long fallow. The blackest and fattest ground yields most of it, though other land affords some, and it is made thus. They make certain trenches which they fill with their saltpetrous earth, and let into them small rivulets, as much water as will serve for its soaking, which may be the more effectually done, they make use of their feet treading it till it become a broth. When the water hath drawn out all the saltpeter which was in the earth, they take the clearest part of it, and dispose it into another trench, where it grows thick, and then they boil it like salt, continually scumming it, and then they put it into earthen pots, wherein the remainder of the dregs goes to the bottom; and when the water begins to thicken, they take it out of these pots, to set it drying in the sun, where it grows hard, and is reduced into that form, wherein it is brought into Europe.' So the German traveller Joseph Albrecht de Mandelslo described the making of rough saltpeter in India in the late 1630s. His account was rendered into English and posthumously published in London in 1662, by which time England had become dependent on saltpeter from India. Contradicting the widely held view that saltpeter occurred naturally in the subcontinent, available for easy taking, Mandelslo described the effort that went into its manufacture from ground enriched with urine and dung of both humans and cattle. A special caste of 'nuniyas' performed the collecting, spreading, leaching, and boiling of saltpeter, in a seasonal *cycle between drought and monsoons, and local merchants sold the unrefined product in bulk to European traders. This rural Indian industrial chemistry, which had long served the 'gunpowder empires' of South Asia, provided the basis for Dutch, French, and British imperial power for almost two hundred years.*[1]

* * *

The English saltpeter enterprise was transformed in the second half of the seventeenth century, as abundant imported supplies rendered the socially contentious practice of digging and boiling unnecessary. The 'vexation and oppression' of the saltpetermen ended in Charles II's reign, not because of social, legal, or technological changes, but because cheap East India saltpeter flooded the market. A few saltpetermen continued to ply their trade, but there was little point in digging when so much came in so cheaply from abroad. Not quite a *deus ex machina,* the new East India commerce procured an unexpected external solution to the country's security problem. Gunpowder-makers and natural philosophers of the Restoration era knew saltpeter primarily as an import item. 'Now East India... and Barbary are the chief places, in many parts of which it is artificially extracted and transported to us,' noted William Clarke in his *Natural History of Nitre* (1670).[2] 'This trade alone furnisheth us with saltpeter, a commodity so necessary that in the late king's time the nation suffered greatly by the want if it,' observed Sir Josiah Child of the East India traffic in 1681.[3] The social 'discommodities' of the saltpeter enterprise disappeared as the Indian trade became ascendant. The gunpowder needs of the state were henceforth assured, and saltpeter scarcity was merely a spectre of the past.

Restoration provisions

Remnants of the old saltpeter interest sought favour and advantage under the newly restored monarch, though the pickings for their toil were thin. Anyone expecting business as usual would be disappointed. Several entrepreneurs offered to make saltpeter for Charles II from domestic sources, while others sought recompense for their losses in the late king's service. A few projectors offered schemes for the better making of saltpeter, or 'to make saltpeter after their own invention', but provided few details. Robert Lindsey and Henry Holden obtained grants in September 1660 to produce saltpeter for the crown, but not to sell it privately. The veteran saltpeterman Richard Bagnall petitioned in November 1660 for the sole making of saltpeter, and claimed he had not been paid for his provisions for Charles I. A few years later the physician Henry Stubbe watched Bagnall's crew 'employed about the making of saltpeter at Warwick and Coventry', and learned from them some of the properties of this mysterious substance.[4]

The diarist John Evelyn, scion of the gunpowder dynasty, secured appointment to the commission 'for the forming and making of saltpeter through the whole kingdom', and in 1666, at the height of the war with the Dutch, he signed warrants for saltpetermen to deliver their quotas, or 'for undertakers to furnish their proportions'. A royal proclamation in that July authorized crown agents 'to search and dig for saltpeter in all convenient places', though it barred them from 'dwelling houses inhabited'. Charles II's saltpetermen would be more scrupulously governed, in principle, than those of his predecessors, though these protocols were never rigorously tested.[5]

The domestic saltpeter enterprise was not yet dead, but was dwindling to insignificance. Ordnance Office receipts show Richard Bagnall delivering five tons of saltpeter in 1660–1661 and nine and a half tons in 1666–1667, but he represented a dying breed. Before the civil war he might have furnished twenty to thirty tons a year. Tower officials tracked 46,051 barrels of gunpowder between 1663 and 1667, of which only 2,147 (less than five per cent) were made of English saltpeter. The same accounts show that powder made from English materials was more expensive, costing up to £1 per barrel more than powder from Indian sources.[6] The royal gunpowder-maker Daniel O'Neale observed in 1663 that 'former powder-makers were always supplied with saltpeter by English saltpetermen', whereas he had to deal with the vagaries of Asian shipping.[7]

By this time the saltpeter trade was a major source of profit to the East India Company. Though the government paid little more than £3 a hundredweight, investors could still secure a fourfold return. The Ordnance Office paid the Company £10,800 in 1662, £37,198 in 1665, and £40,000 in 1669 for saltpeter fit to make gunpowder.[8] Huge shipments came from workings near Patna, inland from the Bay of Bengal, swamping the market for home-made material. More came from the Coromandel coast, and the coasts of Malabar and Bombay. The quality of Bengal saltpeter was generally well regarded, and its consistency improved from 1665 when local workings came under Company supervision. 'If we had the monies, 1000 tons might easily yearly be procured,' wrote one enthusiastic factor. Company agents were quick to intervene if the quality of the product declined.[9]

Charles I in the 1630s had set targets of 240 lasts of saltpeter a year, representing 5,760 barrels or 288 tons, and was hard pressed to achieve those figures. Charles II, by contrast, was importing 1,000 tons a year at various points in his reign. Enemies of the East India Company claimed that their bulk saltpeter was too often contaminated by 'fixed salt, dirt, and rubbish', but their principal customer, the Ordnance Office, seemed generally satisfied. 'Rough' or brown saltpeter went first to 'his majesty's storehouse for saltpeter at Woolwich', and thence to the powder-makers at the Minories (behind the Tower of London) or at Chilworth and Weybridge in Surrey to be refined and processed.[10] Crown and Company together pursued their 'noble...design of making England the magazine for this commodity, which formerly was fetched from our neighbours'.[11]

The Ordnance Office bureaucracy expanded to manage this flow of material and munitions, and was ably managed by Colonel William Legge. Legge had been governor of royalist Oxford and became Lieutenant General of the Ordnance at the Restoration. His son George Legge succeeded to the post in 1672, and was ennobled in 1681 as Baron Dartmouth. Their saltpeter accounts, which document their requisitions for munitions, are divided between the Ordnance Office records in the National Archives and the Dartmouth family papers at the Staffordshire Record Office.[12]

Annual figures for saltpeter imported from Bengal are available from 1664. In that year 589 tons reached London. The East India Company shipped 659 tons of saltpeter in 1665, and 1,037 tons in 1669. Average annual imports in the 1670s topped 632 tons, 733 tons in the 1680s. Most of this Indian saltpeter arrived in bags, individually numbered and weighing from one to one and a half hundredweight. In December 1665 the king's powder-makers at the Minories took delivery of 1,463 bags of saltpeter, a total of some ninety-one tons. In February 1666 they received 1,007 bags, approximately sixty-three tons.[13] Between September 1664 and May 1665 the East India Company delivered 730 tons of saltpeter to the royal stores. Another 603 tons arrived in March 1666.[14] Accounts and calculations no longer counted lasts (twenty-four barrels), but measured saltpeter by the bag and by weight in pounds, quarters, hundredweights, and tons. No longer a matter of 'vexation', the saltpeter enterprise was governed by metrics of capacity and volume, tonnage and profit, stocks and reserves. It was appropriate, in an age of 'political arithmetic', to express strength and resources in numbers, and the remainder of this chapter employs these quantitative measures.

Shipments of saltpeter from India continued to increase across the later seventeenth century, despite interruptions from foreign wars, disputes with local rulers, and famine in some of the source areas. The East India Company had 650 tons ready to ship from Bengal in 1666, and 200 to 250 tons more expected from Patna. In 1668 the Patna plants alone were expected to yield 800 to 1,000 tons.[15] The Company shipped more than 1,000 tons of saltpeter to England in 1669 and 1670. Their order in 1679 was for 1,318 tons, although only 884 tons were actually delivered.[16] A single shipment in September 1682 comprised 6,666 bags, some 400 tons. Another in June 1683 had 17,300 bags, over 1,000 tons. Company records show receipts of £40,463 10s. in July 1683 for saltpeter delivered to the crown. Sometimes the East India Company would buy up an interloper's cargo, it was said, 'to prevent the fall of their own goods'. An East India interloper, Robert Wooley, delivered 3,082 bags weighing just over 185 tons in June 1684.[17]

England's Dutch Wars (1664–1667, 1672–1674) further stimulated demand for munitions. Although these wars dipped deep into powder reserves they also produced occasional windfalls, such as 111 tons of 'prize' saltpeter acquired in 1666, and 156 tons more taken from Dutch ships in 1673.[18] To thwart England's enemies and to guarantee supplies for the realm, the re-export of saltpeter was expressly forbidden by royal proclamation. Each time peace was restored the gunpowder-makers sought permission to trade saltpeter with their former enemies.[19]

Ordnance Office registers indicate the changing scale of saltpeter provision, and the general abundance of supply compared to earlier reigns. The volume of material for munitions available to later Stuart monarchs dwarfed supplies from all previous wars. The tonnage in store varied month by month, as raw shipments arrived from India and the powder-makers drew supplies for their work, but inventories rarely fell below 100 tons. Early in October 1670 England's saltpeter reserve stood at 517 tons, when a huge shipment from India boosted the store to over 977 tons. There were 757 tons of saltpeter at Woolwich and the Tower when war resumed in April 1672, but stocks were run down rapidly to supply fleets and armies. By mid-June 1672 (after the battle of Sole Bay) there were 488 tons on hand, by October only 127, dropping to a low point of forty-three tons in February 1673. Peacetime stocks fluctuated from 685 tons in August 1677 to 475 tons in July 1678 and 680 tons in September 1679.[20]

A detailed account of 'the present state of saltpeter' in July 1684 found 1,962 tons, ten hundredweight, three quarters, and eighteen pounds of saltpeter in Charles II's ordnance stores.[21] This was a vast reserve of almost imperial dimensions, boosted by massive shipments from India. It would grow even larger, to 2,015 tons, by the time of James II's coronation in April 1685. Thereafter stocks dwindled to 1,503 tons in May 1686, 1,091 tons in May 1687, 692 tons in May 1688, and a low point of 219 tons in July 1689.

FIG 16   English merchantmen, *c.*1680
William van de Velde, Yale Center for British Art, Paul Mellon Collection, B.1976.778, detail, reproduced by permission.

Identifying saltpeter as key to 'the strength of war', and recognizing its absolute necessity 'for the defence and safety of this realm', one of James II's last proclamations in July 1689 again prohibited the export of saltpeter without licence.[22] Fresh East India purchases of 500 tons in August 1689 and 1,000 tons in June 1690 brought reserves back into balance, but William III's wars ran them down.[23]

The so-called 'Glorious Revolution' of 1688–1689 removed the catholic James II from his throne and replaced him with his protestant nephew cum son-in-law and daughter, who reigned as William III and Mary II. English foreign policy changed direction now that the Dutch Stadholder William of Orange was king. William's victory in the battle of the Boyne, fought in Ireland in 1690 against French and Jacobite forces, secured this transfer of power; backed by fierce artillery, as many as 60,000 men had taken the field. William III engaged England in relentless competition with Louis XIV of France, with consequent expenditure of munitions. The two countries were at war from 1689 to 1697, and fought again from 1702 to 1713 in the War of the Spanish Succession. Saltpeter was in high demand for these gunpowder conflicts, though politics, finance, and greed caused temporary dislocations of supply.

Commercial restrictions, which had earlier been used to thwart the Dutch, were now employed to safeguard English supplies and to frustrate the French. As allies now, the English and the Dutch could collaborate against King William's enemies. The war with France sometimes disrupted Asian shipping, so that the annual average receipt of Bengal saltpeter dropped below 337 tons in the 1690s. But deficiencies could be made up by purchases from Amsterdam, where Dutch gunpowder, though 'not quite so good', could be obtained cheaper than in London.[24] On three occasions English saltpeter reserves fell below 100 tons: in July 1693, January 1695, and February 1696. In August 1695 the powder-makers blamed the East India Company for their short deliveries, but the Treasury deemed their complaint 'very frivolous'. A printed broadside attributed the 'ill consequence' of 'saltpeter wanting in England' to the East India Company monopoly, 'embezzlements from the king's ships and stores', and 'the buying [of] powder from Holland'.[25]

Mr Long's saltpeter works

Perceiving a crisis of supply and an opportunity for profit, several investors of the 1690s sought to revive plans for a domestic salt-peter industry. Rival groups of projectors again sought privileges to supply the state with home-made saltpeter for gunpowder. One group, announcing 'methods never yet practised by any of their majesties' subjects', promoted a bill in parliament in January 1691 'for the encouragement of making saltpeter here in England'. Another group, the heirs of John Wandesford, an ordnance com-missioner under Charles I, wanted the privilege assigned to them. They claimed to have stockpiled 'hundreds of tons of matter to be formed or turned into nitre' in places near London, and hoped to supply the crown with 100 tons a year. They touted 'an extraordinary way of making saltpeter in great quantities', though they had not yet the means to commence actual production.[26] With more political and financial clout, though little proof of greater technical knowledge, the newly formed 'Company for Making and Refining of Saltpeter' engaged to deliver 200 tons, and fancied they might one day furnish the state with 'one thousand pounds per annum'. Shares moved briskly, to the benefit of early investors, though the company had yet to bring any saltpeter to market.[27] Like the projectors who badgered earlier Tudors and Stuarts, the schemers under William and Mary claimed too much and produced more bluster than serviceable material for munitions.

Accounts survive for 'Mr Long's saltpeter works' from 1693 to 1699, which trace the rise and fall of this commercial endeavour. The joint stock investors engaged Thomas Jett, merchant taylor of London, 'to undertake the whole management and conduct of making saltpeter at the works called Mr Long's saltpeter works' near Covent Garden in the parish of St Mary le Bone. Jett's task was to manufacture 'ninety tons of merchantable saltpeter, equal in goodness and value to the brown saltpeter usually brought from the East Indies'. To this end the company hired carpenters, bricklayers, and plumbers, purchased laboratory equipment including retorts and glass funnels, and twice borrowed saltpeter from the Tower 'for raising mother of nitre for the better expedition of their works'. They seem to have envisaged some sort of forcing house or nitre bed, utilizing London night soil, but unfortunately no usable saltpeter was forthcoming. In April 1695 the shareholders urged Jett 'to make another trial of the earth' and to 'give his final answer of his opinion' of its strength, but the outcome was again failure. Eventually in 1699 the enterprise fell into bankruptcy, its assets were liquidated, and investors were left with debt and recrimination. The nurture and manufacture of saltpeter in England was dead forever.[28]

William III's government could not wait for domestic supplies to be revived. Saltpeter was in urgent demand, and parliament sought to ease its importation. A bill before the Commons in February 1693 sought to free saltpeter imports from the restrictions of the Navigation Acts, and Queen Mary herself pressed for ways to bring more saltpeter into England.[29] A new government contract with the East India Company in 1693 required it to furnish the Ordnance Office with 500 tons of saltpeter a year, at £45 10s. a ton in peacetime and £53 10s. a ton in wartime, with freedom to sell any surplus on the open market. These were bargain rates for the government, though less advantageous to the Company, equivalent to £2 5s. 6d. and £2 13s. 6d. a hundredweight, half the price of saltpeter fifty years earlier. Though they still made profit, Company accountants called this 'a losing price'. Stocks recovered after the Peace of Ryswick (1697), ending the war with France, so much so that a member of parliament could declare in 1698 that 'there was never so great a quantity of gunpowder in store'.[30] None of the saltpeter with which it was composed was made in England. Saltpeter was again plentiful, and nearly all of it arrived by ship from Bengal.

Georgian might

The eighteenth century saw further increases in the scale, range, and duration of Britain's foreign wars, and a concomitant expansion of expenditure on gunpowder. Georgian military presence reached all oceans and hemispheres, with ever more powerful armies and weapons. Whereas twenty-six years of the sixteenth century had been taken up with warfare, and seventeenth century wars at home and abroad covered forty-two years, the wars of the eighteenth century were longer and more frequent, with foreign conflict in fifty-five years. Britain's Royal Navy swelled from 195 ships in 1740 to 375 in 1760, and the number of seamen and marines almost tripled from fewer than 30,000 to more than 86,000. The manpower of the British army more than doubled over those two decades from 41,000 to 99,000 strong. Peacetime forces were smaller, but George III's admirals commanded more than 97,000 mariners by 1780, his generals over 115,000 men at arms.[31]

FIG 17 John Seller, *The Sea Gunner: Shewing the Practical Part of Gunnery as it is used at Sea* (1691), title page. © The British Library Board (8806. aa. 12).

Gunpowder consumption increased with the intensity of conflict, from 14,493 barrels (647 tons) each year in the Seven Years War (1756–1763) to 36,000 barrels year (over 1,600 tons) in the War of American Independence (1775–1783). By 1828 it was assumed that any new war would consume 200,000 barrels of gunpowder (almost 9,000 tons).[32] The world of ordnance had been transformed since the reign of Charles I, when a few hundred tons of gunpowder would have served for any foreign conflict.

Over the first sixty years of the eighteenth century, annual imports of saltpeter varied from a low of 255 tons in 1726 to a high of 2,658 tons in 1743. The variation had as much to do with the East India Company's calculations of profit as with the changing military situation in Europe. Production and market conditions and rainfall in India also affected supply. Annual saltpeter imports into England averaged 538 tons between 1700 and 1709, 664 tons in 1710–1719, 508 tons in 1720–1729, 840 tons in 1730–1739, 1,399 tons in 1740–1749, and 964 tons in 1750–1759. The British takeover of Bengal after the battle of Plassey in 1757 secured control of seventy per cent of the world's saltpeter production. The French were squeezed out, and other European traders suffered eclipse. In addition to Indian supplies, small amounts of saltpeter also trickled into Britain from Russia, the Baltic, and North Africa. The consequences of this dominance were far-reaching. British victories in the Seven Years War owed much to superior supplies of gunpowder, and the French themselves attributed military setbacks to their shortages of saltpeter.[33] British command of the seas secured a constant advantage in munitions, which did not necessarily translate into success on the battlefield. George III's forces enjoyed material superiority over the American rebels: Cornwallis at Yorktown in 1781 was outmanoeuvred, not outgunned.

Britain's Asian saltpeter trade surpassed all records in the later eighteenth century. The volume of saltpeter freight under George III grew three to four times higher than under the first Hanoverians, whose imports dwarfed the earlier Stuart traffic. An East India Company 'account of saltpetre imported and supplied to government' from 1755 to 1792 indicates gross average shipments of 943 tons per year in 1755–1759, 1,731 tons per year in 1760–1769, 1,675 tons per year in 1770–1779, and 2,285 tons per year in 1780–1789. The peak year was 1784, when 4,508 tons came to London.[34] Government statistics yield roughly commensurate figures. A treasury review of British saltpeter imports from 1769 to 1774 noted that 1,648 tons arrived in the year ending Christmas 1770. The figure for 1771 was 1,985 tons, for 1772 it was 2,229 tons, for 1774 2,000 tons, and for 1774 1,837 tons. An analysis by the Board of Trade a few years later found that the East India Company offered the crown on average 30,083 bags of saltpeter (roughly 1,805 tons) a year from 1770 to 1779, and 44,056 bags (2,643 tons) a year from 1783 to 1789. Not all was sold to the government, one in twelve bags being re-exported. The price of saltpeter fell steadily from £4 0s. 6d. a hundredweight in 1783 to £1 18s. 6d. in 1789, but this was not reflected in the price of gunpowder, which remained above £3 10s. a barrel.

The years 1780–1782 were omitted from the Board's analysis, because, they said, in those years 'this country was engaged in a war with America, France, Spain and Holland, the severity of which occasioned an almost total suspension of all commercial operations'. East India Company records reveal shortfalls of supply in 1779 and 1782, that had to be made up through purchases in Europe.[35]

Reserves were dangerously low when the American war ended. George III's government had only 380 tons of saltpeter in store in August 1790, which put the country at risk should a new war with France develop. The French Revolution, which exploded in July 1789, put all of Europe in peril. In these circumstances the government proposed again to ban saltpeter exports, to permit imports from any source, and to double the East India contract to 1,000 tons. In March 1791 the Duke of Richmond, Master-General of the Ordnance, proposed that the Company supply 1,250 tons a year until stores were more comfortably stocked.[36]

Not surprisingly, when war with France resumed, the London price of saltpeter rose precipitously from less than £2 a hundredweight in 1789 to £2 11s. 6d. in March 1792, £3 7s. 10d. in September 1792, to a peak of £5 2s. 2d. in April 1793. Only European purchases kept the government powder mills turning. The East India Company, on which Britain had come to depend, proved a fickle partner. Critics charged that the Company preferred profits from other customers, and offered better terms on saltpeter to the Dutch, French, Germans, Portuguese, Danes, Swedes, and Americans, than to the king's gunpowder-makers in London. Political, military, and commercial considerations stirred the conflict, against the background of contract adjustments and negotiations for a new East India Company charter.[37]

The solution, some advisors suggested, was 'a grand reformation... to preserve to this country the carrying trade to and from India on a permanent footing', which would make London 'the grand depot for Asiatic produce'. If the interests of the Company and the kingdom were more tightly fused, then supplies might be secured 'with a greater quantity... and at a cheaper rate'. The outcome was that 'between 1793 and 1809 the East India Company delivered 25,168 tons of saltpeter to the Ordnance Office, and roughly an equivalent amount to private gunpowder mills in Britain'. Total imports exceeded 3,000 tons a year. Average deliveries to the state were 1,573 tons a year, with as much again going to commercial customers.[38]

Imperial power

Britain's consumption of saltpeter and gunpowder in the nineteenth century grew commensurate with her military reach and global dominance. Every measure indicated further expansion. Expenditure on ordnance for Wellington's armies rose from £1.1 million in 1803 to £4.3 million in 1812, the cost of Nelson's navy rising in those same years from £10.2 million to £20.5 million.[39] At the height of the Napoleonic War in 1812 the British army could call on 342,273 soldiers, her navy counting 116,923 seamen and marines. A peacetime army establishment of 88,848 men in 1830 expanded again to 100,011 by 1840, and to 153,483 by 1890. The emergency of the Crimean War (1853–1856) saw more than 223,000 men in arms, the Boer War (1899–1902) 430,000. The Royal Navy similarly expanded again from 29,000 men in 1830 to 39,000 in 1840, 68,880 in 1890, and over 114,000 by 1900. Mid-Victorian Britain mounted 1,664 guns in fortresses and batteries at home, and 4,812 more in garrisons throughout the empire.[40] All of these weapons relied on gunpowder. In the Peninsula War in 1812 the British used 74,978 pounds of gunpowder (33.5 tons) in 30 hours at the siege of Cuidad Rodrigo, 228,830 pounds (102.2 tons) in 104 hours at the storming of Badajoz, roughly a ton per hour of heavy action.[41] The siege of Sebastopol (1854–1855) so depleted reserves that 'the government had to send to the colonies for powder, and to employ merchants to purchase gunpowder and saltpeter wherever it could be obtained'.[42]

A parliamentary analysis in 1828 found that the crown had 279,602 barrels of gunpowder in store in its forts and magazines at home and in the colonies (12,482 tons, assuming a barrel of 100 pounds). This was a comfortable reserve, though it would be depleted in short order should any new war break out. Military planners called for a new manufacturing capacity of 180,000 barrels of gunpowder a year (8,036 tons). To meet this requirement, and the even greater demands of imperial Victorian Britain, saltpeter imports would expand yet again and gunpowder production would be industrialized. Facilities at Waltham Abbey, which processed 960 tons of saltpeter a year in the 1830s, had doubled their capacity to 1,880 tons by the 1890s.[43] Other gunpowder mills at Faversham and elsewhere similarly expanded.

To meet these needs the production of saltpeter in India's Bengal region rose from 14,000 tons a year in the 1830s to 25,000 tons in the 1850s, and the bulk of this came to Britain. The Bengal trade in saltpeter flattened somewhat to 20,000 tons a year in the 1890s, but still exceeded 18,000 tons a year in the first decade of the twentieth century.[44] London was indeed 'the grand depot for Asiatic produce' that eighteenth-century promoters had projected, but not all the saltpeter went to British government purposes. Almost a quarter was re-exported. The American Civil War stimulated sales, and in November 1861 the du Pont company of Delaware purchased 2,000 tons of saltpeter in London and arranged to buy more inbound from India.[45] Parliamentary figures from the early 1860s show England importing 18,640 tons of saltpeter a year, and re-exporting 4,255 tons.[46] Though much of the remaining 14,385 tons went for gunpowder, a considerable amount found civilian, commercial, agricultural, industrial, or pharmacological uses. 'Villainous saltpeter' had become an imperial commodity of diverse applications, at the very time that the new industrial chemistry began to challenge its centrality for military explosives.[47]

Empress Victoria's armed forces remained gunpowder-dependent, despite improvements in chemistry and ballistics. Only towards the end of the nineteenth century did new propulsives and explosives edge out the old. Even the industrialized warfare of the early twentieth century retained a place for gunpowder. The First World War was fought with coal-tar products, toluol, phenol, trinitrotoluene, and nitrated glycerine,[48] but gunpowder remained on shipboard and the battlefield. An advisor to Lloyd George's war cabinet in 1917 observed that 'nothing has yet been found to take the place of gunpowder as an igniting charge for smokeless powder for naval and military purposes...indeed, not a single round of cordite can be fired without the use of black powder'. The advisor was Major T. G. Tulloch of the Chilworth Gunpowder Company, who had both commercial and patriotic interests at stake. Tulloch urged the government to attach geologists or chemists to British armies in Palestine and Mesopotamia, to prospect for 'essential salts and minerals', rather like overseas adventurers under Elizabeth I. The proposal reached Winston Churchill, then Minister of Munitions, and gained some momentum despite advice from his ministry that 'the supply of Indian nitrate of potash is quite sufficient for our gunpowder production'.[49]

Production was phased out after the First World War, as synthetic materials replaced traditional propellants. The works at Chilworth, Surrey, closed in 1920, after a 400-year history that stretched back to the Evelyns. The gunpowder factory at Faversham, Kent, closed in 1934. Work continued at the Royal Gunpowder Factory at Waltham Abbey, Essex, until a German bomb brought production to a halt in 1941. Today these are heritage sites, where visitors can marvel at gunpowder's tortuous past. Gunpowder procurement has become a historical curiosity, but for several hundred years it determined the fate of the world.

8

The New World and the
Ancien Régime

J OHN Adams of Massachusetts, who would later succeed George
Washington as president of the United States, argued in 1775 that
liberty and independence could only be won by securing supplies of
saltpeter. Virtue alone was not enough. American self-sufficiency in munitions was the only counter to British military might. In his words 'the
unum necessarium', the one thing necessary for victory, was saltpeter. In
letter after letter, speech after speech, Adams urged families, communities,
and colonies to experiment with saltpeter production, to learn and share
the secrets of the art, and to contribute to the revolutionary war effort. 'We
want nothing but saltpeter...now is the critical time...it must be
had...every stable, dove house, cellar, vault, etc. is a mine of saltpeter.'[1]
Making saltpeter for gunpowder, Adams believed, was 'as simple as making soap'. In enlightened American hands the instructions would be 'short,
plain and simple, so that Dick, Tom, and Joan may understand 'em'. His
own wife, Abigail Adams, was among hundreds of patriot enthusiasts who
experimented with backyard saltpeter production in the opening crisis of
the American Revolution.[2] The earth of Massachusetts meeting houses,
like the churches of early modern England, proved especially rich in potassium nitrate. South Carolina's delegates to the Continental Congress
recommended digging under 'negro houses and barns'.[3] In the event, however,
American victory came not through home-made munitions but with war

supplies from France, which had recently overcome its own saltpeter crisis through science and ingenuity.

* * *

Seventeenth-century English enthusiasts for America hoped that the New World would supply them with profitable commodities. If America yielded gold and silver, why not saltpeter too? Promoters imagined that nitre from America could prove even 'more valuable than the mines of Peru or Mexico'.[4] Colonial projectors looked for these resources in the king's American dominions, though their optimism was unrewarded. In 1633, for example, Governor Sir John Harvey of Virginia promised the Privy Council at Whitehall that great quantities of saltpeter would soon be found, although no such mine was discovered for over a hundred years.[5] In the mid-seventeenth century John Winthrop, Jr, the savant of New London, conceived of saltpeter works in Connecticut that would produce a 'returnable merchandize' for the New England colonies, but the scheme foundered through lack of finance. The lack of native saltpeter thwarted plans to establish a gunpowder mill in Stuart, Massachusetts, though Governor Leverett hoped in 1675, yet again, to 'raise it amongst us'.[6] The best prospect seemed to lie in New England's offshore islands, where accumulations of bird dung could be extracted at little charge. Further inland was said to be 'strong soil ... where pigeons usually frequent', another possible source of 'strong saltpeter'. Thomas Offley petitioned the king in 1690 for exclusive rights to exploit these North American resources, but nothing came of his plan.[7]

Other prospectors turned to the island colonies, hoping to find 'great store of saltpeter' in Barbados, St Christopher, or Antigua. After it fell to the English in 1655, Jamaica too was believed to be endowed with saltpeter 'as good and as plentifully as any place in the world'. A more thorough report in 1685 concluded that Antigua did indeed have saltpeter, and Jamaica too had deposits, though not enough to be profitable. Attempts to make gunpowder on Antigua were abandoned when the works 'was unfortunately blown up' and their sponsor 'suddenly' died.[8]

Eighteenth-century optimists dreamed of saltpeter fortunes, though few did any digging or boiling until brought to it by the pressures of revolution. Describing saltpeter as 'a commodity infinitely valuable in Europe...in its proportion as sure a wealth as gold itself', Daniel Defoe in 1726 imagined South America as a gunpowder eldorado.[9] Promoters of the new colony of Georgia in 1740 likewise thought they had found the ideal environment for a saltpeter enterprise. American saltpeter, they hoped, could 'secure to the British nation a perpetual magazine of the principal ingredient of gunpowder, in case of war, without going so far as the East Indies for it'.[10] Another treatise, in 1750, announced opportunities 'for collecting and manufacturing saltpeter' in the northern colonies close to Canada. There was said to be 'an inexhaustible fund in the Mohawks country, from the dung of those innumerable flocks of wild pigeons which breed there', but these opportunities, like most others, went unfulfilled.[11]

Only a few colonists made experiments with saltpeter, because it was easier to shop for the material than to make it from muck and dung. Imperial Britain controlled most of India's saltpeter, and the search for alternative supplies was less pressing. 'Mr Jeremiah Brown's method of making saltpeter' from the scrapings of Virginia tobacco barns was published in London in 1764, but very few planters attempted the operation.[12] Mature colonial America purchased its gunpowder from London, or from royal magazines left over from the Seven Years War. Only when the crisis of revolution forced them to fend for themselves did Americans think about home-made munitions. George III's order in October 1774 forbidding gunpowder exports to the American colonies precipitated a crisis of military supply and a flurry of interest in saltpeter self-sufficiency.[13] A Boston columnist had already suggested that 'a manufactory of nitre might doubtless be established in America to as much advantage as that of France, notwithstanding several attempts of this kind have miscarried'.[14] A Pennsylvania writer in 1774 extolled 'the usefulness of nitre or saltpeter' and recommended its manufacture, remarking on the 'small progress...hitherto made in these American colonies'.[15]

A craze for saltpeter accompanied the opening phase of the American Revolution.

Saltpeter, 'the unum necessarium'

Facing war with Great Britain, the Continental Congress at Philadelphia in 1775 revived the almost forgotten art of localized saltpeter provision. Like Tudor and Stuart regimes of the early modern era, they sought to provide for their security without 'the expensive, uncertain and dangerous necessity of relying on foreign importations'. Like the earlier government of Queen Elizabeth I, the Congress understood the equation of saltpeter and survival.[16] Virtue alone would not suffice. All major reserves of powder and munitions were in British imperial hands, so the rebels would have to improvise. As one Massachusetts merchant remarked with reference to the saltpeter problem, 'necessity is the mother of invention'. Another told John Adams, 'your maxim, "God helps those who help themselves," recurs to mind'. Since saltpeter was 'so necessary for defence and...so extensively useful', its provision would require 'public patronage' as well as 'the attention of individuals'. Promoting the manufacture of this commodity, said Congress, would secure 'the salvation and prosperity of America' and the 'lives, liberties, and estates' of American citizens. As the Virginia delegates advised the Committee of Safety at Williamsburg in October 1775, 'the wicked activity and power on the sea of our enemies renders it so essential and indispensable a duty...to push the making of saltpeter with unremitting diligence...Without this internal and essential security the liberty and rights of America rest on doubtful ground.'[17] 'Infinite security' still depended upon saltpeter for gunpowder.

The problem was well understood, but its solution posed practical difficulties. The colonies had no local saltpeter tradition, and expertise was in short supply. Imperial Britain, by contrast, commanded close to 2,000 tons a year imported from India, and could afford to be profligate with firepower. To combat this monster would require a mobilization of knowledge, ingenuity, and effort, to make American soil yield serviceable raw materials. The colonial press helpfully published accounts of saltpeter manufacture in Europe, and solicited practical wisdom, 'that the country may have the benefit of its publication'.[18] The *Royal American Magazine* of Boston reprinted the 1764 report on saltpeter experiments in Virginia in January 1775, and the *Virginia Gazette* and *Pennsylvania Mercury* followed suit in August.[19] Other colonial newspapers circulated recipes, instructions, tips, and commentaries that brought discourse on the manufacture of saltpeter into the revolutionary public sphere.

Acutely aware of America's powder shortage, the Continental Congress appointed a committee in June 1775 'to devise ways and means for introducing the manufacture of saltpeter into these colonies'. In July they encouraged colonists everywhere 'to apply themselves to the manufacture of saltpeter'. The warehouses and yards of the tobacco colonies, they believed, were 'particularly and strongly impregnated with nitre'. Drawing on the American scientific community, immigrant knowledge, and homespun ingenuity, and mobilizing the colonial press and its readers, Congress attempted to popularize the 'several methods of making saltpeter'. The powder problem remained on the revolutionary agenda throughout 1776, when Congress several times discussed 'further ways and means of promoting the manufacture of saltpeter'.[20]

American scientists and virtuosi lent their knowledge to this patriotic effort. Benjamin Franklin dug out notes of his travels in Germany and described the manufacture of saltpeter at Hanover in 1766. So simple was the process, he assured colleagues, 'that it was carried on entirely by an illiterate old man and his wife'. At greater length and with more sophistication, Benjamin Rush summarized European understandings of the chemistry of saltpeter, and supplied detailed accounts of nitre operations in Germany and France. The Germans, said Rush, had 'great success' from 'lime, rubbish of all kinds, garden mould, and ashes... mixed together and moistened from time to time with urine'. In France they used plant stalks, 'sharp and bitter herbs... the leaves that fall

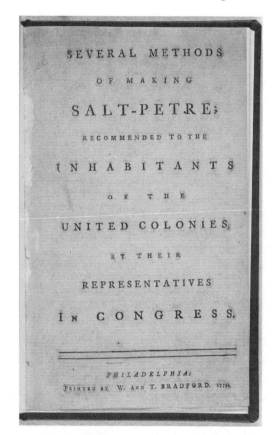

SEVERAL METHODS

OF MAKING

SALT-PETRE;

RECOMMENDED TO THE

INHABITANTS

OF THE

UNITED COLONIES,

BY THEIR

REPRESENTATIVES

IN CONGRESS.

PHILADELPHIA:
PRINTED BY W. AND T. BRADFORD. 1775.

FIG 18 Methods for making saltpeter, 1775

Several Methods of Making Salt-Petre; Recommended to the Inhabitants of the United Colonies by their Representatives in Congress (Philadelphia, 1775), title page (Huntington Library, rare book 88785, reproduced by permission of the Huntington).

from the trees...pigeons' dung, hens' dung, birds' and hens' feathers, the ashes which women generally make their lees with...hogs' hair, the horns of oxen and cows, and the bones the dogs eat not of'. Americans could surely make use of such easily available resources, as well as 'the earth under the floor of old stables, mixed with a quantity of ashes'. Suitably moistened with urine, it was thought, these materials, 'putrifying together, do put on the nature and property of saltpeter'. Even tobacco stalks could yield nitre, according to Rush, for 'a number of experiments' showed tobacco to be replete with nitrous salts. A process of leaching and boiling, separation and purification would yield acceptable weapons-grade saltpeter, though the problem of contamination by common salt was not fully solved. Rush concluded that the manufacture of saltpeter 'may be carried on in this country with as great advantages as in France, Germany, or the East Indies'.[21]

Describing in detail how that might be accomplished, the Committee of Safety at Philadelphia published an account of 'the process for extracting and refining saltpeter' which it recommended to 'every family in the country'. Patriots would search the floors of 'sheep, horse or cow stables and sheds, in old out-houses, in cellars, and under barns where any animals usually shelter', and subject the excavated material to soaking, leaching, boiling, crystallizing, and refining. By one calculation, if 20,000 families made five pounds of saltpeter, 'which may be made in as many days', it would 'afford a stock of gunpowder for a large army, leaving a sufficiency for cannon both for forts and batteries, and for the field'. Such an effort would yield forty-five tons a week, and would tilt the military balance in the Americans' favour. Congress thought the project suitable for 'private families', and by early 1776 the manufacture of saltpeter was said to be 'spreading...in the family way'.[22]

John Adams of Massachusetts, chairman of the Board of War, became the most vigorous advocate for saltpeter independence. Saltpeter, he declared, was 'the *unum necessarium*' for American survival and victory. In letter after letter, speech after speech, Adams urged his colleagues to find sources of saltpeter and gunpowder: 'We must, and God willing, we will have them...we want nothing but saltpeter...now is the critical time.' In October 1775 he avowed, 'I am determined never to have saltpeter out of my mind, but to insert some stroke or other about it in every letter for the future. It must be had.' He advised whoever would listen to spread the word, 'that every stable, dove house, cellar, vault, etc. is a mine of saltpeter'.[23]

Massachusetts had begun to search for saltpeter as early as February 1775. Meeting at Cambridge, the Provincial Congress of

Massachusetts appointed a committee 'to draw up directions, in an easy and familiar style, for the manufacturing of saltpeter', and ordered copies to be printed and sent to every town and district. Inhabitants would make military supplies for the public good, and the state would pay £14 a hundredweight for this emergency saltpeter—this at a time when the British were paying £4 a hundredweight for saltpeter from India.[24] Local technical skill was hard to find, however, so Massachusetts sent Dr William Whiting to New York in June to obtain 'the most minute, particular, and intelligible account relative to the manufacturing of saltpeter', and to recruit 'some ingenious person, who has been used to work in the business of making saltpeter', if such an expert could be found.[25]

During the summer of 1775 Whiting travelled through six of the united colonies 'in quest of knowledge in the manufacturing of saltpeter'. He found success near White Plains, New York, where Dr Graham, 'by means of a German servant whom he bought and found to be good for nothing else', had once turned out 'between eight and nine hundredweight of good saltpeter in one season'. Here was another model for Americans to follow. Instead of using earth from stables, Graham dug soil from under old buildings, preferring 'such as smelled strong and had somewhat of a bitterish or alum taste upon the tongue'. He trickled water through tubs of this earth and boiled the resultant liquid, filtered it through ashes, and then boiled it again to a concentrate, from which crude saltpeter would crystallize. Further refinement produced saltpeter in cake form, 'fit to pack up for sale'. Reporting these findings in print, Whiting wished 'that every gentleman who heartily desires the salvation and prosperity of America' would devote himself to similar projects. Here was 'an easy, simple, and successful method' of making saltpeter that others would find to be 'easy and infallible'. A Massachusetts merchant who heard of this process described it as 'simplicity itself'. 'A good account' was expected from 'the meeting house earth of Great Barrington', where a pound of saltpeter was said to be furnished from every bushel of soil.[26]

Trials and experiments sprang up throughout the colonies in the opening months of the revolution. A promising start was made in Philadelphia, where, John Adams informed Josiah Quincy in July 1775, he had seen both saltpeter and gunpowder 'of our own make'. Captain Pryor and Thomas Paine conducted experiments in Philadelphia to demonstrate 'some easy, cheap, and expeditious method of making saltpeter in private families'. Nicholas Cooke of Providence, Rhode Island, shared reports 'that Dr Franklin and Dr Rush of Philadelphia had set up a saltpeter manufactory in which they had made a small experiment which turned out far beyond their expectation'. Eventually, backers hoped, they would make enough saltpeter for gunpowder 'to last all America in a war of seven years duration'.[27] Franklin learned in September 1775 that Baltzer Moody and George Garver of York County, Pennsylvania, had 'dug in stables, outhouses, etc'. and produced 117 pounds of saltpeter, which was 'perhaps as good as that imported from Europe'. Later that year he informed a French correspondent, 'we are using the utmost industry in endeavouring to make saltpeter, and with daily increasing success'.[28]

John Adams heard from Connecticut in September 1775 'that two persons of the names of De Witt, of Dutch extraction, one in Norwich, the other in Windham, have made saltpeter with success...and propose to make a great deal'. In December he learned of more 'critical experiments' in Massachusetts, some 'as simple as making soap'.[29] Reports came in November 'that skilful persons sent to Virginia, and employed there in a public saltpeter work...may, with sufficient assistance, produce a considerable quantity of that article'. Congress urged each of the United Colonies to follow suit, 'to work up such earth as is now fit for making saltpeter, and to collect together and place in beds or walls under sheds, all such earth and composition of materials as are suitable to produce saltpeter'. Patriotic enthusiasm was widespread, but despite these efforts, 'our saltpeter does not come in fast enough', observed Thomas Lynch in November 1775.[30]

It would be a work of freedom, not oppression or vexation, to supply the revolution with home-sourced material for munitions.

'Country gentlemen', advised one official publication, 'will find an agreeable and profitable amusement in erecting works of this kind.' The labour, wrote another enthusiast, would be 'an agreeable amusement, which every well-wisher to his country ought to encourage or practice'. The work was voluntary, collaborative, and cooperative, with an open exchange of knowledge among the various colonies. 'The knowledge of making saltpeter engages the attention of a number, who at this critical time are zealous for the country's good,' declared the *Essex Journal* in December 1775.[31] American patriotic volunteerism contrasted strongly with the oppressive and unpopular state saltpeter enterprise that had troubled early modern England before the era of East Indian imports. Rather than resisting the intrusions of the hated saltpetermen, revolutionaries would turn saltpetermen themselves.

Printed pamphlets showered Americans with tips on saltpeter-making. Anyone nurturing a nitre bed 'must pour into the pit the urine gathered in his house, and that he may have enough, he must get as much as he can from his neighbours', advised one publication. 'Where stables are constantly used, you must take the earth that lies near the manger, otherwise it will have too great a mixture of the urine and dung of the animals, which will produce sal-ammoniac instead of saltpeter,' recommended another. 'The north east winds in North America are generally accompanied with moisture which render them improper for the formation of saltpeter. The house that contains our saltpeter materials should therefore, in this country, be exposed to the north west wind.' And so on. The basic instructions, claimed John Adams, were 'short, plain and simple, so that Dick, Tom, and Joan may understand 'em', though this was over-optimistic.[32] In January 1776 Robert Treat Paine sent Philip Schuyler 'a newspaper containing a simple and I think intelligible method of making saltpeter', suggesting that some of the previous advice was too complicated. More newspapers followed in April 'which contain the successful making of it in New England', which Paine urged Schuyler to distribute 'with your authoritative injunctions to put it into immediate and vigorous execution'.[33]

Abigail Adams and her Massachusetts neighbours were among patriots experimenting with this backyard chemistry. Writing to her husband in April 1776, she described saltpeter projects in their part of New England, and offered to send to John Adams a manuscript 'describing the proportions for the various sorts of powder, such as fit for cannon, small arms and pistols'. She herself had not yet been successful with saltpeter, but Mr Tertias Bass 'has got very near an hundredweight which has been found to be very good'.[34] Saltpeter production 'flourish[ed] abundantly' across New England in the spring and summer of 1776, as manufacturers overcame initial difficulties. Reporting to John Adams in May 1776, Samuel Cooper marvelled, 'fourteen tons had been taken into the province store, and the bounty paid. Has any colony exceeded this?'[35]

Progress can be traced in Massachusetts records. Residents who offered their material for military use had to swear before a justice of the peace 'that the manufacture of the saltpeter now presented...was begun, carried on, and finished within the limits of this colony, and that no foreign saltpeter is mixed thereunto'. Surviving certificates to this effect show a burgeoning local enterprise, with deliveries from February to July 1776 ranging from several pounds to several hundredweight. Enoch Bagley, Henry Quimby, and James Bayley of Amesbury, Massachusetts, for example, combined in February 1776 to produce three hundredweight of merchantable saltpeter. Nathaniel Felt of Salem brought in eight pounds in May, and Elijah Sheldon of Bernardston just one. That Abigail Adams was not the only woman attempting to make saltpeter is shown by the certificates of Hannah Mead of Worcester, that the nine pounds of saltpeter she exhibited in May 'was of her own manufacturing', and of Mary Leonard of Hampshire County, whose twenty-one pounds of saltpeter reached the military store in June 'in a cotton small bag'.[36]

Frontier prospectors further south found promising sources of 'saltpeter rocks' in Virginia's Blue Ridge Mountains. Peyton Randolph informed John Adams in October 1775 that 'many gentlemen of Virginia, cautious, incredulous men, of strict honour and veracity', had tested the material and found it productive. Charles Lynch of Bedford, Virginia, (for whom 'lynch law' is named) was quick to set up a powder mill to exploit this saltpeter outcropping. A contributor to the *Virginia Gazette* in December 1775 offered further advice on the mixing of gunpowder, derived from the *New Chymical Dictionary*, translated from the French.[37] Seeking to make 'good merchantable saltpeter' within their province, the Congress of North Carolina sent to Virginia to obtain 'instructions and information how the process may be most beneficially conducted'. An experimental saltpeter works at Halifax, North Carolina, began work in April 1776 but was abandoned eighteen months later.[38] Delegates from South Carolina recommended digging under 'negro houses and barns'.[39]

Several states offered bounties and rewards for saltpeter manufactured within their jurisdiction, and appointed assayers or inspectors to weed out 'impure and unfit supplies'. Entrepreneurs across the colonies took up the challenge. James Cargill of Orange County, New York, was one who asked for exemption from military duty in August 1776, because it 'breaks in on his time of manufacturing saltpeter'. Another, David Gelston, had made almost half a ton on Long Island before the British moved in. Saltpeter makers in East Hadham, Sharon, Durham, and Pomphrett, Connecticut, also attracted attention in May 1777 because their paperwork was out of order. They had produced from 120 to 360 pounds of saltpeter, 'pure, clean and dry', and sued to be paid their bounties.[40]

America had created a domestic saltpeter enterprise, virtually from scratch, in hopes of securing gunpowder independence. 'The safety, freedom and wealth of the United Colonies' depended upon it, so Congress pronounced in March 1776. It was 'an object of the greatest concern that private families should be induced to make it ... when the method is once understood'. Saltpeter, wrote Oliver Wolcott, 'will procure us an Independency on which we may rely'.[41] But the work was more difficult than amateur enthusiasts envisaged, and the output suffered from poor quality control. Despite the spate of information and advice, skill and experience remained limited. Domestic supplies came in slower than anticipated, and the home-made saltpeter had high contaminations of common salt. Small-scale experiments did not translate well into industrial production. A few hundred pounds here and there, however promising, could not provision a revolutionary army.

Persistence, however, produced success. Massachusetts produced forty-five tons of saltpeter by midsummer 1776, and Connecticut had made thirty tons. Though still only a fraction of the total military need, it demonstrated that America could rise to the challenge. 'Twelve months ago we were distressed, to a degree that posterity will scare credit, for powder. This is now over,' John Adams declared in June 1776.[42] 'But without great care it will be all spoilt in making gunpowder,' warned Robert Treat Paine in September, since much of the locally milled powder was 'miserable trash'. How ironic, what 'cruel vexation in the day of decision for Liberty or Slavery, to have the scale turn against us merely through the defect of our own powder'.[43]

Attention now turned to technologies of gunpowder manufacture, with a search for expertise similar to the earlier campaign for making saltpeter. The problem was only partially resolved by the arrival in 1777 of Nicolas Fouquet from France, 'a person perfectly well acquainted with the process of extracting and refining saltpeter, making powder, constructing powder-mills on the best principles, and in short everything which relates to the manufacturing of powder'. Innovations associated with the work of Antoine Laurent de Lavoisier's Régie des Poudres, the newly formed and highly efficient French gunpowder administration, would help put the American explosives industry on a firmer scientific footing.[44]

In the event, however, these local efforts proved unnecessary, because the French were happy to supply England's enemies with all the gunpowder they needed. Much of this French powder was staged through the West Indies. The Dutch and Spanish too were willing to ship munitions through their island colonies, with Sint Eustatius a major entrepôt. As much effort went into beating blockades as into making saltpeter, with much more immediate success. In February 1776, while local production remained meagre and experimental, 120 tons of foreign saltpeter arrived in Philadelphia, with thirty more expected. All told, more than 213 tons of imported saltpeter and 649 tons of European gunpowder reached the American rebels before autumn 1777, the bulk of it coming to Philadelphia. Despite the upsurge of effort and enthusiasm, no more than ten per cent of America's gunpowder used to fight the British was derived from indigenous sources. Though the rebels still faced critical material shortages, successful importation gave them ammunition enough for victory.[45]

In later years the independent United States continued to build its military strength, though more by trade than industry. France remained an important source of supply, but American merchants turned increasingly to Asia, where the British munitions programme was sourced. One ship alone, the *Hydra* of Rhode Island, delivered 168 tons of Bengal saltpeter in one voyage in 1788.[46] Not surprisingly, British interests sought to exclude Americans from the Indian saltpeter trade lest they rival the forces of the crown. Because 'their own country [is] so scantily supplied with saltpeter', the Americans would 'have great inducement to go to India for it', so British observers feared in the 1790s. With their advantageous ability to trade metals, masts, spars, and other 'natural produce of their soil', the fledgling United States would 'totally eclipse the British', if not counteracted.[47] (An exception to this was the Committee of Trade's permission in July 1791 for Ward Nicholas Boylston to export thirty tons of saltpeter to the United States.)[48]

British restrictions gave further stimulus to American saltpetermen, who undertook the extracting, crystallizing, and refining of saltpeter at home. Israel Aber of Morris County, New Jersey, writing in 1796, revived the claim that an American saltpeter enterprise, 'if propagated and practiced as it might be', would 'produce a source of wealth equal to the mines of Peru'. Like the pamphleteers of 1776, he linked saltpeter to liberty as well as profit; and like the saltpeter projectors of Tudor and Stuart

England, his scheme was mostly derivative puffery.[49] American saltpeter manufacture languished after the urgent efforts of the mid-1770s, and by January 1780 was said to be 'in a dangerous way'.[50]

America's domestic explosives industry remained backward and under-developed, until the arrival in 1800 of Eleuthère Irénée du Pont de Nemours (1771–1834), who had learned his chemistry from Lavoisier in France. The du Pont company, founded in 1802, became the leading supplier of gunpowder, smokeless powder, dynamite, and nitroglycerine, before diversifying and becoming a multinational chemistry-based giant. Du Pont saltpeter, however, came mostly from India, either directly or re-imported from Britain.[51] Only in the South in the American Civil War was serious consideration again given to the local manufacture of saltpeter.[52] By the end of the nineteenth century American importation of saltpeter from India surpassed that of Britain herself.[53]

Salpêtriers and men of science

They ordered things differently in France, and the Gallic saltpeter trail took distinctive turnings. The French took an alternative path to saltpeter independence, with consequences for international security, commerce, and science.

France was more powerful than England for most of the early modern period, with a larger population and greater military capacity. Her appetite for saltpeter and gunpowder grew even faster than England's. The French army of the mid-fifteenth century needed only ten tons of powder and forty qualified gunners for its artillery, but by 1500 the equivalent figures were sixty tons and a hundred gunners. By the mid-sixteenth century, at the death of Francis I, the French crown employed 275 gunners and expended 250 tons of gunpowder per year. French fleets and French armies expanded through the seventeenth century, to make the forces of Louis XIV the most formidable in Europe.[54]

In sixteenth- and seventeenth-century France, as in early modern England, the state guarded its monopoly of munitions manufacture, and sent royal officials to fetch nitrous earth from barns, cellars, bird houses, and private dwellings. Kings of France claimed rights to requisition necessary supplies, and their agents and commissioners ensured a flow of saltpeter and gunpowder to the crown. Major towns owed the king approximately a pound of saltpeter per household. The French saltpeter enterprise was nationally centralized, with the same territorial divisions as the tax system, the *taille* (a land tax) and the *gabelle* (a tax on salt). A national allocation of 1544 demanded 803 *milliers* (almost 400 tons) of saltpeter from 300 *salpêtriers* who obtained their material from local sources. Inevitably, there were corruptions, exceptions and evasions, but from Francis I (r. 1515–1547) to Louis XV (r. 1715–1774) a pyramid of power from the local *salpêtriers* to the Grand Master of the Artillery helped France to secure its territory and project its military power.[55]

With no tradition of common law, and few proponents of individual rights, landowners in France could do little to resist the demands of the state. As the English author Henry Stubbe observed in 1670, 'In France there is a commission given to the principal officers of the artillery, dispersed through that vast kingdom, to enter all houses private and public, to find out such saltpeter earth; and the private persons are forced to be patient because it is for the service of the king.' The royal *salpêtriers* could enter any property, dig in any dwelling, and take what fuel they needed, in order to meet their quotas. Their operatives wore the sash of the saltpeterman 'with the Royal Arms and those of the Grand Master about his waist'. As privileged servants of the crown, the French saltpetermen themselves were exempt from paying the *taille*. Only the nobility and clergy were exempt from their intrusions. The system was modified under Louis XIV when gunpowder 'farmers' or monopoly lessees were awarded the *droit de fouille*, the privilege of searching and digging for usable saltpeter.[56]

French technicians had access to the same international expertise as their English counterparts, and drew on the same range of publications. It was, ironically, an Englishman, Francis Malthus, who served as Commissaire Général des Feux et Artifices de l'Artillerie de France under Louis XIV, whose treatise *Pratique de la guerre* explained saltpeter and its uses.[57] A finely illustrated account by Pierre Surirey de Saint-Rémy, *Mémoires d'artillerie* (Paris, 1697; Amsterdam, 1702), describes the manufacture of saltpeter at the Paris Arsenal, where 126 leaching tubs were in operation. The goal was to produce 'good saltpeter' that is 'hard, white, clear and transparent, clear of grease and well-purged of salt', for delivery to the royal powder works. Because the purification of saltpeter yields salt, and salt was highly taxed in France, the process gave opportunities for illicit profit. The closely guarded saline by-product was supposed to be drowned in the river.[58] Though projectors often dreamed of it, there was no English saltpeter plant of this concentration, intensity, and scale.

The French, like the English, also sought alternative supplies overseas, and had early eighteenth-century successes in India. Their shipments never matched those of the English or Dutch, but the French East India Company established warehouses at Port-Louis and Lorient on the Breton Atlantic coast to handle imports of saltpeter. French ships were trading in Bengal by the end of the seventeenth century, and the Compagnie des Indes was well established by the 1720s. Gunpowder-makers in France came to depend increasingly on imported Asian material, and the domestic enterprise was neglected. In the second half of the eighteenth century, however, British military power excluded French interests from the Indian trade, and cut off their supplies of saltpeter. The battle of Plassey in 1757 signalled the shift in imperial control. France was weakened, and the French themselves attributed defeat in the Seven Years War (1756–1763) to shortages of gunpowder.[59]

Exclusion from the world's major source of saltpeter forced the French to reorganize as domestic producers, and to improve both their technology and science. The baron Anne-Robert-Jacques Turgot, Controller-General to Louis XVI, undertook reform of the French saltpeter programme in 1775, and tightened government control of its operations. He sought assistance from the Académie Royale des Sciences to unlock 'this secret of nature', and recruited

Antoine Laurent de Lavoisier (1743–1794), France's foremost chemist and a principal of the Académie, to improve saltpeter production. Lavoisier became a *régisseur* or director of the new Régie des Poudres, the gunpowder administration, and devoted himself to the science and technology of explosives and combustion.[60] It was one of his assistants, Nicolas Fouquet, who was sent to America in 1777 to assist the rebels with their munitions production.[61]

Lavoisier's publication in 1777, *Instruction sur l'établissement de nitières et sur la fabrication du salpêtre*, offered detailed instructions on leaching and refining, including the use of a hydrometer to test crucial liquids. Precise measurement and careful recording were hallmarks of Lavoisier's proceedings. Lavoisier supervised the award of the 'extraordinary prize' that Turgot had persuaded the Académie to offer for understanding of how saltpeter was formed and how to extract it most efficiently. He collected and eventually published his *Recueil de mémoires sur la formation et sur le fabrication du salpêtre* (1786), which put France's saltpeter enterprise on a solid scientific footing. Along the way he created the modern science of industrial chemistry.[62] These developments coincided with the quickening of interest in saltpeter among Americans, who were hungry for materiel and expertise.

Besides conducting experiments in his laboratory at the Arsenal, Lavoisier supervised saltpeter refineries in more than a dozen French cities. He proposed a system of beds and sheds that would make the intrusive *fouille* less necessary, and prohibited his saltpetermen from entering wine cellars and private residences. He even lifted the restriction on digging in noble properties, though this did him little good at the Revolution. Through administrative ingenuity and path-breaking science Lavoisier raised French saltpeter production from 1.7 million livres (roughly 832 tons) in 1775 to 2 million livres (979 tons) in 1777, to 2.6 million livres (1,273 tons) in 1784. Some accounts credit Lavoisier with quintupling French nitrate production. French gunpowder reserves reached 5 million livres (almost 2,500 tons), and its quality was among the best in the world. This transformation took place precisely at the time

FIG 19 French saltpeter works, 1702

Pierre Surirey de Saint-Rémy, *Mémoires d'artillerie où, il est traité des mortiers, petards, arque-buses à croc, mousquets, fusils, &c.* (Amsterdam, 1702), following p. 100 (Huntington Library, rare book 16395, vol. 2, reproduced by permission of the Huntington).

when France was assisting the American revolutionaries, justifying Lavoisier's remark in 1789 that North America owed its freedom to French saltpeter and French gunpowder. Most of the munitions that Americans used to win independence originated in France.[63] As the British recognized with alarm, when yet another foreign war threatened in 1791, 'France produces much more saltpeter than is necessary for its own consumption', and had supplies in hand for four or five years.[64]

The aristocrat Lavoisier was arrested in 1793, the same year that his Académie des Sciences was abolished and Louis XVI guillotined. Revolutionary France was at war with the British and Dutch, and needed all available weaponry, but the brain behind its gunpowder programme was in prison. Lavoisier was guillotined in 1794, but the supply of French munitions did not immediately suffer. As the royal system of procurement foundered it gave way to a free-for-all in which any citizen could exploit saltpeter, and the *salpêtriers sans-culottes* produced more than the discredited Régie des Poudres. A painting by the Lesueur brothers shows revolutionary workers cheerfully engaged in 'fabrication du salpêtre'. Who needs academic chemistry, asked the leaders of the Terror, when you have 'la chimie du peuple'? The revolution would rely on citizen saltpeter, at least in the short run, and a

FIG 20   Making saltpeter, *c.*1790

Brothers Lesueur, 'Fabrication du salpêtre' ('Making saltpeter') *c.*1790. © Private Collection/Giraudon/The Bridgeman Art Library.

patriotic drive would furnish the arms of the republic. As the American William Jackson observed in France in 1794 at the height of the Terror, 'every consideration is sacrificed to public exigence...where reluctance may exist, terror supplies the absence of patriotism, and operates its full effect. Age and infancy are employed in extracting from the earth (and by a late refinement in chemistry, from vegetables) the thunders which youth and manhood are to direct.' Revolutionary saltpeter supplied the substance of those thunders, which reverberated worldwide into the Napoleonic era.[65] British gunpowder, made from Indian saltpeter, would go shot for shot with *poudre française*, derived from the soil of *la patrie*.

CONCLUSION

The saltpeter trail, as we have followed it, leads to unexpected connections between the social, legal, political, economic, scientific, and military histories of early modern England. It intersects the scholarship of many sub-specialities and illuminates such matters as the calculus of cannonry and the economy of human waste. It is a project with alchemical, philosophical, material, and even mystical dimensions. Just as saltpeter, for chemical savants, broke boundaries and challenged categories, so for historians it assumes a multibranched character, connecting the 'military revolution', the 'scientific revolution', and the revolutions of the Stuart realms. More than just a simple substance or commodity, like salt or sugar, saltpeter implicated the royal prerogative, and affected agrarian relations, cosmopolitan commerce, and imperial expansion. It furnished firepower and made the nation safe.

At the heart of the matter lay the vitalizing power of urine and excrement, and the miracle of nitrous-rich soil, whether in India or in Essex. Equally important was the ingenuity of making that soil yield the mother of gunpowder, the formidable potassium nitrate. Of crucial concern was the harnessing of organic material in the national security interest, without too much social, political, or financial cost. To secure indispensable supplies the government engaged in technology transfer through cosmopolitan experts, extended patronage to scientists and saltpetermen, and risked the wrath of its citizens by intruding onto their lands and homes. England's saltpeter enterprise tested royal authority against individual rights and hastened the formation of a centralized power. Its practitioners explored the limits of private, public, domestic, and even ecclesiastical space. Seen from multiple perspectives, through the eyes of Privy Councillors and common lawyers, artillerymen and military planners, natural philosophers and grubbing projectors, kings and subjects, the saltpeter economy could prove mysterious and miraculous, villainous and vexatious, profitable and indispensable, a foundational experience of the early modern state.

The period between the accession of Henry VIII and the death of William III saw England transformed from a condition of vulnerability and deficiency in military explosives to one of munitions abundance. The eighteenth and nineteenth centuries saw the rise to global dominance of a well-armed imperial industrial power. The transformation was accompanied by an outpouring of speculative enquiry, slow advances in chemical theory, and ingenious applications of practical problem-solving that have only begun to be noted.

Saltpeter dependence grew with the expansion of England's power, and was variously satisfied from domestic, European, North African, or East Indian sources. The saltpeter budget of the Ordnance Office soared from less than 100 tons a year in the sixteenth century to more than 1,000 tons in the eighteenth century. By the mid-nineteenth century British imports exceeded 20,000 tons a year. The demand for saltpeter energized a system of procurement and processing from Patna to Putney, from the Ganges to the Thames. But as the scale of the enterprise expanded, its deleterious social consequences lessened. An oppressive nuisance became a major imperial commodity.

Elizabethan and early Stuart governments pressed hard to secure saltpeter at home, but overseas merchants furnished the bulk. As much as ninety per cent of England's saltpeter was imported in the opening decade of Queen Elizabeth's reign, mostly from north-west Europe. Energetic saltpetermen raised the home-produced proportion from about ten per cent in the 1560s to perhaps thirty per cent by the 1590s, fifty per cent by the 1600s, and as much as seventy per cent in peak years in the 1630s, before East Indian shipments altered the balance. Domestic saltpetermen produced less than ten per cent of the nation's needs in the 1660s, and by the end of the seventeenth century almost all saltpeter in England arrived from Asia. The century-long effort to derive weapons-grade saltpeter from English earth was abandoned.

These shifts in the source and method of saltpeter procurement had profound consequences for England's wealth and safety, but they also helped shape her politics. The Elizabethan quest for 'infinite security' and the early Stuart demand for that 'inestimable treasure' caused strains between the crown and its subjects and tested the limits of royal authority. At its height in the reign of Charles I, the domestic saltpeter enterprise brought vexation to many and profit to a few, until East Indian imports relieved householders of that imposition. The saltpetermen who dug in private properties and the projectors who offered schemes to replace them could be grasping and aggressive, enterprising and odious, venal and corrupt, and sometimes exhibited all these qualities combined. 'Necessary varlets', as the playwright Thomas Middleton named them, or 'undermining two-legged moles' in Robert Boyle's characterization, the saltpetermen of early modern England had few friends and no successors. When William Pitt the elder declaimed so eloquently in 1763 that 'an Englishman's home is his castle…the King of England cannot enter', the government had long ceased digging for dung beneath his floors.

Our exploration of the quest for saltpeter has focused on early modern England and pre-industrial Britain, with comparative glances at America and France. It has shown how the changing dimensions of military conflict pressed planners to build up supplies of munitions and to procure the 'habiliments for the war'. This led to aggressive efforts to secure saltpeter, which constituted most of the bulk and even more of the value of gunpowder, without which no musket or cannon could be fired. Successive saltpeter projects embraced a social universe of operatives and administrators, subjects of the crown, whose dealings and frustrations shaped policy, business, and law. The two diagrams in the Appendix indicate the range and linkage of these interconnections.

Shifting to a wider gaze brings larger questions into view. What comparative lessons might be learned from this history about the social, legal, and political consequences of the pursuit of national security? Where do the rights of the individual end, and how far may the power of the state extend? At what price does the government equip itself with the necessary means of defence? Legal theorists and practical politicians such as Sir William Cecil, Sir Edward Coke, and the framers of Interregnum ordinances were among those exercised by these matters, as were the makers of the American and French revolutions. Alert citizens worry about them today.

More might be learned about relationships between science and warfare, and the intellectual consequences of government arms programmes. How did the procurement procedures of the munitions industry in the past affect basic science and technology, and how has that relationship changed? How connected were the worlds of saltpetermen, artillery engineers, and post-alchemical natural philosophers, and how did they share their knowledge? Were the gunpowder states of the early modern period best served by secrecy or openness, and how should such expertise be controlled? In what ways do demands of national security constrain or stimulate development of ideas, technology, and society? These are questions for continuing conversation, and topics for further research.

APPENDIX

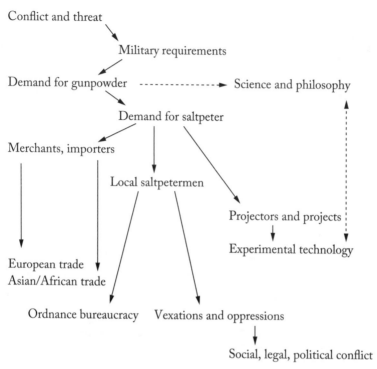

DIAGRAM I The Saltpeter System

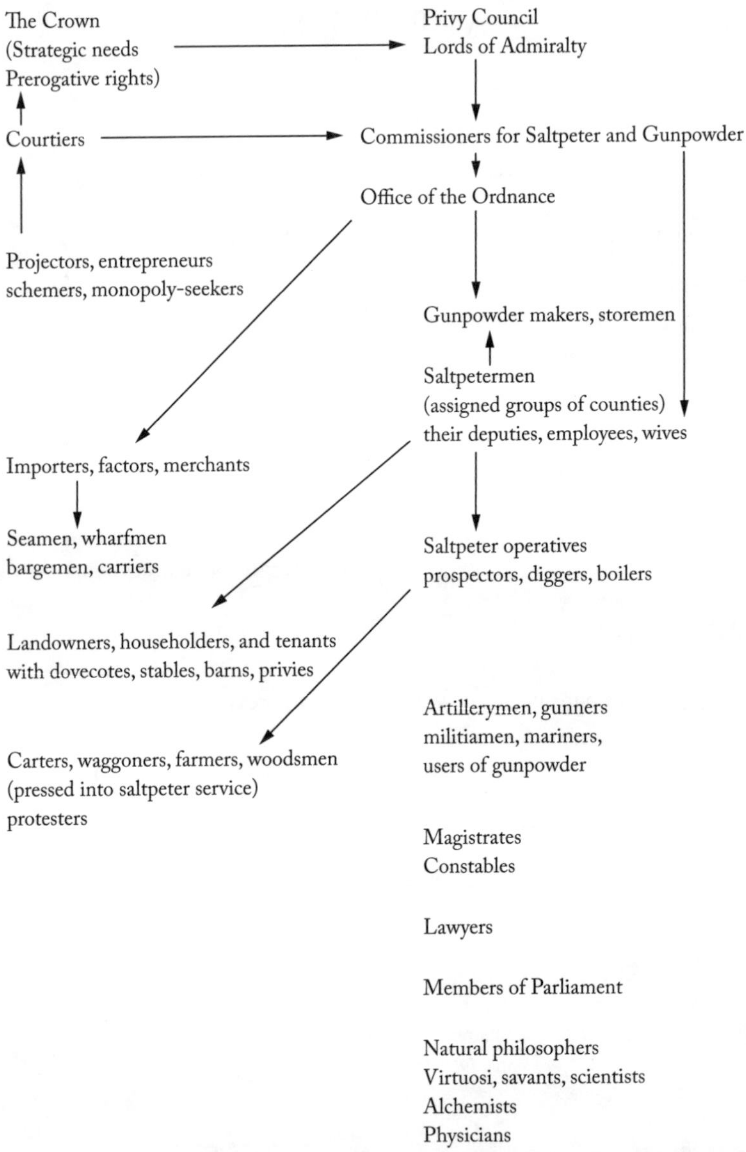

The Crown   Privy Council
(Strategic needs   Lords of Admiralty
Prerogative rights)

Courtiers   Commissioners for Saltpeter and Gunpowder

                                       Office of the Ordnance

Projectors, entrepreneurs
schemers, monopoly-seekers

                                       Gunpowder makers, storemen

                                       Saltpetermen
                                       (assigned groups of counties)
                                       their deputies, employees, wives

Importers, factors, merchants

Seamen, wharfmen   Saltpeter operatives
bargemen, carriers   prospectors, diggers, boilers

Landowners, householders, and tenants
with dovecotes, stables, barns, privies

                                       Artillerymen, gunners
                                       militiamen, mariners,
                                       users of gunpowder

Carters, waggoners, farmers, woodsmen
(pressed into saltpeter service)
protesters   Magistrates
                                       Constables

                                       Lawyers

                                       Members of Parliament

                                       Natural philosophers
                                       Virtuosi, savants, scientists
                                       Alchemists
                                       Physicians

DIAGRAM 2 The Saltpeter Universe: governors, processors, users, and victims of
the early modern saltpeter enterprise

NOTES

Preface

1. Ronald Edward Zupko, *A Dictionary of English Weights and Measures from Anglo-Saxon Times to the Nineteenth Century* (Madison, Wis., and London, 1968); Ronald Edward Zupko, *British Weights and Measures: A History from Antiquity to the Seventeenth Century* (Madison, Wis., 1977).
2. TNA, SP 12/209/37, f. 53.
3. K. N. Chaudhuri, *The Trading World of Asia and the English East India Company 1660–1760* (Cambridge, 1978), 472.

Introduction

1. John Bate, *The Mysteryes of Nature and Art* (1634), 55.
2. William Bourne, *The Arte of Shooting in Great Ordnaunce* (1587), 5–7; Nathaniel Nye, *The Art of Gunnery* (1647), 4–9, 19.
3. *By the King. A Proclamation for the better making of Saltpeter within this Kingdome*, 2 January 1627; TNA, SP 12/275/76, f. 125.
4. *Remonstrance of the State of the Kingdom* (1641), nos. 29, 36.
5. Thomas Henshaw, 'The History of the Making of Salt-Peter', in Thomas Sprat, *The History of the Royal-Society of London, For the Improving of Natural Knowledge* (1667), 274.
6. William Shakespeare, *Henry IV, Part I*, Act 1, scene 3. This is Hotspur reporting the womanly words of a popinjay lord.
7. William Harrison, *The Description of England*, ed. Georges Edelen (Ithaca, N.Y., 1968), 362, 364; TNA, SP 12/286/42, f. 102; *By the King. A Proclamation for the maintenance and encrease of the Mines of Saltpeter, and the true making of Gunpowder, and reforming abuses concerning the same*, 13 April 1625.
8. TNA, CAB 21/120. See also E. A. Brayley Hodgetts (ed.), *The Rise and Progress of the British Explosives Industry* (1909).
9. Gerald Aylmer, *The King's Servants: The Civil Service of Charles I, 1625–1642* (1961), 284–5.
10. Kelly DeVries, 'Sites of Military Science and Technology', in Katherine Park and Lorraine Daston (eds.), *The Cambridge History of Science. Vol. 3. Early Modern Science* (Cambridge, 2006), 311.
11. TNA, SP 1/10, f. 154; C 1/1193/73–75. *Letters and Papers, Foreign and Domestic, of the Reign of Henry VIII*, vol. 2, pt. 1, 111.
12. *CSP Foreign 1562–1563*, 228–9, 239.

13. Robert J. Taylor (ed.), *Papers of John Adams*, 15 vols. (Cambridge, Mass., 1977–2010), vol. 3, 221; Paul H. Smith (ed.), *Letters of Delegates to Congress 1774–1789*, 26 vols. (Washington, D.C., 1976–2000), vol. 2, 121.

Chapter 1

1. *The Correspondence of Robert Boyle. Vol. 1. 1636–61*, ed. Michael Hunter, Antonio Clericuzio, and Lawrence M. Principe (2001), 42–4; Robert Boyle, 'A Physico-Chymical Essay, Containing an Experiment, with some Considerations Touching the Differing Parts and Redintegration of Salt-Petre', in Robert Boyle, *Certain Physiological Essays* (1661), 108.

2. Gábor Ágoston, *Guns for the Sultan: Military Power and the Weapons Industry in the Ottoman Empire* (Cambridge, 2005); Weston F. Cook, Jr, *The Hundred Years War for Morocco: Gunpowder and the Military Revolution in the Early Modern Muslim World* (Boulder, San Francisco, and Oxford, 1994); Yar Muhammad Khan, 'Bārūd', *Encyclopedia of Islam*, (2nd edn., Leiden, Brill Online, http://www.paulyonline.brill.nl, accessed May 2009); William H. McNeill, *The Pursuit of Power: Technology, Armed Force, and Society since A.D. 1000* (Chicago, 1982); Arnold Pacey, *Technology in World Civilization: A Thousand-Year History* (Oxford, 1990), 73–91; Geoffrey Parker, *The Military Revolution: Military Innovation and the Rise of the West, 1500–1800* (2nd edn., Cambridge, 1996); Clifford J. Rogers (ed.), *The Military Revolution Debate: Readings on the Military Transformation of Early Modern Europe* (Boulder, 1995); Jan Glete, *Warfare at Sea 1500–1650: Maritime Conflicts and the Transformation of Europe* (1999). For criticism of the term 'gunpowder empires' see Stephen F. Dale, *The Muslim Empires of the Ottomans, Safavids, and Mughals* (Cambridge, 2010), 5–6.

3. For the history of gunpowder and explosives see, E. A. Brayley Hodgetts (ed.), *The Rise and Progress of the British Explosives Industry* (1909); J. R. Partington, *A History of Greek Fire and Gunpowder* (Cambridge, 1960; 2nd edn., Baltimore, Md., 1998); Joseph Needham, *Science and Civilisation in China. Vol. 5. Chemistry and Chemical Technology, Part 7: Military Technology: The Gunpowder Epic* (Cambridge, 1986); Brenda J. Buchanan (ed.), *Gunpowder: The History of an International Technology* (Bath, 1996); Glenys Crocker, *The Gunpowder Industry* (2nd edn., Princes Risborough, 1999); Brenda J. Buchanan, '"The Art and Mystery of Making Gunpowder": The English Experience in the Seventeenth and Eighteenth Centuries', in Brett D. Steele and Tamera Dorland (eds.), *The Heirs of Archimedes: Science and the Art of War through the Age of Enlightenment* (Cambridge, Mass., 2005), 233–74; Robert A. Howard, 'Realities and Perceptions in the Evolution of Black Powder Making', in Brenda J. Buchanan (ed.), *Gunpowder, Explosives and the State: A Technological History* (Aldershot, 2006), 22–5. For some of its cultural resonances see J. R. Hale, *Renaissance War Studies* (1983), 389–410. For gunpowder recipes see Niccolò Tartaglia, *Quesiti et inventioni diverse* (Venice, 1546), sig. L; Nathaniel Nye, *The Art of Gunnery* (1647), 4–9; Thomas Henshaw, 'The History of Making Gun-Powder', in Thomas Sprat, *The History of the Royal-Society of London,*

For the Improving of Natural Knowledge (1667), 278; Henry Stubbe, *Legends no Histories: Or, A Specimen of Some Animadversions Upon the History of the Royal Society* (1670), 94–5, 114–19. For accessible accounts of burning rates, shockwaves, physico-chemical phenomena, and combustion reactions, see E. Gray, H. Marsh, and M. McLaren, 'A Short History of Gunpowder and the Role of Charcoal in its Manufacture', *Journal of Materials Science*, 17 (1982), 3385–400; Jaime Wisniak, 'The History of Saltpeter Production with a Bit of Pyrotechnics and Lavoisier', *Chemical Educator*, 5 (2000), 205–9.

4. Roger Bacon in the 1260s, quoted in Robert Friedel, *A Culture of Improvement: Technology and the Western Millennium* (Cambridge, Mass., 2007), 85, 87. Cf. Francis Bacon, *The New Organon*, ed. Lisa Jardine and Michael Silverthorne (Cambridge, 2000), 166–7, on the 'marvellous conflict' that caused the 'blasting flames and fiery winds' of a gunpowder explosion. For the ranges of early modern European ordnance, see John Smith, *An Accidence for the Sea* (1636), 50, and William Eldred, *The Gunners Glasse* (1646), 90. Battlefields, of course, varied enormously in size, but a commonly used demi-culverin needed nine pounds of gunpowder to fire a nine-pound shot over half a mile. A heavy cannon could shoot an iron projectile as far as 1,950 yards with a muzzle velocity of 500 feet per second, James Raymond, *Henry VIII's Military Revolution: The Armies of Sixteenth-Century Britain and Europe* (London and New York, 2007), 27.

5. Friedel, *Culture of Improvement*, 86. See, however, Tadeusz Urbanski, *Chemistry and Technology of Explosives*, 3 vols. (New York, 1964–7), vol. 3, 322–42; Seymour H. Mauskopf, 'Bridging Chemistry and Physics in the Experimental Study of Gunpowder', in Frederick L. Holmes and Trevor H. Levere (eds.), *Instruments and Experimentation in the History of Chemistry* (Cambridge, Mass., 2000), 335–65.

6. *Oxford English Dictionary*, 'serpentine', noun, 2 and 6; William Bourne, *The Arte of Shooting in Great Ordnaunce. Contayning very Necessary Matters for all sortes of Servitoures eyther by Sea or by Lande* (1587), 6; William Clarke, *The Natural History of Nitre: or, a Philosophical Discourse of the Nature, Generation, Place, and Artificial Extraction of Nitre, with its Vertues and Uses* (1670), 88; Bert S. Hall, 'The Corning of Gunpowder and the Development of Firearms in the Renaissance', in Brenda J. Buchanan (ed.), *Gunpowder: The History of an International Technology* (Bath, 1996), 87–120, esp. 94–5. Corned powder was moistened to a paste and pressed through a sieve to improve its granular and surface properties. See also John F. Guilmartin, 'The Earliest Shipboard Gunpowder Ordnance: An Analysis of its Technicalities, Parameters and Tactical Capabilities', *Journal of Military History*, 71 (2007), 649–69.

7. Peter Whitehorne, *Certain Waies for the orderyng of Souldiers in battelray…And moreover, howe to make Saltpeter, Gunpoulder, and divers sortes of Fireworkes*, appended to his translation of Niccolò Machiavelli's *Arte of Warr* (1562), f. 27v.

8. Robert Norton, *The Gunner: Shewing the Whole Practise of Artillerie* (1628), 145, 149.

9. C. G. Cruickshank, *Army Royal: Henry VIII's Invasion of France 1513* (Oxford, 1969), 79; Thomas Binning, *A Light to the Art of Gunnery* (1703), 129.

10. Whitehorne, *Certain Waies for the orderyng of Souldiers*, f. 28.

11. BL, Add. Ms. 29303, f. 10v, on the composition of gunpowder in the time of James I; Norton, *Gunner*, 144; Nye, *Art of Gunnery*, 4–9, 19. Tartaglia, *Quesiti et inventioni diverse*, sig. L, listed twenty-three different recipes. See also Stubbe, *Legends no Histories*, 94–5, 114–16, for various continental formulae; Partington, *History of Greek Fire and Gunpowder*, 324–5; Howard, 'Realities and Perceptions in the Evolution of Black Powder Making', 22–5; Andrew Ure, *A Dictionary of Arts, Manufactures, and Mines: Containing a Clear Exposition of their Principles and Practice*, 2 vols. (4th edn., Boston, 1853), vol. 1, 976–8; Arthur Pine Van Gelder and Hugo Schlatter, *History of the Explosives Industry in America* (New York, 1927), 20. For the repair of powder that was decayed or spoiled, see Norton, *Gunner*, 146; William Salmon, *Seplasium. The Compleat English Physician* (1693), 95.

12. Henshaw, 'History of the Making of Gun-powder', 278. Henshaw was a close friend of John Evelyn, the descendant of gunpowder manufacturers, and had ample opportunity to learn their craft.

13. For the manufacture of charcoal, see John Evelyn, *Sylva: or, A Discourse of Forest-Trees* (1664), 100–3. Norton, *Gunner*, 144, recommended charcoal from 'hazel, alder, willow or birch...without bark or knots therein'. Salmon, *Seplasium*, 91, preferred charcoal made from hazel, ash, or juniper.

14. William Harrison, *The Description of England*, ed. Georges Edelen (Ithaca, N.Y., 1968), 289, 362. Advisors to the Muscovy Company in 1580 recommended their merchants to carry 'brimstone, to try the vent of the same, because we abound of it in the realm', Richard Hakluyt, *Divers Voyages Touching the Discoverie of America, and the Ilands adjacent unto the Same* (1582), sig. I4.

15. On the 'subterranean treasures' belonging to the crown by royal prerogative, see Sir John Pettus, *Fodinae regales. Or the History, Laws and Places of the Chief Mines and Mineral Works in England, Wales, and the English Pale in Ireland* (1670) 5, 21, 28. The royal mines were primarily of gold and silver, but Pettus included saltpeter among 'minerals and other products...beneficial to the kingdom'.

16. For the furnishing of saltpeter in continental Europe see Walter Panciera, 'Saltpetre Production in the Republic of Venice from the Sixteenth to the Eighteenth Century', *Icon: Journal of the International Committee for the History of Technology*, 3 (1977), 155–66; Bengt Åhslund, 'The Saltpetre Boilers of the Swedish Crown', in Brenda J. Buchanan (ed.), *Gunpowder: The History of an International Technology* (Bath, 1996), 163–81; John U. Nef, *Industry and Government in France and England, 1540–1640* (Philadelphia, 1940), 58–68, 97–8; Surirey de Saint-Rémy, 'The Manufacture of Gunpowder in France (1702). Part 1: Saltpetre, Sulphur and Charcoal', ed. and trans. David H. Roberts, *Journal of the Ordnance Society*, 5 (1993), 47; Robert P. Multhauf, 'The French Crash Program for Saltpeter Production, 1776–94', *Technology and Culture*, 12 (1971), 163–81.

17. Salmon, *Seplasium*, 90. Modern scholarship concludes that ancient 'nitre' was most likely soda (i.e. sodium carbonate) and that the properties of saltpeter

were unknown, Partington, *History of Greek Fire and Gunpowder*, 298–314. R. Abraham Portaleone, *Shilte ha-Gibborim* [Shields of the Heroes] (Mantua, 1612; Jerusalem, 1970), ch. 41, claims that ancient Hebrews were familiar with gunpowder artillery, a reference I owe to Matt Goldish.

18. William Eamon, *Science and the Secrets of Nature: Books of Secrets in Medieval and Early Modern Culture* (Princeton, 1994); Tara Nummedal, *Alchemy and Authority in the Holy Roman Empire* (Chicago and London, 2007); William R. Newman, 'From Alchemy to "Chymystry"', in Katherine Park and Lorraine Daston (eds.), *The Cambridge History of Science. Vol. 3. Early Modern Science* (Cambridge, 2006), 497–517; *The Hartlib Papers* (University of Sheffield, CD-ROM, 2nd edn., 2002), 13/223A; 39/1/11B; Boyle, 'Physico-Chymical Essay', 108.

19. Whitehorne, *Certain Waies for the orderyng of Souldiers*, fos. 21v–22.

20. Joseph Duchesne [as Iosephus Quersitanus], *The Practise of Chymicall, and Hermeticall Physicke, for the Preservation of Health*, trans. Thomas Timme (1605), sig. Pv; Allen G. Debus, *The Chemical Philosophy: Paracelsian Science and Medicine in the Sixteenth and Seventeenth Centuries* (New York, 1977), 432; Allen G. Debus, 'The Paracelsian Aerial Niter', *Isis*, 55 (1964), 43–61; Anna Marie Roos, *The Salt of the Earth: Natural Philosophy, Medicine, and Chymistry in England, 1650–1750* (Leiden and Boston, 2007).

21. Norton, *Gunner*, 7, 142.

22. Francis Bacon, *Sylva sylvarum or A Naturall History in Ten Centuries* (1627), 10; Francis Bacon, *The Historie of Life and Death* (1638), 158.

23. Boyle, 'Physico-Chymical Essay', 107–35.

24. Stubbe, *Legends no Histories*, 45; Henshaw, 'History of the Making of Gunpowder', 274–5; Clarke, *Natural History of Nitre*, 19, 53; Herman Boerhaave, *A New Method of Chemistry, Including the Theory and Practice of that Art* (1727), 109.

25. *Elements of the Theory and Practice of Chymistry* (translated from the French of Pierre-Joseph Macquer, Edinburgh, 1777), 182.

26. J. W. Leather and Jatindra Nath Mukerji, *The Indian Saltpetre Industry* (Calcutta, 1911), 14.

27. H. Lee and J. H. Quastel, 'Biochemistry of Nitrification in Soil', *Biochemical Journal*, 40 (1946), 803–28; J. H. Quastel and P. G. Scholefield, 'Biochemistry of Nitrification in Soil', *Bacteriological Reviews*, 15 (1951), 1–53. I am grateful to Gideon Fraenkel, Newman Professor of Chemistry at Ohio State University, and to Margaret Mathies, Weinberg Professor Emerita in Joint Science at the Claremont Colleges, for advice on this topic.

28. Vannoccio Biringuccio, *De la pirotechnia* (Venice, 1540); Cyril Stanley Smith and Martha Teach Gnudi (eds.), *The Pirotechnia of Vannoccio Biringuccio* (New York, 1942).

29. Georgius Agricola, *De re metallica* (Basel, 1556); Herbert Clark Hoover and Lou Henry Hoover (eds.), *Georgius Agricola, De re metallica. Translated from the First Latin Edition of 1556* (New York, 1950), 561–4.

30. TNA, SP 12/16/29; A. R. Williams, 'The Production of Saltpetre in the Middle Ages', *Ambix: The Journal of the Society for the History of Alchemy and Chemistry*, 22 (1975), 128–30. See below, Chapter 3.

31. Whitehorne, *Certain Waies for the orderyng of Souldiers*, fos. 21v–28v; reprinted 1574 and 1588.

32. Whitehorne, *Certain Waies*, fos. 21v–25.

33. Whitehorne, *Certain Waies*, fos. 21v–22.

34. Whitehorne, *Certain Waies*, fos. 22–3.

35. Whitehorne, *Certain Waies*, fos. 26–27v.

36. Whitehorne, *Certain Waies*, fos. 26–27v.

37. Williams, 'Production of Saltpetre in the Middle Ages', 127; Partington, *History of Greek Fire and Gunpowder*, 314–16.

38. Cyprian Lucar, *Colloquies Concerning the Arte of Shooting in Great and Small Peeces of Artillerie* (1588), Appendix, 5–11.

39. Lucar, *Colloquies*, Appendix, 5–11.

40. Bourne, *Arte of Shooting in Great Ordnaunce*. 5–7. For similar concerns among later artillerymen, see Norton, *Gunner*, 144–7, and Nye, *Art of Gunnery*, 19–20. William Cecil had earlier been informed that in Germany 'their cattle be kept with straw for the most part in the house, and of the ground where they stand is made the great plenty of saltpeter which the English lack', *CSP Foreign 1547–1553*, 96.

41. TNA, SP 12/106/53; SP 15/30, f. 213, and examples in Chapters 3 and 5, below.

42. See, for example, Nye, *Art of Gunnery*, 9–17.

43. *Lazarus Ercker's Treatise on Ores and Assaying translated from the German edition of 1580*, trans. Anneliese Grünhaldt Sisco and Cyril Stanley Smith (Chicago, 1951), 291–310. First published in Prague in 1574, the work was reprinted in Frankfurt in 1580, 1598, 1629, and 1672. Much of Ercker is translated in Sir John Pettus, *Fleta minor. The Laws of Art and Nature* (1683; reprinted 1685 and 1686). His treatise on 'the manner of boiling saltpeter' also appears in John Rudolph Glauber, *The Works of the Highly Experienced and Famous Chymist John Rudolph Glauber* (1689). According to Henry Stubbe, *Legends no Histories*, 87–8, Henshaw's 'History of the Making of Salt-Peter' was also heavily plagiarized from Ercker. See also R. J. W. Evans, *Rudolf II and his World: A Study in Intellectual History 1576–1612* (1997), 215.

44. HMC, *Calendar of the Manuscripts of the Most Hon. the Marquis of Salisbury, Preserved at Hatfield House*, 14 (1923), 339; Salisbury Ms. 276, no. 5, in Folger Shakespeare Library microfilm 164.70, partially transcribed in Gary C. Grassl, 'Joachim Gans of Prague: The First Jew in English America', *American Jewish History*, 86 (1998), 195–217, appendix. See below, Chapter 3, on Joachim Gaunz in Elizabethan England.

45. Charles Webster, *The Great Instauration: Science, Medicine and Reform 1626–1660* (New York, 1975), 378–81; Charles Webster, 'Benjamin Worsley: Engineering for Universal Reform from the Invisible College to the Navigation Act', in Mark Greengrass, Michael Leslie, and Timothy Raylor (eds.), *Samuel Hartlib and Universal Reformation: Studies in Intellectual Communication* (Cambridge, 1994), 215–17; Boyle, 'Physico-Chymical Essay', 107–8, 125; Robert Boyle, *The Sceptical Chymist* (1661), in *The Works of the Honourable Robert Boyle*, 6 vols. (1772), vol. 1, 566; Michael Hunter, *Boyle between God and Science* (New

Haven and London, 2009), 104–20; Thomas Leng, *Benjamin Worsley (1618–1677): Trade, Interest and the Spirit in Revolutionary England* (Woodbridge, 2008), 18–25. See also Samuel Worsley, 'De nitro theses quaedam', in *Hartlib Papers*, 39/1/16A, and 'Animadversions upon the fore-said observations', 39/1/11B.

46. Henshaw, 'History of the Making of Salt-Peter' and 'History of the Making of Gun-powder', in Sprat, *History of the Royal-Society*, 260–76, 277–83. Henshaw's account was popularized in John Houghton (ed.), *A Collection for the Improvement of Husbandry and Trade* (1696 and later editions), and repeated in subsequent collections of Royal Society transactions.

47. Henshaw, 'History of the Making of Salt-Peter', 266. See below, Chapter 5, for digging for saltpeter in churches.

48. Henshaw, 'History of the Making of Salt-Peter', 274–5.

49. Stubbe, *Legends no Histories*, 44, 76.

50. Joseph M. Levine, *Between the Ancients and the Moderns: Baroque Culture in Restoration England* (New Haven and London, 1999), 28.

51. Stubbe, *Legends no Histories*, 81, 87–8. *The Compleat Gunner* (1672), another Restoration compendium on gunpowder, drew on 'Casimir, Diego, Ussano, Hexam, and other authors', and based its treatment of ballistics on 'Galiaeus and Torricellio…with some excellent observations out of Mersennus and other famous authors', title page.

52. Thomas Chaloner, *A Shorte Discourse of the Most Rare and Excellent Vertue of Nitre* (1584), fos. 2–22.

53. Boyle, 'Physico-Chymical Essay', 115, describing the practice of 'that profound naturalist Lord Verulam' (Francis Bacon).

54. *Evening Post*, 17 October 1745; *St. James's Evening Post*, 14 November 1745; *London Evening Post*, 29 September 1747, on saltpeter for horned cattle.

55. Robert Lovell, *Panoryktologia. Sive Pammineralogicon. Or An Universal History of Mineralls* (Oxford, 1661), 45–7.

56. William Thraster, *The Marrow of Chymical Physic; or, The Practice of Making Chymical Medicines* (1669; 1679 edn.), 111–15.

57. Clarke, *Natural History of Nitre*, epistle dedicatory, 15, 19, 20, 23–31. 51–9, 65, 68–9, 71, 86, 91–2. See also Edward Jorden, *A Discourse of Naturall Bathes, and Minerall Waters* (1673), 44–57; John Mayow, *Tractatus quinque medico-physici. Quorum primus agit de sal-nitro, et spiritu nitro-aereo* (Oxford, 1674).

58. TNA, PC 2/46, 126; *CSPD 1665–1666*, 354.

59. Salmon, *Seplasium*, 50–3, 90–5.

60. George Wilson, *A Compleat Course of Chemistry* (1699), 'to the reader', 160–1; Nicolas Lémery, *A Course of Chymistry: Containing the Easiest Manner of Performing those Operations* (1677).

61. Boerhaave, *New Method of Chemistry*; Godfrey Smith, *The Laboratory, or School of Arts* (1738); George Wilson, *A Course of Practical Chemistry* (1746); [Macquer], *Elements of the Theory and Practice of Chymistry* (Edinburgh, 1777); Peter Shaw, *Chemical Lectures* (1734); Richard Watson, *Chemical Essays* (1781).

62. *Several Methods of Making Salt-Petre, Recommended to the Inhabitants of the United Colonies, by the Honorable Continental Congress, and Re-published by*

Order of the General Assembly of the Colony of Massachusetts (Watertown, Mass., 1775), 20.

63. BL, Add. Ms. 49093, Napier Papers, vol. 8, fos. 3–14.
64. W. C. D., *Considerations on the Importance of the Production of Saltpetre in England and its Dependencies* (1783), 5, 16, 32.
65. TNA, BT 6/184/36. See below, Chapter 8.
66. Multhauf, 'French Crash Program for Saltpeter Production', 163–81; Tony Travis, 'Revolutions and Gunpowder: Antoine Lavoisier', *Chemistry and Industry*, 9 (1994), 333–8; Jean-Pierre Poirier, *Lavoisier: Chemist, Biologist, Economist* (Philadelphia, 1996), 89–96; Arthur Donovan, *Antoine Lavoisier: Science, Administration, and Revolution* (Cambridge, 1996), 190–7; Seymour H. Mauskopf, 'Gunpowder and the Chemical Revolution', *Osiris,* 2nd ser., 4 (1988), 92–118. On the backwardness of English academic chemistry see Jan Golinski, *Science as Public Culture: Chemistry and Enlightenment in Britain, 1760–1820* (Cambridge, 1992), 129–36.
67. TNA, SUPP 5/762/6.
68. Seymour H. Mauskopf, '"From an Instrument of War to an Instrument of the Laboratory: the Affinities do not Change": Chemists and the Development of Munitions, 1785–1885', *Bulletin of the History of Chemistry*, 24 (1999), 1–15; Arnold Burgen, 'An Explosive Story', *European Review*, 12 (2004), 209–15; Stephen R. Bown, *A Most Damnable Invention: Dynamite, Nitrates, and the Making of the Modern World* (Toronto and London, 2005).
69. Jean L'hirondel and Jean-Louis L'hirondel, *Nitrate and Man: Toxic, Harmless or Beneficial?* (Wallingford and New York, 2002).
70. George W. Rich and David F. Jacobs, 'Saltpeter: A Folkloric Adjustment to Acculturation Stress', *Western Folkore*, 32 (1973), 164–79; Jeff Schogol, 'Are New Recruits Secretly Given Saltpeter?' *Stars and Stripes* (http:www.stripes.com/blogs/the-rumor-doctor, accessed June 2010).
71. Burgen, 'Explosive Story', 209–15; William D. Steers, 'Viagra—After One Year', *Urology*, 54 (1999), 12–17.

Chapter 2

1. TNA, C 1/1120/52. For a map of early Tudor Shrewsbury showing the river and barges, see BL, Royal Ms. 18 DIII, f. 90.
2. For Bosworth battlefield archaeology, see *Guardian*, 28 October 2009. For late-medieval ordnance see Bert S. Hall, *Weapons and Warfare in Renaissance Europe: Gunpowder, Technology, and Tactics* (Baltimore, Md., 1997); Michael Prestwich, *Armies and Warfare in the Middle Ages: The English Experience* (New Haven and London, 1996), 287–93; Kelly DeVries, 'Sites of Military Science and Technology', in Katherine Park and Lorraine Daston (eds.), *The Cambridge History of Science. Vol. 3. Early Modern Science* (Cambridge, 2006), 308–11; Mark Charles Fissel, *English Warfare 1511–1642* (2001), 44, 52. Cf. Geoffrey Parker (ed.), *The Cambridge Illustrated History of Warfare: The Triumph of the West* (Cambridge, 1995), 115.
3. Kelly DeVries, 'Gunpowder Weaponry and the Rise of the Early Modern State', *War in History*, 5 (1998), 127–45, quote from 130; James Raymond, *Henry*

VIII's Military Revolution: The Armies of Sixteenth-Century Britain and Europe (London and New York, 2007), 3, 28; Fissel, *English Warfare*, 44.

4. Steven Gunn, 'Archery Practice in Early Tudor England', *Past and Present*, no. 209 (2010), 75–7.

5. Fissel, *English Warfare*, 4–16; C. G. Cruickshank, *Army Royal: Henry VIII's Invasion of France 1513* (Oxford, 1969), 76; Raymond, *Henry VIII's Military Revolution*, 30, 44; Paul E. J. Hammer, *Elizabeth's Wars: War, Government and Society in Tudor England, 1544–1604* (Basingstoke and New York, 2003), 18.

6. C. S. Knighton and D. M. Loades (eds.), *The Anthony Roll of Henry VIII's Navy* (Navy Records Society, 2000), 41–106; Geoffrey Parker, 'The *Dreadnought* Revolution of Tudor England', *Mariner's Mirror*, 82 (1996), 270; N. A. M. Rodger, *The Safeguard of the Sea: A Naval History of Britain 660–1649* (1997), 485.

7. TNA, C 1/108/61; C 1/308/71; *Letters and Papers, Foreign and Domestic, of the Reign of Henry VIII*, vol. 1, pt. 2, 206, 334, 400, 401.

8. *Letters and Papers...Henry VIII*, vol. 1, pt. 1, 670; vol.1, pt. 2, 404, 588; TNA, SP 1/8, f.1.

9. *Letters and Papers...Henry VIII*, vol.1, pt. 2, 2, 6, 13, 18, 20, 21, 23, and passim; TNA, SP 1/4, f. 66; SP 1/8, f. 1.

10. *Calendar of the Patent Rolls...1485–1494* (1914), 395; *Calendar of the Patent Rolls...1494–1509* (1916), 233; A. R. Williams, 'The Production of Saltpetre in the Middle Ages', *Ambix: The Journal of the Society for the History of Alchemy and Chemistry*, 22 (1975), 126. See TNA, SP 1/3, fos. 64, 75, and SP 1/229, f. 32, for payment to Arthur Somerset for making gunpowder in 1510, and to Thomas Hart for making gunpowder at Portchester castle in 1511 and 1512.

11. TNA, STAC 2/15, fos. 23–31; *Letters and Papers...Henry VIII*, vol. 3, pt. 1, 478, for reference to Fawkener, deceased.

12. *Letters and Papers...Henry VIII*, vol. 1, pt. 1, 670. Other contemporary saltpeter accounts refer to John Stangate of London.

13. *Letters and Papers...Henry VIII*, vol. 2, pt. 1, 1111; TNA, SP 1/10, f. 154. Hans Wolf's receipt for saltpeter, brimstone, and coal powder (i.e. charcoal) in 1514 is in SP 1/7, fos. 168–72.

14. *Letters and Papers...Henry VIII*, vol. 5, 153.

15. TNA, C 1/1120/52. The case can be dated no more precisely than April 1544 to February 1547.

16. TNA, C 1/1193/73–75.

17. Niccolò Tartaglia, *Quesiti et inventioni diverse* (Venice, 1546), 'Libro Terzo. Delle specie di salnitrii et delle varie compositioni delle polvere'; *Letters and Papers...Henry VIII*, vol. 21, pt. 1, 739.

18. *Letters and Papers...Henry VIII*, vol. 20, pt. 2, 16; B. H. St J. O'Neil, 'Stefan von Haschenperg, an Engineer to King Henry VIII, and his Work', *Archaeologia*, 91 (1945), 137–55; Williams, 'Production of Saltpetre in the Middle Ages', 125–6.

19. *Letters and Papers...Henry VIII*, vol. 3, pt. 2, 1394; TNA, SP 1/102, f. 31.

20. *APC 1542–1547*, 332.
21. *Letters and Papers... Henry VIII*, vol. 19, pt. 2, 12, 382, 426; TNA, SP 1/191, ff. 40, 191, 230; SP 1/195, f. 138, also SP 1/216, f. 84, in April 1546.
22. TNA, C 1/1159/30-32.
23. TNA, E 315/255, f. xxiii.
24. *CSP Foreign, Edward VI*, 34; *APC 1547–1550*, 500.
25. *CSP Foreign, Edward VI*, 96.
26. *CSP Foreign, Mary*, 190, 197, 201, 363, 368.

Chapter 3

1. BL, Lansdowne Ms. 24, fos. 137, 139; Lansdowne Ms. 25, f. 138.
2. *APC 1577–1578*, 140, 142, 159–61, 170–1; BL, Lansdowne Ms. 28, fos. 13, 23, 141, 145, 147, 149, 152; E. C. Wrey, 'Saltpetre House, Ashurst Wood, Colbury', *Papers and Proceedings of the Hampshire Field Club and Archaeological Society*, 18 (1954), 335–6.
3. *CSP Foreign 1559–1560*, 557; John William Burgon, *The Life and Times of Sir Thomas Gresham*, 2 vols. (1839), vol. 1, 294; Paul E. J. Hammer, *Elizabeth's Wars: War, Government and Society in Tudor England, 1544–1604* (Basingstoke and New York, 2003), 56.
4. Geoffrey Parker, *The Military Revolution* (2nd edn., Cambridge, 1996); Clifford J. Rogers (ed.), *The Military Revolution Debate: Readings on the Military Transformation of Early Modern Europe* (Boulder, 1995).
5. Geoffrey Parker, 'The *Dreadnought* Revolution of Tudor England', *Mariner's Mirror*, 82 (1996), 273; N. A. M. Rodger, *The Safeguard of the Sea: A Naval History of Britain 660–1649* (1997), 486–7. For more on the guns of' 1588, see Colin Martin and Geoffrey Parker, *The Spanish Armada* (1988); Paul E. J. Hammer, *Elizabeth's Wars* (Basingstoke and New York, 2003), 149, where Elizabeth's thirty-four ships sport 883 cannon; Huntington Library, Ellesmere Ms. 6206b, fos. 15v–16, 20v–21, for the 1578 survey; BL, Royal Ms. 17 AXXXI, fos. 25v–26, for the survey of 1603. The queen's ships also carried large numbers of arquebuses and hand guns, with appropriate gunpowder.
6. William Bourne, *The Arte of Shooting in Great Ordnaunce* (1587), 72–3; Richard Winship Stewart, *The English Ordnance Office 1585–1625: A Case Study in Bureaucracy* (Woodbridge, 1996), 92–3.
7. 'Munition requisite to be provided and kept always in store for 1000 men', in *Cabala, sive Scrinia sacra: Mysteries of State and Government... Second Part* (1691), 97.
8. Stewart, *English Ordnance Office*, 80–95; TNA, SP 12/275/76, for 'infinite security'.
9. *CSPD 1547–1580*, 117; TNA, SP 12/1/31, f. 66.
10. *CSP Foreign 1558–1559*, 201.
11. *CSPD 1547–1580*, 117; *CSP Foreign 1558–1559*, 582.
12. *CSPD 1547–1580*, 172; TNA, SP 12/1/31, f. 66; *CSP Foreign 1561–1562*, 1–2, 22.
13. *CSP Foreign 1558–1559*, 28, 61, 121, 153; *CSP Foreign 1559–1560*, 48, 338, 434, 436, 544; *CSP Foreign 1560–1561*, 49, 677, 155; Hammer, *Elizabeth's Wars*, 56.

14. *CSP Foreign 1558–1559*, 121; *CSP Foreign 1561–1562*, 2.

15. *CSP Foreign 1562–1563*, 228–9, 239.

16. TNA, SP 12/228, f. 101, SP 12/253 f. 149, *CSP Foreign 1559–1560*, 18, 544; *CSP Foreign 1561–1562*, 319; *Oxford Dictionary of National Biography*, sub 'Stephen Borough'.

17. TNA, SP 15/24 f. 141; E. W. Bovill, 'Queen Elizabeth's Gunpowder', *Mariner's Mirror*, 33 (1947), 179–86; 'The Ambassage of M. Edmund Hogan' (to Morocco) in Richard Hakluyt, *The Principal Navigations Voyages Traffiques & Discoveries of the English Nation*, 12 vols. (Glasgow, 1903), vol. 6, 290–1. On English dealings with Morocco, see N. I. Matar, *Britain and Barbary, 1589–1689* (Gainesville, Fla., 2005).

18. HMC, *Calendar of the Manuscripts of the Most Hon. the Marquis of Salisbury, Preserved at Hatfield House*, 23 vols. (1883–1973) (hereafter HMC, *Salisbury*), vol. 2, 394; W. H. Overall and H. C. Overall (eds.), *Analytical Index to the Series of Records known as the Remembrancia* (1878), 406.

19. TNA, SP 12/223, f. 77. 'The Description of the Countrey of Russia' (1588), in Hakluyt, *Principal Navigations*, vol. 3, 369, notes that 'saltpeter they make in many places…but want skill to refine it.'

20. BL, Cotton Ms. Galba, D XIII, f. 90; *CSPD 1591–1594*, 99, 158; *CSPD 1595–1597*, 152.

21. *CSP Venice*, vol. 8, no. 811.

22. TNA, SP 12/275/76.

23. TNA, SP 12/275/76; SP 15/24, f. 141.

24. TNA, SP 12/16/28, f. 55.

25. TNA, SP 12/16/30, f. 59; BL, Lansdowne Ms. 5, f. 98; *Calendar of the Patent Rolls 1560–1563* (1948), 98, 104.

26. Peter Whitehorne, *Certain Waies for the orderyng of Souldiers in battelray*, appended to his translation of Niccolò Machiavelli's *Arte of Warr* (1562), fols. 21v–27. See also, Bourne, *Arte of Shooting in Great Ordnaunce*, 5. See above, Chapter 1, for the science and technology of saltpeter extraction.

27. The Master, Lieutenant, and Surveyor of the Ordnance supervised a staff of gunners and gun-founders, engineers and saltpeter-makers. A table of fees c.1578 showed the Master of the Ordnance was paid £151 11s. 4d a year, and the saltpetermaker 6d. per diem or £9 2s. 6d. a year, Huntington Library, Ellesmere Ms. 6206b, f. 40.

28. TNA, SP12/286/42, f. 100; SP 12/21, fos. 106, 107; SP 12/229, f. 54.

29. TNA, SP 12/83, f. 102; SP 12/224/114, f. 175.

30. BL, Lansdowne Ms. 57, f. 144.

31. Surrey History Centre, Guildford, More Molyneux Correspondence, 6729/10/13; 2/91/44, f. 99.

32. TNA, E 101/64/8.

33. TNA, SP 12 106/53, f. 115.

34. *CSPD 1547–1580*, 53, 68; *CSPD 1581–1590*, 4; TNA, SP 12/106/1, f. 115; SP 15/24/68, f. 175; SP 12/147/42, f. 88; BL, Lansdowne Ms. 80, f. 93; HMC, *Salisbury*, vol. 13, 597.

35. TNA, SP 12/83, f. 102.

36. TNA, SP 15/24/50, f. 141.

37. BL, Lansdowne Ms. 24, f. 143; TNA, SP 12/228/38, f. 101.

38. BL, Lansdowne Ms. 24, fos. 137, 139; Lansdowne Ms. 25, f. 138; *APC 1577–1578*, 171.

39. Hatfield House, Cecil Papers 9/110.

40. *APC 1577–1578*, 140, 142, 159–61, 170–1; BL, Lansdowne Ms. 25, f. 138; BL, Lansdowne Ms. 28, fos. 13, 23, 141, 145, 147, 149, 152.

41. *CSPD 1547–1580*, 658; TNA, SP 12/139/1; BL, Lansdowne Ms. 30, f. 6, 7.

42. Wrey, 'Saltpetre House, Ashurst Wood', 335–6; Brenda Buchanan, '"The Art and Mystery of Making Gunpowder": The English Experience in the Seventeenth and Eighteenth Centuries', in Brett D. Steele and Tamera Dorland (eds.), *The Heirs of Archimedes* (Cambridge, Mass., 2005), 238; Brenda J. Buchanan, 'Saltpetre: a Commodity of Empire', in Brenda J. Buchanan (ed.), *Gunpowder, Explosives and the State* (Aldershot, 2006), 71.

43. TNA, SP 12/161/11 f. 30.

44. TNA, SP 12/286/42, f. 101; *By the Queene. A Proclamation for the calling in and frustrating all commissions for the making of salt-peeter*, 13 January 1590.

45. TNA, SP 12.225/55, f. 89; SP 12/227/3, f. 5.

46. *By the Queene. A Proclamation for the calling in and frustrating all Commissions for the making of Salt-peter*, 13 January 1590; Stewart, *English Ordnance Office*, 86–7.

47. See note 5, above.

48. TNA, SP 12/209/37, f. 53; SP 12/219/7, f. 18.

49. *CSPD 1591–1594*, 1, 95.

50. TNA, SP 12/225/47, f. 76; SP 12/225/55, f. 89.

51. BL, Lansdowne Ms. 57, f. 144.

52. TNA, SP 15/30, f. 213; BL, Lansdowne Ms. 58, f. 150.

53. HMC, *Salisbury*, vol. 14, 339; Hatfield House, Cecil Papers, 276/5; Folger Shakespeare Library, Washington, D.C., microfilm 164.70, partially transcribed in Gary C. Grassl, 'Joachim Gans of Prague: The First Jew in English America', *American Jewish History*, 86 (1998), pp. 195–217, appendix. See *CSPD 1581–1589*, 617, and TNA, SP 12/226/40, for reports from Bristol that Joachim Gaunz, now residing at Blackfriars, London, denied Christ to be son of God and thereby showed himself 'a most wicked infidel, and not meet to be suffered among Christians'.

54. TNA, SP 12/224/114, f. 175; SP 12/227/4, f. 8.

55. *APC 1590–1591*, 21.

56. HMC, *Salisbury*, vol. 4. 263; *CSPD 1595–1597*, 153; TNA, SP 12/255/63, f. 96.

57. Hugh Plat, *The Jewell House of Art and Nature* (1594), 76; Malcolm Thick, *Sir Hugh Plat: The Search for Useful Knowledge in Early Modern London* (Totnes, 2010), 255, 259, 278–9, 293.

58. HMC, *Salisbury*, vol. 14, 238–9; HMC, *Salisbury*, vol. 12, 542.

59. BL, Lansdowne Ms. 103, no. 44, f. 104; TNA, SP 12/275/76, f. 125.

60. *CSPD 1547–1580*, 511; *CSPD Addenda 1566–1579*, 495; TNA, SP 15/24/50, f. 141; BL, Lansdowne Ms. 31, f. 188; Lansdowne Ms 57, f. 144.

61. BL, Lansdowne Ms. 24, f. 139.

62. BL, Lansdowne Ms. 58, f. 150.

63. Surrey History Centre, More Molyneux Correspondence, 6729/7/39, correspondence concerning the 'willful and headstrong' saltpeterman Mr Cresswell.

64. BL, Lansdowne Ms. 61, no. 72.

65. BL, Lansdowne Ms. 84, no. 63, fos. 145–6.

66. *Calendar of the Patent Rolls 1560–1563*, for the 1561 patent; TNA, SP 12/91/44, f. 99, for the 1573 commission.

67. *By the Queene. A Proclamation for the calling in and frustrating all commissions for the making of salt-peeter*, 13 January 1590.

68. TNA, SP 12/225/63, f. 96; *APC 1595–1596*, 11; Overall and Overall (eds.), *Analytical Index to the...Remembrancia*, 214.

69. HMC, *Salisbury*, 14, 1596–1597, 238; TNA, SP 12/275/76, transcribed in the appendix to this chapter.

70. *APC 1599–1600*, 818.

71. TNA, SP 12/225/47, f. 76/55, f. 89/56, f. 91/57, f.92; BL, Lansdowne Ms. 103, no. 44, fos. 104, 104v.

72. TNA, SP 12/225/61, f. 96; SP 12/226/31, f. 35; SP 12/224/114, f. 175; SP 12/227, f. 8.

73. BL, Lansdowne Ms. 113, f. 167; TNA, E 133/7/1045–8. Further complaints against Powell for his mismanagement of the ordnance stores are in E 133/71052 and 1071. George Evelyn allegedly said 'that the queen's majesty did take not part with any but with beggars, as the king of Navarre and such like, and that it was pity that her highness had no better counsel, and that the Spaniards living in his house in Queen Mary's time were good men and bountiful, or words to that effect'. For accounts of 'decayed and unserviceable gunpowder and saltpeter...new wrought and made good' by John and Robert Evelyn, 1595–1603, see TNA, E 351/2708.

74. *By the Queene. A Proclamation for the reformation of many abuses and misdemeanours committed by Patentees*, 28 November 1601; HMC Salisbury, vol. 12, 63–4.

75. TNA, SP 12/286/42. Another version is in BL, Cotton Ms. Ortho E VII, fos. 94–9, 105–105v. A court case in 1602 confirmed the royal privilege of digging saltpeter for the defence of the realm: *Darcy v. Allen*, King's Bench, Easter 1602, in Sir Francis Moore, *Cases Collect & Report* (1688), 672.

76. TNA, SP 12/286/42, SP 16/275/76.

77. TNA, SP 16/275/76. An abbreviated version appears in *CSPD 1598–1601*, 470–2.

Chapter 4

1. Thomas Middleton, *A Faire Quarrell* (1617), Act 1, scene 1.

2. BL, Royal Ms. 17 A XXXI, fos. 31-31v; Yale Center for British Art, New Haven, B. 1977.14.17888; John Nichols (ed.), *The Progresses, Processions, and Magnificent Festivities of King James the First*, 4 vols. (1828), vol. 1, 63, 66.

3. BL, Royal Ms. 17 A XXXI, f. 4v.

4. *CSP Venetian*, vol. 9, 1155; *CSP Venetian*, vol.10, 35, 274, 313. The Venetian Senate instructed its ambassador in England to pay as much as 130 ducats a ton for refined saltpeter, 'consigned to our arsenal at Venice'.

5. *CSPD Addenda 1580–1625*, 522; BL, Cotton Ms. Ortho E VII, f. 78.

6. David Cressy, *Bonfires and Bells: National Memory and the Protestant Calendar in Elizabethan and Stuart England* (1989), 87–9; *The Mariage of Prince Fredericke, and the Kings Daughter, the Lady Elizabeth* (1613), sig. A.

7. *CSPD 1603–1610*, 6; TNA, SP 14/1/64.

8. BL, Add. Ms 41613, f. 111v; BL, Royal Ms. 17 A XXXI, f. 29v; TNA, SP 14/11/68; *CSPD 1603–1610*, 156. Richard Evelyn's account book includes 'a bill of the charges for the making of saltpeter, 1611', with payments for labour and equipment, BL, Add. Ms. 78278, fos. 4–4v.

9. Folger Shakespeare Library, Washington, Ms. Z.e.26, saltpeter receipts January–June 1605.

10. David Harris Willson (ed.), *The Parliamentary Diary of Robert Bowyer 1606–1607* (Minneapolis, 1931), 131–2, 156; Wallace Notestein, *The House of Commons, 1604–1610* (New Haven and London, 1971), 168; Sir Robert Johnson to Secretary Cecil, October 1606, HMC, *Salisbury*, vol. 18, 335–6.

11. BL, Harley Ms. 6070, f. 413v.

12. *By the King. A Proclamation for prevention of future abuses in Purveyance*, 23 April 1606.

13. BL, Add. Ms. 41613, fos. 111v–114.

14. Sir Edward Coke, *The Twelfth Part of the Reports* (1656), 12–15; Sir Edward Coke, *The Third Part of the Institutes of the Laws of England* (1644), 162; Sir Edward Coke, *Quinta pars relationum... The Fift Part of the Reports* (1612), fos. 91–92, citing Semayne's Case. See also Henry Rolle, *Les reports de Henry Rolle* (1675), 182, citing a finding in 1606 'per touts justices, l'officiers del Roy ne poient enfreinder le inner mese d'un subject pur saltpeeter etsi soit pur le bien publique, mes outer mese ils potent'. These Jacobean judgments were recited in parliament in 1628 when grievances against the saltpetermen were again in debate, Robert C. Johnson, Maija Jansson Cole, et al. (eds.), *Commons Debates 1628*, 6 vols. (New Haven, 1977–1983), vol. 1, 110; vol. 2, 46; vol. 3, 71. See also 'The Lord Cookes charge given at Norwiche Assizes the 4 of August 1606 against the abuses and corruptions of officers, amongst whom saltpeter menn', BL, Harley Ms. 6070, f. 413v.

15. HMC, *Salisbury*, vol. 18, 335–6; BL, Cotton Ms. Ortho E VII, f. 102–102v.

16. HMC, *Salisbury*, vol. 24, 135–6; *CSPD 1603–1610*, 356; W. H. Overall and H. C. Overall (eds.), *Analytical Index to the Series of Records known as the Remembrancia* (1878), 218, 219. See TNA, SP 16/189/10 for a review of the saltpeter patent, looking back from 1630.

17. *CSPD 1619–1623*, 179, 205; *APC 1619–1621*, 188; *CSPD 1623–1625*, 286, 300.

18. TNA, SP 14/118/73 & 74.

19. HMC, *Salisbury*, vol. 24, 136.

20. *APC 1619–1621*, 177, 188; *CSPD 1623–1625*, 25.

21. HMC, *Salisbury*, vol. 21, 365; *APC 1617–1619*, 248.

22. *CSPD 1610–1623*, 79; TNA, SP 14/110/67.

23. *CSPD 1619–1623*, 189; *APC 1619–1621*, 177.

24. Middleton, *Faire Quarrell*, Act 1, scene 1.

25. *APC 1617–1619*, 248; *APC 1619–1621*, 323, 330, 341.

26. *CSPD 1619–1623*, 216; TNA, SP 14/119/45.

27. *By the King. A Proclamation for prevention of abuses touching Gunpowder and Saltpeter*, 16 January 1623.

28. *APC 1623–1625*, 215; TNA, SP 16/361/9; Richard Winship Stewart, *The English Ordnance Office 1585–1625* (Woodbridge, 1996), 88–92.

29. *By the King. A Proclamation for the preservation of Grounds for making of Salt-Peeter, and to restore such Grounds which now are destroyed*, 26 December 1624.

Chapter 5

1. *CSPD 1637*, 61, 187, 259; TNA, SP 16/355/55; SP 16/361/8; SP 16/362/101.

2. *CSPD 1637*, 353, 531; *CSPD 1637–1638*, 37, 144–5; TNA, SP 16/371/67; SP 16/378/21.

3. *By the King. A Proclamation for the maintenance and encrease of the Mines of Saltpeter, and the true making of Gunpowder, and reforming abuses concerning the same*, 13 April 1625; *APC 1625–1626*, 14, 18; *CSPD 1625–1626*, 4, 9.

4. TNA, SP 16/31/14; L. E. Harris, *The Two Netherlanders: Humphrey Bradley and Cornelius Drebbel* (Leiden, 1961), 194; Gerrit Tierie, *Cornelius Drebbel (1572–1633)* (Amsterdam, 1932), 10–11, 72–3.

5. Richard W. Stewart, 'Arms and Expeditions: the Ordnance Office and the Assaults on Cadiz (1625) and the Isle of Rhé (1627)', in Mark Charles Fissel (ed.), *War and Government in Britain, 1598–1650* (Manchester and New York, 1991), 118, 125; Andrew Thrush, 'The Ordnance Office and the Navy, 1625–40', *Mariner's Mirror*, 77 (1991), 339–54.

6. *By the King. A Proclamation for the better making of Saltpeter within this Kingdome*, 2 January 1627.

7. TNA, SP 16/11/24.

8. *CSPD 1625–1626*, 214; *APC 1625–1626*, 375–6.

9. TNA, SP 16/19/63; E 44/431.

10. *CSPD 1627–1628*, 452; *APC September 1627–June 1628*, 250.

11. TNA, SP 16/11/24.

12. *The Register of the Privy Council of Scotland…1627–1628*, 332, 333; *CSPD 1628–1629*, 16. *CSPD 1625–1649*, 307; *CSPD 1628–1629*, 436; *CSPD 1633–1634*, 433; *CSPD 1637–1638*, 273; *CSP Colonial, America*, vol. 1, 112–14, 156; TNA, SP 16/126/54; SP 16/259/42.

13. *APC July 1628–April 1629*, 395, also *APC May 1629–May 1630*, 154; *CSPD 1629–1631*, 84; *CSPD 1633–1634*, 493; *CSPD 1635*, 45, 246; *CSPD 1636–1637*, 354; *CSP Colonial, East Indies, 1630–1634*, 256, 329; *CSPD 1639–40*, 101; K. N. Chaudhuri, *The English East India Company: The Study of an Early Joint-Stock Company 1600–1640* (New York and London, 1965), 189–90.

14. TNA, SP 16/82/2; SP 16/292, fos. 36, 38; *APC 1627 January–August*, 261, 263, 360; *APC June 1630–June 1631*, 202; *CSPD 1640*, 326.

15. HMC, *Report on the Manuscripts of Earl Cowper*, 3 vols. (1888–89), vol. 1, 231; TNA, SP 16/306/85; BL, Add. Ms. 72419, fos. 17–21; Dorset Record Office, Dorchester, D/BOC/Box 22, 48 (Diary of Dennis Bond); *CSPD 1636–1637*, 440; *CSPD 1637*, 11; *CSPD 1637–1638*, 8.

16. *CSPD 1637*, 507–8; *The Works of the Most Reverend Father in God, William Laud*, ed. James Bliss, 7 vols. (Oxford, 1853), vol. 5, 372. For more on 'the Barbary business', see *CSPD 1638*, 130, 281, 501. On the scale and dynamics of North African slavery see Robert Davis, *Christian Slaves, Muslim Masters: White Slavery in the Mediterranean, the Barbary Coast and Italy, 1500–1800* (Basingstoke and New York, 2003).

17. *CSPD 1625–6*, 206; *CSPD 1635–36*, 34.

18. TNA, SP 16/11/24.

19. Parliamentary Archives, House of Lords Main Papers, HL/PO/JO/10/1/31, 22 April 1626.

20. Thomas Russell, *To the Kings most Excellent Maiestie, the Lords Spirituall and Temporall, and the Commons in this Present Parliament* (1626), broadsheet.

21. William B. Bidwell and Maija Jansson (eds.), *Proceedings in Parliament 1626*, 4 vols. (New Haven, 1991–6), vol. 1, 197, 208; Robert C. Johnson, Maija Jansson Cole, et al. (eds.), *Commons Debates 1628*, 6 vols. (New Haven, 1977–1983), vol. 4, 388 note, citing *Calendar of Patent Rolls*; *By the King. A Proclamation for the better making of Saltpeter within this Kingdome*, 2 January 1627; *CSPD 1627–1628*, 303.

22. *CSPD 1627–1628*, 263–4; TNA, SP 16/71/54.

23. *By the King. A Proclamation for the maintaining and increase of the Mines of Saltpeter, and the true making and working of Saltpeter and Gunpowder, and reforming of all abuses concerning the same*, 23 July 1627.

24. *APC September 1627–June 1628*, 192–3; TNA, SP 16/180/4; Johnson, Cole, et al. (eds.), *Commons Debates 1628*, vol. 4, 390, 396.

25. *CSPD 1629–1631*, 382, 483, 554; TNA, SP 16/175/58.

26. BL, Add. Ms. 4458, f. 48, undated.

27. *CSPD 1634–1635*, 29; TNA, SP 16/268/24.

28. *CSPD 1637–1638*, 371.

29. Thomas Leng, *Benjamin Worsley (1618–1677): Trade, Interest and the Spirit in Revolutionary England* (Woodbridge, 2008), 18–25, and below, Chapter 6.

30. TNA, SP 16/1/15.

31. *APC 1625–1626*, 14, 18; *CSPD 1625–1626*, 4, 9; *By the King. A Proclamation for the maintenance and encrease of the Mines of Saltpeter, and the true making of Gunpowder, and reforming abuses concerning the same*, 13 April 1625.

32. *By the King. A Proclamation for the maintenance and encrease of the Mines of Saltpeter, and the true making of Gunpowder, and reforming abuses concerning the same*, 13 April 1625.

33. Russell, *To the Kings most Excellent Maiestie*; *By the King. A Proclamation for the better making of Saltpeter within this Kingdome*, 2 January 1627; *APC July 1628–April 1629*, 235–6, 241; *APC May 1629–May 1630*, 19–20.

34. TNA, SP 16/70/12; PC 2/39, 100–1; *APC 1627 January–August*, 408; *APC July 1628–April 1629*, 339–40; *CSPD 1637–1638*, 96. Cf. George Peirce's complaint to the king's secretary when saltpetermen dug his stables and damaged his dovecotes at Richmond, Surrey, TNA, SP 16/236/35.

35. TNA, SP 16/101/46.

36. Johnson, Cole, et al. (eds.), *Commons Debates 1628*, vol. 2, 41, 387; vol. 3, 623, 629; vol. 4, 347, 350, 353, 355; *CSPD 1629–1631*, 206, 386; TNA, SP 16/162/40; SP 16/169/46.; SP 16/169/47. For William Laud's reaction to 'sacrilegious abuse' by saltpetermen in Wales in 1624, see his diary in Laud, *Works*, vol. 3, 155.

37. *APC 1625–1626*, 482.

38. For example, Oxfordshire Record Office, Oxford, PAR 207/4/F1/1, fos. 116, 182, for 'the pissing place' at St Martin's, Oxford, a reference I owe to John Craig. A saltpeter warrant of April 1631 urging 'restraint of digging in churches' is in BL, Harley Ms. 1576, f. 164v. The natural philosopher Henry Stubbe later explained that unpaved floors of churches or 'seats that are loosely boarded' could be rich in saltpeter because those places allowed 'long putrefication' where 'the earth be animated and impregnated by the air', Henry Stubbe, *Legends no Histories: Or, A Specimen of Some Animadversions Upon the History of the Royal Society* (1670), 51, 85.

39. Johnson, Cole, et al. (eds.), *Commons Debates 1628*, vol. 3, 629; vol. 4, 347.

40. Johnson, Cole, et al. (eds.), *Commons Debates 1628*, vol. 2, 46; vol. 3, 623, 629; vol. 4, 348, 350. Coke's view, first articulated in 1605, was also rehearsed at length in the 'Resolutions of all the Judges of England concerning digging of Saltpeter', dated 24 June 1625. Here it was insisted that 'the king's ministers… cannot dig the floor of any mansion houses which serve for the habitation of man', and 'in all places where they dig they ought to make the places as commodious for the owner as the same were before', BL, Sloane MS 1039, fos, 93-93v.

41. *CSPD 1628–1629*, 540; TNA, SP 16/142/32 and 42.

42. Essex Record Office, Q/SR 267/18 (1629), Q/SR 269/13 (1630), and similarly Q/SR300/34, Q/SBa 2/30 (1638); Essex Record Office, T/A 418/107/20 (1630).

43. TNA, SP 46/77, f. 33 (Bayning papers, 1637). Suffolk, Record Office, Ipswich, FC 101/E2/19, Framlingham accounts.

44. *CSPD 1625–1649*, 464; *CSPD 1629–1631*, 188; TNA, SP 16/161/1. Hilliard's saltpeter warrant also included Cheshire, Lancashire, Cumberland, and Westmorland, TNA, PC2/39, 258.

45. TNA, SP 16/163/40; SP 16/171/79; BL, Harley Ms. 1576, fos. 186-7. See also Gloucestershire Archives, Gloucester, D7115/1, 36, for another copy of Bond's complaint.

46. TNA, SP 16/165/38; Gloucestershire Archives, D7115/1, 38.

47. *APC July 1628–April 1629*, 235; *CSPD 1629–1631*, 219, 238.

48. TNA, SP 16/169/46.; SP 16/169/47; *CSPD 1629–1631*, 386.

49. *CSPD 1629–1631*, 318; TNA, SP 16/171/79; BL, Harley Ms. 1576, f. 186v.

50. *CSPD 1628–1629*, 101; *CSPD 1629–1631*, 193; *CSPD 1628–1629*, 386; *CSPD 1629–1631*, 539; TNA, SP 16/121/10; SP 16/186/102; PC 2/39, 257-8.

51. TNA, PC 2/42, 19-20.

52. *CSPD Addenda 1625–1649*, 340; TNA, SP 16/530/45. For new saltpeter warrants in May 1629 see *APC May 1629–May 1630*, 19-20 and SP 16/142/42. For similar assignments in 1630 see SP 16/165/51-54; SP 16/180/1-2.

53. TNA, SP 16/180/3 and 10.

54. *CSPD 1631–1633,* 29, 50, 62, 97; *CSPD 1633–1634,* 457; TNA, SP 16/189/89; SP 16/192/89.

55. *CSPD 1631–1633,* 109; *CSPD 1625–1649,* 373.

56. *APC May 1629–May 1630,* 318; *CSPD 1631–1633,* 76, 152, 365, 371; *CSPD 1633–1634,* 299, 451; TNA, PC 2/39, 707; SP 16/193/83; SP 16/260/21; SP 16/169/46.

57. *CSPD 1633–1634,* 451; TNA, SP 16/260/20 and 21; BL, Add. Ms. 11764, fos. 6v–8; BL, Harley Ms. 4022, f. 2v.

58. *CSPD 1631–1633,* 557–8, 573; *CSPD 1633–1634,* 85, 98, 108, 120; TNA, SP 16/233/23; SP 16/240/21; SP 16/241/71–73.

59. *CSPD 1633–1634,* 282, 402–3, 436.

60. TNA, PC 2/47, 341. For problems in Norfolk see TNA, SP 16/535/108; for similar disputes in Hampshire see Kevin Sharpe, *The Personal Rule of Charles I* (New Haven and London, 1992), 492.

61. *CSPD 1634–1635,* 502; TNA, SP 16/283/18.

62. *CSPD 1635,* 33, 449; TNA, SP 16/300/49; SP 16/300/63; SP 16/301/61 for Bagnall's 'hindrances and losses'; SP 16/318/40; J. P. Ferris, 'The Salpetremen in Dorset, 1635', *Proceedings of the Dorset Natural History and Archaeological Society,* 85 (1963), 158–63.

63. TNA, SP 16/282/103.

64. TNA, SP 16/259/42.

65. *CSPD 1634–1635,* 36, 58, 62, 71, 294, 304, 339, 368, 388, 479, 582; *CSPD 1635,* 33, 58, 449, 459, 476, 511; Eric Kerridge, *The Agricultural Revolution* (1967), 240, 242.

66. On the economic benefits and manorial privileges of pigeon-keeping, see John McCann, 'Dovecotes and Pigeons in English Law', *Transactions of the Ancient Monuments Society,* 44 (2000), 25–50. The Berkshire landowner Robert Loder earned more than £10 from his pigeons in 1620, including forty-five shillings from their dung, G. E. Fussell (ed.), *Robert Loder's Farm Accounts 1610–1620* (Camden Society, 3rd series, vol. 53, 1936), 186. It was widely believed that pigeon dung produced 'the best nitre of all others', Joseph Duchesne [as Iosephus Quersitanus], *The Practise of Chymicall, and Hermeticall Physicke,* trans. Thomas Timme (1605), sig. P2. However, pigeon dung was in fact a poorer source for potassium nitrate than saltpeter enthusiasts believed.

67. TNA, SP 16/292, ff. 38-38v; *CSPD 1637–38,* 242; J. R. Powell, *The Navy in the English Civil War* (1962), 7–9; Brian Quintrell, 'Charles I and his Navy in the 1630s', *Seventeenth Century,* 3 (1988), 159–79; Kenneth R. Andrews, *Ships, Money and Politics: Seafaring and Naval Enterprise in the Reign of Charles I* (Cambridge, 1991), 7, 143, 152; Thrush, 'Ordnance Office and the Navy', 339–54. James Scott Wheeler, *The Making of a World Power: War and the Military Revolution in Seventeenth-Century England* (Stroud, 1999), 32–8, shows naval expenditure rising from £174,596 a year 1625–29 to £209,395 a year 1635–39.

68. James F. Larkin and Paul Hughes (eds.), *Stuart Royal Proclamations. Volume II. Royal Proclamations of King Charles I 1625–1646* (Oxford, 1983), 180–2; *CSP Venice, 1632–1636,* 483; BL, Egerton Ms. 2716, f. 227, Anthony Mingay to Framlingham Gawdy, 1 December 1635.

69. TNA, E 44/46; SP 16/292, f. 36v. By February 1640 Samuel Cordewell could estimate that 'home-made saltpeter falls short about 80 lasts to make 240 lasts yearly', *CSPD 1639–40*, 424.

70. *By the King. A Proclamation for preservation of Grounds for making of Saltpeter, and to restore such grounds as are now destroyed, and to command Assistance to be given to His Majesties Saltpeter-Makers*, 14 March 1635; John U. Nef, *Industry and Government in France and England, 1540–1640* (Philadelphia, 1940), 65; *CSPD 1637*, 34.

71. *CSPD 1635*, 511, 568, 596; *CSPD 1635–1636*, 410, 449; *CSPD 1636–1637*, 217, 294; TNA, SP 16/292, f. 52v; SP 16/320/40; SP 16/354/4.

72. *CSPD 1635*, 605; *CSPD 1635–1636*, 150, 152; TNA, SP 16/303/56; SP 16/305/2; SP 16/305/64; SP 16/311/27. Salpetermen also excavated the town hall at Leicester in 1628, and the borough had to pay for its 'levelling,' *Records of the Borough of Leicester... 1603–1688*, ed. Helen Stocks and W. H. Stevens (Cambridge, 1923), 248.

73. TNA, SP 16/535/108. See also 'the general complaint of the county' against the practices of the saltpetermen in 1637, in Walter Rye (ed.), *State Papers Relating to Musters, Beacons, Shipmoney, etc. in Norfolk* (Norwich, 1907), 232–3.

74. *CSPD 1637*, 129, 222–3; TNA, SP 16/361/110 and 112; SP 16/320/40 and 41; SP 16/320/30; SP 17/D/19 (saltpeter commission 30 November 1637).

75. *CSPD 1635–1636*, 359; *CSPD 1636–1637*, 28; TNA, SP 16/327/100.

76. *CSPD 1635–1636*, 567.

77. *CSPD 1635–1636*, 448; *CSPD 1636–1637*, 238, 372, 431, 458; TNA, SP 16/376/146; Sharpe, *Personal Rule of Charles I*, 195. See also Richard Cust, *Charles I: A Political Life* (Harlow, 2005), 186, on the crown's willingness to 'make sacrifices' in this regard.

78. *CSPD 1636–1637*, 53, 449; TNA, SP 16/328/31.

79. *CSPD 1636–1637*, 437, 449–50; *CSPD 1637*, 202, 222; TNA, SP 16/292, fos. 23, 29.

80. *CSPD 1637*, 61, 187, 259; TNA, SP 16/355/55; SP 16/361/8; SP 16/362/101.

81. *CSPD 1637*, 353, 531; *CSPD 1637–1638*, 37, 144–5; SP 16/371/67; SP 16/378/21.

82. *CSPD 1639*, 157; TNA, SP 16/420/146.

83. *CSPD 1639–1640*, 594; SP 16/449/25. *CSPD 1640*, 62; SP 16/450/36 and 45; SP 16/451/25.

84. *CSPD 1637–1638*, 159, 174, 180, 190, 344, 372, 375, 453, 513, 589; *CSPD 1639*, 262–3; *CSPD 1640*, 91–2, 348; TNA, SP 16/335/54 and 59, and SP 16/361/110, for more complaints.

85. *CSPD 1639–1640*, 176, 473; TNA, SP 16/445/79.

86. *CSPD 1638*, 118, 448, 472; *CSPD 1639*, 12; *CSPD 1639–1640*, 102, 424; *CSPD 1640–1641*, 313.

87. *CSPD 1640*, 439, 507, 523, 562.

88. *CSPD 1637–38*, 242; TNA, SP 292, ff. 38-38v.

89. *CSPD 1637*, 547; *CSPD 1637–1638*, 396; *CSPD 1638–1639*, 85; *CSPD 1639–40*, 68; *CSPD 1640*, 439, 507, 523, 562; BL, Add. Ms. 21506, f. 18.

90. *CSPD 1640–1641*, 240; *CSPD 1641–1643*, 152.

91. *CSPD 1638*, 443; *CSPD 1639–40*, 424.

92. Late in 1640 gunpowder sold in England for £6, then £5 a barrel, *CSPD 1640*, 523, 561. Royal armourers reckoned the price of gunpowder at 18d. a pound in 1638, Bodleian Library, Ms. Clarendon 14, f. 160. In Leicestershire the Earl of Huntington paid 1s. 2d. for half a pound of gunpowder, equivalent to more than £11 a barrel, Huntington Library, HA Misc. Box 12 (3), f. 18v. By October 1640, however, William Le Neve could report that 'powder is here at the Tower at 12d. a pound', or £5 a barrel, BL, Add. Ms. 21506, f. 11v. The Staffordshire county magazine secured four barrels of powder in January 1641, 'with a great deal of trouble...in regard of the scarceness at that time'. This premium-priced gunpowder cost 21d. a pound, almost £9 a barrel, Staffordshire Record Office, Q/SR/245/1.

93. *APC 1625–1626*, 240; TNA, SP 16/11/24.

94. *CSPD 1625–1626*, 236; *APC 1626*, 186.

95. *CSPD 1625–1626*, 490; *CSPD 1627–1628*, 493; *CSPD 1628–1629*, 118.

96. *CSP Colonial, East Indies, 1622–1624*, 202, 240, 476; *CSP Colonial, East Indies, 1630–1634*, 315–19; TNA, SP/39/19/13; PC 2/42, 286, 294.

97. *CSPD 1631–1633*, 347; SP 16/165/52.

98. *CSPD 1633–1634*, 244, 282; TNA, SP 16/165/54, 193/83; SP 16/219/36.

99. TNA, E 44/464; *CSPD 1636–37*, 153; *CSPD 1639–40*, 67.

100. *CSPD 1625–1649*, 595–6; *CSPD 1638*, 134, 460; *CSPD 1639*, 84; *CSPD 1639–1640*, 11; *CSPD 1640*, 523; TNA, SP 16/292, f. 44.

101. *CSPD 1638*, 253, 259; *CSPD 1639*, 203, 389; TNA, SP 16/292, ff. 45, 47v.

Chapter 6

1. *CSPD 1625–1649*, 595–6; *CSPD 1638*, 134, 460; *CSPD 1639*, 84; *CSPD 1639–1640*, 118. *CSPD 1640*, 523; TNA, SP 16/292, f. 44; Ian Roy (ed.), *The Royalist Ordnance Papers 1642–1646*, Oxfordshire Record Society, vol. 43 (1964) and vol. 49 (1975); Peter Edwards, 'Logistics and Supply', in John Kenyon and Jane Ohlmeyer (eds.), *The Civil Wars: A Military History of England, Scotland and Ireland 1638–1660* (Oxford, 1998), 243; Peter Edwards, 'Gunpowder and the English Civil War', *Journal of the Arms & Armour Society*, 15 (1995), 114–17; Peter Edwards, *Dealing in Death: The Arms Trade and the British Civil Wars, 1638–52* (Stroud, 2000), 115–17; Brenda J. Buchanan, '"The Art and Mystery of Making Gunpowder": The English Experience in the Seventeenth and Eighteenth Centuries', in Brett D. Steele and Tamera Dorland (eds.), *The Heirs of Archimedes* (Cambridge, Mass., 2005), 242–5; Stephen Bull, *The Furie of the Ordnance: Artillery in the English Civil War* (Woodbridge, 2008), 77–8, 185. For Baber's Restoration-era claims, *CSPD 1660–1661*, 154, 493; *CSPD November 1667–September 1668*, 177; *Calendar of Treasury Books 1660–1667*, 97; TNA, SP 29/232/193.

2. Parliamentary Archives, London, HL/PO/JO/1/52, 24 February 1641.

3. Lambert B. Larking (ed.), *Proceedings Principally in the County of Kent, in Connection with the Parliaments called in 1640* (Camden Society, 1852), 48–9.

4. Thomas Brugis, *The Discovery of a Projector: Shewing the Beginning, Progresse, and End of the Projector and his Projects* (1641).

5. Maija Jansson (ed.), *Proceedings in the Opening Session of the Long Parliament*, 7 vols. (Rochester, N.Y., 2000–7), vol. 2, 306, 308, 309; *Remonstrance of the State of the Kingdom* (1641), nos. 29, 36.

6. *CSPD 1640–1641*, 521; Jansson (ed.), *Proceedings in the Opening Session*, vol. 2, 309, 637; vol. 4, 302.

7. Jansson (ed.), *Proceedings in the Opening Session*, vol. 6, 17; *Statutes of the Realm*, vol. 5 (1819), 131; Parliamentary Archives, HL/PO/JO/10/1/68; *CSPD 1641–1643*, 66.

8. *CSPD 1641–1643*, 103, 152. Gunpowder reserves at the Tower and Portsmouth actually rose in late 1640 and early 1641, due to continuing imports and the end of the Scottish war, but thereafter became depleted, *CSPD 1640–1641*, 131, 241, 293, 405, 451, 486, 528.

9. Jansson (ed.), *Proceedings in the Opening Session*, vol. 6, 564, 569, 608, 613.

10. *CSPD 1641–1643*, 152, 280.

11. *CSPD 1641–1643*, 269, 280.

12. David Cressy, *England on Edge: Crisis and Revolution 1640–1642* (Oxford, 2006), 419.

13. Edwards, *Dealing in Death*, 92; Bull, *Furie of the Ordnance*, xix.

14. Edwards, 'Gunpowder and the English Civil War', 113–14; Edwards, 'Logistics and Supply', 243; Edwards, *Dealing in Death*, 110–15. Bull, *Furie of the Ordnance*, 78, estimates a peak parliamentary production of 4,825 barrels a year in 1645, approximately 200 lasts.

15. Roy (ed.), *Royalist Ordnance Papers*; Edwards, 'Logistics and Supply', 243; Edwards, 'Gunpowder and the English Civil War', 114–17; Edwards, *Dealing in Death*, 115–17; Malcolm Wanklyn and Frank Jones, *A Military History of the English Civil War, 1642–1646* (Harlow, 2005), 13, 86, 97; Buchanan, '"Art and Mystery of Making Gunpowder"', 242–5.

16. Charles Carlton, *Going to the Wars: The Experience of the British Civil Wars 1638–1651* (1992), 208.

17. Bodleian Library, Oxford, Tanner Ms. 63, f. 3.

18. C. H. Firth and R. S. Rait (eds.), *Acts and Ordinances of the Interregnum*, 3 vols. (1911) vol. 1, 320–1; TNA, SP 46/95, f.1–5; *CSPD 1645–1647*, 411, 431.

19. TNA, SP 46/95, f. 11.

20. *The Hartlib Papers* (University of Sheffield, CD-ROM, 2nd edn., 2002), 71/11/12A, 'Certaine Propositions in the behalf of the kingdome concerning Salt-Peter'.

21. *CSPD 1645–1647*, 493.

22. *The Correspondence of Robert Boyle. Vol. 1. 1636–61*, ed. Michael Hunter, Antonio Clericuzio, and Lawrence M. Principe (2001), 42–4; Robert Boyle, 'A Physico-Chymical Essay, Containing an Experiment, with some Considerations Touching the Differing Parts and Redintegration of Salt-Petre' (1661), in *The Works of the Honourable Robert Boyle*, 6 vols. (1772), vol. 1, 359; Charles Webster, *The Great*

Instauration: Science, Medicine and Reform 1626–1660 (New York, 1976), 61, 379–80.

23. *CSPD 1644*, 94, 129; *CSPD 1644–1645*, 51, 25; Edwards, 'Gunpowder and the English Civil War', 121. See Bal Krishna, *Commercial Relations between India and England (1601 to 1757)* (1924), 66, 68, for the Courten or Courteen company.

24. Firth and Rait (eds.), *Acts and Ordinances*, vol. 1, 578–9; *CSPD 1648–1649*, 35.

25. James Scott Wheeler, 'Logistics and Supply in Cromwell's Conquest of Ireland', in Mark Charles Fissel (ed.), *War and Government in Britain, 1598–1650* (Manchester and New York, 1991), 38–56.

26. J. R. Powell, *The Navy in the English Civil War* (1962), 7–9; Arthur W. Tedder, *The Navy of the Restoration* (Cambridge, 1916), 12–14, based on Bodleian Library, Carte Ms. 73; James Scott Wheeler, *The Making of a World Power: War and the Military Revolution in Seventeenth-Century England* (Stroud, 1999), 45–6.

27. Webster, *Great Instauration*, 61, 374, 378–81; Charles Webster, 'Benjamin Worsley: Engineering for Universal Reform from the Invisible College to the Navigation Act', in Mark Greengrass, Michael Leslie, and Timothy Raylor (eds.), *Samuel Hartlib and Universal Reformation: Studies in Intellectual Communication* (Cambridge, 1994), 213–35; Thomas Leng, *Benjamin Worsley (1618–1677): Trade, Interest and the Spirit in Revolutionary England* (Woodbridge, 2008), 18–25; *Hartlib Papers*, 15/2/5A; 39/1/16A; 53/26/6A.

28. *Hartlib Papers*, 15/2/5B; 53/26/2A and 7A; 71/11/12A.

29. *CSPD 1649–1650*, 227.

30. Firth and Rait (eds.), *Acts and Ordinances*, vol. 2, 699–702; *Hartlib Papers*. 39/1/25A (28 March 1653); 39/1/11A and B (18 May 1653). See also William R. Newman and Lawrence M. Principe, *Alchemy Tried in the Fire: Starkey, Boyle, and the Fate of Helmontian Chymistry* (Chicago, 2002), 239–53, for intellectual excitement about saltpeter in the 1650s.

31. *CSPD 1649–1650*, 226; Firth and Rait (eds.), *Acts and Ordinance*, vol. 2, 699–702, 1043–8.

32. *CSP Colonial, East Indies, 1617–1621*, 69, 112, 127.

33. *CSP Colonial, East Indies, 1622–1624*, 202, 240, 476. For the Dutch East India saltpeter trade, see Tristan Mostert, *Chain of Command: The Military System of the Dutch East India Company 1655–1663* (M.A. thesis, University of Leiden, 2007; http:vocwarfare.net, accessed April 2011), 35–6.

34. *APC July 1628–April 1629*, 395; *CSPD 1635*, 45, 246; K. N. Chaudhuri, *The English East India Company: The Study of an Early Joint-Stock Company 1600–1640* (New York and London, 1965), 189–90.

35. *A Calendar of the Court Minutes etc. of the East India Company, 1644–1649*, ed. William Foster and Ethel Bruce Sainsbury (Oxford, 1912), 112, 152, 290, 346, 349, 350; J. R. Partington, *A History of Greek Fire and Gunpowder* (Cambridge, 1960), 322–3; James W. Frey, 'The Indian Saltpeter Trade, the Military Revolution, and the Rise of Britain as a Global Superpower', *The Historian*, 71 (2009), 507–54; Jagdish Narayan Sarkar, 'Saltpetre Industry of India in the Seventeenth

Century', *Indian Historical Quarterly*, 14 (1938), 680–91; R. Balasubramiam, 'Saltpetre Manufacturing and Marketing in Medieval India', *Indian Journal of History of Science*, 40 (2005), 663–72.

36. *CSPD 1649–1650*, 74, 246, 306, 317, 548; *CSPD 1651*, 396; Foster and Sainsbury (eds.), *Calendar of the Court Minutes… 1644–1649*, 343, 355, 378, 382, 385.

37. *Oxford Dictionary of National Biography*, sub 'Sir William Rider, d. 1669, merchant'.

38. *The English Factories in India 1646–1650*, ed. William Foster (Oxford, 1914), 299, 332, 337; *The English Factories in India 1651–1654*, ed. William Foster (Oxford, 1915), 45, 119, 196; *The English Factories in India 1655–1660*, ed. William Foster (Oxford, 1921), 206, 308; Brenda J. Buchanan, 'Saltpetre: A Commodity of Empire', in Brenda J. Buchanan (ed.), *Gunpowder, Explosives and the State: A Technological History* (Aldershot, 2006), 77.

Chapter 7

1. 'The Voyages & Travels of J. Albert de Mandelslo', in Adam Olearius, *The Voyages & Travels of the Ambassadors Sent by Frederick Duke of Holstein, to the Great Duke of Muscovy, and the King of Persia*, trans. John Davies (1662), separate pagination, 84. See also *Travels in India by Jean-Baptiste Tavernier*, ed. William Crooke, 2 vols. (Oxford, 1925), vol. 2, 10; Jagdish Narayan Sarkar, 'Saltpetre Industry of India in the Seventeenth Century', *Indian Historical Quarterly* 14, (1938), 680–91; Brenda J. Buchanan, 'Saltpetre: A Commodity of Empire', in Brenda J. Buchanan (ed.), *Gunpowder, Explosives and the State* (Aldershot, 2006), 78–81; R. Balasubramiam, 'Saltpetre Manufacturing and Marketing in Medieval India', *Indian Journal of History of Science*, 40 (2005), 663–72; James W. Frey, 'The Indian Saltpeter Trade, the Military Revolution, and the Rise of Britain as a Global Superpower', *The Historian*, 71 (2009), 522–4.

2. William Clarke, *The Natural History of Nitre: or, a Philosophical Discourse of the Nature, Generation, Place, and Artificial Extraction of Nitre, with its Vertues and Uses* (1670), 19.

3. Sir Josiah Child *A Treatise Wherein is Demonstrated, I. That the East-India Trade is the most National of all Foreign Trades* (1681), 6.

4. *CSPD 1660–1661*, 282, 385; *CSPD 1661–1662*, 46, 562; Henry Stubbe, *Legends no Histories: Or, A Specimen of Some Animadversions Upon the History of the Royal Society* (1670), 36.

5. *CSPD 1661–1662*, 662; *CSPD 1665–1666*, 400; E. S. De Beer (ed.), *The Diary of John Evelyn*, 6 vols. (Oxford, 1955), vol. 3, 443, 445, 446; *By the King. A Proclamation For the effectual prosecution of His Majesties Commission for the Providing and Making of Salt-peter and Gun-powder*, 16 July 1666.

6. Staffordshire Record Office, Stafford, D (W) 1778/V/1393; D 742/M/1/94, papers of William Legge, Lt. General of Ordnance, 1660–1672.

7. *Calendar of Treasury Books 1660–1667*, 189; *CSPD 1660–1661*, 369; *CSPD 1663–1664*, 69; TNA, SP 29/69/32.

8. *Calendar of Treasury Books 1660–1667*, 360, 648; *Calendar of Treasury Books 1669–1672*, 153, 294; BL, India Office Records H/42, 29–31.

9. William Foster (ed.), *The English Factories in India 1665–1667* (Oxford, 1925), 139; BL, India Office Records E/3/102.

10. Staffordshire Record Office, D 742/M/1/24A; D (W) 1778/V/1394.

11. BL, India Office Records H/42, 109.

12. H. C. Tomlinson, *Guns and Government: The Ordnance Office under the Later Stuarts* (1979); TNA, WO 44–55; Staffordshire Record Office, D 742/M/1/24A; D (W) 1778/V/1394.

13. K. N. Chaudhuri, *The Trading World of Asia and the English East India Company 1660–1760* (Cambridge, 1978), 531; Buchanan, 'Saltpetre: A Commodity of Empire', 79; TNA, WO 55/1671.

14. Staffordshire Record Office, D (W) 1778/V/1393.

15. Foster (ed.), *English Factories in India 1665–1667*, 257; William Foster (ed.), *The English Factories in India 1668–1669* (Oxford, 1927), 169.

16. Chaudhuri, *Trading World,* 531; Tomlinson, *Guns and Government,* 112; Frey, 'Indian Saltpeter Trade', 521–2.

17. TNA, WO 55/1759; BL, Add. Ms. 38393, f. 12; *CSPD January 1686–May 1687,* 342. The Company's own ships were significant consumers of gunpowder, and seventy-gun East Indiamen were not uncommon. See also Child, *Treatise,* 6; John Fryer, *A New Account of East India and Persia. Being Nine Years' Travels, 1672–1681,* ed. William Crooke, Hakluyt Society, 2nd series, 19 (1909), 7.

18. Staffordshire Record Office, D (W) 1778/V/1393 and 1394; *Calendar of Treasury Books 1672–1675,* 402.

19. *CSPD 1663–1664,* 517; *By the King. A Proclamation Prohibiting the Exportation of Saltpeter,* 17 March 1664; Staffordshire Record Office, D 742/M/1/24A; B. L., IOR, H/42, 150.

20. Staffordshire Record Office, D (W) 1778/V/1393.

21. Staffordshire Record Office, D 3074/J/1/1.

22. *CSPD 1689–1690,* 195; *A Proclamation to Prohibit the Exportation of Salt Petre,* 25 July 1689.

23. TNA, WO 55/1759; Staffordshire Record Office, D 3074/J/1/2-6; D (W) 1778/V/1395.

24. *Calendar of Treasury Books 1693–1696,* 1426.

25. TNA, WO 55/1758 and 9; Tomlinson, *Guns and Government,* 135; *Calendar of Treasury Papers 1556–1696,* 459–60; *Saltpetre Wanting in England to a Great Degree* (1695), broadside.

26. *CSPD 1690–1691,* 219; *CSPD 1691–1692,* 277; *Journal of the House of Commons,* vol. 10 (1802), 648: January–February 1692.

27. *Journal of the House of Commons,* vol. 10, 818. *CSPD 1691–1692,* 148, 178, 249, 277.

28. TNA, E 101/635/49; E 101/636/1, 2, 3, 6, 14, 36; E 214/1124; E 219/437; E 214/949; LR 9/130; *CSPD 1693,* 20; *CSPD 1694–1695,* 6. See, however, the suggestion in 1767 that the government 'take effectual measures for re-establishing saltpeter works in all parts of England', in case war should imperil East India supplies, *London Magazine, or Gentleman's Monthly Intelligencer,* 36 (1767), 640. Another author in 1783 identified saltpeter as a key material 'on which

our existence as a great people so much depends', but his urging of a domestic system of saltpeter manufacture gained no support, W. C. D., *Considerations on the Importance of the Production of Saltpetre in England and its Dependencies* (1783), 19.

29. *Journal of the House of Commons*, vol. 10, 818; *CSPD 1693*, 282.

30. TNA, BT 6/184/7; BL, Add Ms. 38393, f. 13; *CSPD 1698*, 134.

31. Chris Cook and John Stevenson, *British Historical Facts 1760–1830* (1980), 97–102; N. A. M. Rodger, *The Command of the Ocean: A Naval History of Britain 1649–1815* (New York and London, 2005), 607–8, 636–9; Stephen Conway, *War, State, and Society in Mid-Eighteenth-Century Britain and Ireland* (Oxford, 2006), 281.

32. Jenny West, *Gunpowder, Government and War in the Mid-Eighteenth Century* (Woodbridge, 1991), 163, 212, 224–7; TNA, BT 6/184/19; TNA, SUPP 5/762, 72.

33. Figures recalculated from Chaudhuri, *Trading World*, 531–2, and compared to Bal Krishna, *Commercial Relations between India and England (1601 to 1757)* (1924), 201, 307–8; Frey, 'Indian Saltpeter Trade', 509, 526, 529, 531, 540. On French reactions, see below Chapter 8.

34. BL, IOR, H/49, 62–4.

35. TNA T 64/276B/351; TNA, BT 6/184/5 and 10; BL, IOR, H/49, 63. Calculations of tonnage, where not given in the sources, assume an average bag of 1.2 cwt. Similar figures appear in the *Report of the Committee of Warehouses, on a Memorial from the Manufacturers of Gunpowder, and of other Commodities made from Saltpetre* (1793), 23–4.

36. TNA, BT 6/184/19; TNA, BT 6/184/32; BL, Add Ms. 38393, 28, 34v, 35, 44; 31 Geo. III c. 42; Edmund Hill, *Hints from the Manufacturers of the Raw Material of Saltpetre into Gunpowder, Oil of Vitriol, etc.* (1793), 2.

37. Hill, *Hints from the Manufacturers*, 1–3.

38. BL, Add. Ms. 38393, f. 35; East India Company Charter Act 1793, 33 Geo. III c. 52; Hill, *Hints from the Manufacturers*, 4, 6; Frey, 'Indian Saltpeter Trade', 551.

39. Philip J. Haythornthwaite, *The Armies of Wellington* (1998), 9–10.

40. Figures from Cook and Stevenson, *British Historical Facts 1760–1830*, 97–102; Chris Cook and Brendan Keith, *British Historical Facts 1830–1900* (1975), 185; Hew Strachan, *From Waterloo to Balaclava: Tactics, Technology, and the British Army, 1815–1854* (Cambridge, 1985), 101; Rodger, *Command of the Ocean*, 639–45. The Royal Navy had 361 ships in 1860, including twenty-seven battleships and fifty frigates or corvettes.

41. Robert Wilkinson-Latham, *British Artillery on Land and Sea 1790–1820* (Newton Abbot, 1973), 21 and appendices.

42. *Hansard, House of Commons*, 3rd. series, vol. 145 (29 May 1857), speech by Col. Henry Boldero.

43. TNA, SUPP 5/762, 6, 68, 72; SUPP 5/128.

44. Buchanan, 'Saltpetre: A Commodity of Empire', 79, citing John Stephenson, *Treatise on the Manufacture of Saltpetre* (Calcutta, 1835), 88–96; *Hansard, House*

of Commons, 3rd. series, vol. 176 (21 July 1864), speech by Robert Crawford; J. W. Leather and Jatindra Nath Mukerji, *The Indian Saltpetre Industry* (Calcutta, 1911), 1.

45. Arthur Pine Van Gelder and Hugo Schlatter, *History of the Explosives Industry in America* (New York, 1927), 117.

46. *Parliamentary Papers* (1864), vol. 57, 605, 'An Account of the Quantities of Saltpetre Imported into, and Exported from, the United Kingdom in the years 1860–1863 inclusive, and 1864 to the present time, distinguishing the Countries from which the Saltpetre was Imported, 24 June 1864.'

47. British saltpeter imports totalled 7,806 tons in 1855, 14,985 in 1856, 16,730 in 1857, and 10,360 tons in 1858. Two decades later the figures were 12,810 tons in 1875, 10,500 in 1876, 8,580 in 1877, 9,620 in 1878, and 10,390 in 1879. Prices fluctuated with supply and demand, and with receipt of 'warlike news from the Continent'. *The Economist*, no. 544, 28 January 1854, 101; no. 801, 1 January 1859, 297; no.1897, 3 January 1880, 20.

48. *History of the Ministry of Munitions. Vol. 7, The Control of Materials* (1922, reprinted 2008), part 4; Stephen R. Bown, *A Most Damnable Invention: Dynamite, Nitrates, and the Making of the Modern World* (Toronto and London, 2005).

49. TNA, CAB 21/120. See also E. A. Brayley Hodgetts (ed.), *The Rise and Progress of the British Explosives Industry* (1909).

Chapter 8

1. *Papers of John Adams*, ed. Robert J. Taylor, 15 vols. (Cambridge, Mass., 1977–2010), vol. 3, 28, 50, 61, 101, 168, 169, 193, 225, 227, 336, 363; *Letters of Delegates to Congress 1774–1789*, ed. Paul H. Smith 26 vols. (Washington, D.C., 1976–2000), vol. 1, 545–6.

2. *Essays upon the Making of Salt-Peter and Gun-Powder* (New York, 1776), 11, 23–4; *Several Methods of Making Salt-Petre, Recommended to the Inhabitants of the United Colonies, by the Honorable Continental Congress, and Re-published by Order of the General Assembly of the Colony of Massachusetts* (Watertown, Mass., 1775), 9; *The Process for Extracting and Refining Salt-Petre, According to the Method practiced at the Provincial Works in Philadelphia* (Philadelphia, 1776), 8; Massachusetts Historical Society, Boston, Adams Family Papers, 5 April 1776 (http://www.masshist.org/digitaladams/, accessed 18 May 2009).

3. *Letters of Delegates to Congress*, ed. Smith, vol. 2, 532.

4. *Process for Extracting and Refining Salt-Petre*, 8.

5. *CSP Colonial, America and West Indies*, vol. 1, 112–14, 156–60.

6. *Winthrop Papers Volume VI. 1650–1654*, ed. Malcolm Freiberg (Boston, 1992), 8; Arthur Pine Van Gelder and Hugo Schlatter, *History of the Explosives Industry in America* (New York, 1927), 30–3.

7. Staffordshire Record Office, Stafford, D 742/M/1/73; *CSP Colonial, America and West Indies*, vol. 12, 1685–8, 123–35; *CSPD 1691–1692*, 26, 41.

8. *CSP Colonial, America and West Indies*, vol. 1, 436–40; *The Hartlib Papers* (University of Sheffield, CD-ROM, 2nd edn., 2002), 39/1/23A;

Mercurius Politicus, no. 269 (2–9 August 1655); Staffordshire Record Office, D 742/M/1/73.

9. Daniel Defoe, *A General History of Discoveries and Improvements* (1726), 296.

10. *General Evening Post,* 26 February 1740.

11. Archibald Kennedy, *Observations on the Importance of the Northern Colonies* (New York, 1750), 15.

12. *The Annual Register, or a View of the History, Politics, and Literature, for the Year 1763* (1764), 121–2. 'The Method of Making Gun-Powder' described in Ames's *Boston Almanack* of 1775 assumed that the 'nitre or saltpeter...comes to us from the Indies' rather than local sources, facsimile in Van Gelder and Schlatter, *History of the Explosives Industry,* 48.

13. Orlando W. Stephenson, 'The Supply of Gunpowder in 1776', *American Historical Review,* 30 (1925), 271–81; David L. Salay, 'The Production of Gunpowder in Pennsylvania during the American Revolution', *Pennsylvania Magazine of History and Biography,* 99 (1975), 422–5; Van Gelder and Schlatter, *History of the Explosives Industry,* 36–40. The report on saltpeter experiments in Virginia in 1764 was reprinted in the *Royal American Magazine* (Boston, January 1775), 18.

14. 'The Nature, Properties, and Use of Nitre or Salt-Petre', *Royal American Magazine* (Boston, August 1774), 284.

15. *Dunlap's Pennsylvania Packet or, the General Advertiser,* no. 162, 28 November 1774.

16. *Several Methods of Making Salt-Petre,* 3; E. Wayne Carp, *To Starve the Army at Pleasure: Continental Army Administration and American Political Culture 1775–1783* (Chapel Hill, 1984), 22–3. On Elizabeth England, see above, Chapter 3.

17. *Several Methods of Making Salt-Petre,* 3, 4, 15, 20; *Correspondence and Journals of Samuel Blachley Webb. Vol. 1. 1772–1777,* ed. Worthington Chauncey Ford (New York, 1983), 113–14, Joseph Barrell to Joseph Green, 3 November 1775; *Papers of John Adams,* ed. Taylor, vol. 3, 221, James Warren to John Adams, 20 October 1775; *Letters of Delegates to Congress,* ed. Smith, vol. 2, 121.

18. *Boston Evening Post,* no. 2049, 2 January 1775; *Boston Gazette or Country Journal,* no. 1029, 2 January 1775; *Connecticut Gazette,* no. 583, 13 January 1775; *Pennsylvania Gazette,* no. 2405, 25 January 1775; *Connecticut Courant,* no. 549, 3 July 1775. Further reports of French and German saltpeter processes appeared in *Newport Mercury,* no. 882, 31 July 1775, and *Pennsylvania Mercury,* no. 18, 4 August 1775.

19. *Royal American Magazine,* January 1775, 18; *Virginia Gazette,* 4 August 1775; *Pennsylvania Mercury and Universal Advertiser,* 18 August 1775.

20. *Journals of the Continental Congress 1774–1789,* ed. Worthington Chauncey Ford et al., 37 vols. (Washington, D.C., 1904–37), vol. 2, 107, 218–19; vol. 3, 296, 345, 347, 349; vol. 4, 170–1; *Letters of Delegates to Congress,* ed. Smith, vol. 1, 477, 478, 481, 483.

21. 'Account of the Manufactory of Salt-Petre', *Pennsylvania Magazine: Or, American Monthly Museum* (June 1775), 266–9; *Several Methods of Making Salt-Petre,* 7–14. Benjamin Rush, a member of the Second Continental

Congress, had spent three years in Europe before becoming professor of chemistry at the College of Philadelphia.

22. *Process for Extracting and Refining Salt-Petre,* 1–7, 8; *Essays upon the Making of Salt-Peter and Gun-Powder,* 32; *Papers of John Adams,* ed. Taylor, vol. 3, 391, Robert Treat Paine to Joseph Palmer, 1 January 1776; *Papers of John Adams,* ed. Taylor, vol. 4, 4, Resolution of Congress, 23 February 1776.

23. *Papers of John Adams,* ed. Taylor, vol. 3, 28, 50, 61, 101, 168, 193, 225, 227; *Letters of Delegates to Congress,* ed. Smith, vol.1, 545–6.

24. *The Journals of Each Provincial Congress of Massachusetts in 1774 and 1775* ed. William Lincoln (Boston, 1838), 98, 100, 101. The Continental Congress offered half a dollar per pound for saltpeter in June 1775, two-fifths of a dollar per pound in November 1775, *Journals of the Continental Congress,* ed. Ford, vol. 2, 219; vol. 3, 347.

25. *Journals of Each Provincial Congress of Massachusetts,* ed. Lincoln, 417, 421; *Report of the Committee of Warehouses, on a Memorial from the Manufacturers of Gunpowder, and of other Commodities made from Saltpetre* (1793), 23–4.

26. *Several Methods of Making Salt-Petre,* 17–20; *Correspondence and Journals of Samuel Blachley Webb,* ed. Ford, vol. 1., 113–14, Joseph Barrell to Joseph Green, 3 November 1775; *Papers of John Adams,* ed. Taylor, vol. 3, 221, 225; *The Massachusetts Spy: or, American Oracle of Liberty,* 12 January 1776; *Letters of Delegates to Congress,* ed. Smith, vol. 2, 310, 333.

27. *Papers of John Adams,* ed. Taylor, vol. 3, 101; *Letters of Delegates to Congress,* ed. Smith, vol.1, 676–7; *New London Gazette,* 8 December 1775; *The Papers of General Nathanael Greene. Vol. 1. December 1766–December 1776,* ed. Richard K. Showman (Chapel Hill, 1976), 96; *Essays upon the Making of Salt-Peter and Gun-Powder,* 34; *Process for Extracting and Refining Salt-Petre,* 1–8; Salay, 'Production of Gunpowder', 426–7.

28. *The Papers of Benjamin Franklin,* ed. William B.Willcox, 39 vols. (New Haven, 1959–2008), vol. 22, 207, 289.

29. *Papers of John Adams,* ed. Taylor, vol. 3, 169, 336, 363.

30. *Journals of the Continental Congress,* ed. Ford, vol. 3, 345, 347; *Letters of Delegates to Congress,* ed. Smith, vol. 2, 311, 364.

31. *Essays upon the Making of Salt-Peter and Gun-Powder,* 7; Israel Aber, *The Art of Manufacturing Saltpeter, by Cheap, Easy, and Expeditious Methods* (Newark, NJ, 1796), sig. A2. *Essex Journal,* 15 December 1775.

32. *Essays upon the Making of Salt-Peter and Gun-Powder,* 11, 23–4; *Several Methods of Making Salt-Petre,* 9; *Process for Extracting and Refining Salt-Petre,* 8; *Papers of John Adams,* ed. Taylor, vol. 3, 336.

33. *Letters of Delegates to Congress,* ed. Smith, vol. 3. 20, 477.

34. Massachusetts Historical Society, Adams Family Papers, 5 April 1776 (Electronic Archive, accessed May 2009).

35. *Papers of John Adams,* ed. Taylor, vol. 4, 216.

36. Massachusetts State Archives, Boston, vol. 274, Certificates 1705–1781, nos. 231–351.

37. *Papers of John Adams,* ed. Taylor, vol. 3, 226–7; *The Papers of Thomas Jefferson. Vol. 1. 1760–1776,* ed. Julian P. Boyd (Princeton, 1950), 263; *Revolutionary Virginia.*

The Road to Independence. Vol. VII part 1. Independence and the Fifth Convention, 1776, ed. Brent Tarter (Charlottesville, Va., 1983), 149; Donald E. Reynolds, 'Ammunition Supply in Revolutionary Virginia', *Virginia Magazine of History and Biography*, 73 (1965), 57–8.

38. Van Gelder and Schlatter, *History of the Explosives Industry*, 40; William L. Saunders (ed.), *The Colonial Records of North Carolina*, (Raleigh, N.C., 1890), vol. 10, 216, 537; vol. 12, 373. North Carolina offered a bounty of £25 per hundredweight of saltpeter produced by March 1776, reduced to £20 per hundredweight in the following six months.

39. *Letters of Delegates to Congress*, ed. Smith, vol. 2, 532.

40. Charles L. Hoadly (ed.), *The Public Records of the State of Connecticut, From October, 1776, to February, 1778, Inclusive* (Hartford, 1894), 9, 11, 280, 294, 300, 302; *Calendar of Historical Manuscripts, Relating to the War of the Revolution, in the Office of the Secretary of State, Albany, NY* (2 vols., Albany, 1868), vol. 1, 447, 577, 640. See also vol. 2, 67, for saltpeter makers in Orange County seeking exemption from military duty.

41. *Letters of Delegates to Congress*, ed. Smith, vol. 3, 427, 455.

42. *Letters of Delegates to Congress*, ed. Smith, vol. 4, 305, 339.

43. *Letters of Delegates to Congress*, ed. Smith, vol. 5, 238–9.

44. *Letters of Delegates to Congress*, ed. Smith, vol. 8, 96; *Journals of the Continental Congress*, vol. 15, 1152–4, 1164. For Lavoisier's contribution, see later in this chapter.

45. *Papers of General Nathanael Greene*, ed. Showman, 96; *Papers of Benjamin Franklin*, ed. Willcox, vol. 22, 343; Stephenson, 'Supply of Gunpowder', 277, showing 478,259 pounds of saltpeter and 1,454,210 pounds of gunpowder imported. See also Neil L. York, 'Clandestine Aid and the American Revolutionary War Effort: A Re-Examination', *Military Affairs*, 43 (1979), 26–30. Charles Coulston Gillispie, *Science and Polity in France: The End of the Old Regime* (Princeton, 2004), 65, has 1,700,000 pounds of French gunpowder going to the United States in 1776 and 1777. James A. Huston, *The Sinews of War: Army Logistics 1775–1953* (Washington, D.C., 1966), 24, has 2,347,000 pounds (1,048 tons) of gunpowder used in the revolutionary war, of which 90 per cent was imported from Europe. For the French gunpowder experts, Nicolas and Mark Fouquet, see *Journals of the Continental Congress*, vol. 15, 1152–4, 1164; Salay, 'Production of Gunpowder', 437–8. See also David Hackett Fischer, *Washington's Crossing* (Oxford, 2004), 155, and John Ferling, *Almost a Miracle: The American Victory in the War of Independence* (Oxford, 2007), 181, on American sufficiency in firearms and gunpowder.

46. *An Abstract of the Cargo of the Ship HYDRA, from Bengal* (Newport, R.I., 1788), single sheet, listing 376,196 pounds of saltpeter, plus thousands of pieces of textiles.

47. Edmund Hill, *Hints from the Manufacturers of the Raw Material of Saltpetre into Gunpowder, Oil of Vitriol, etc.* (1793), 4.

48. BL, Add. Ms 38393, f. 114.

49. Aber, *Art of Manufacturing Saltpeter*, title page.

50. *Letters of Delegates to Congress*, ed. Smith, vol. 14, 363.

51. René Dujarric de la Rivière, *E.I. du Pont, élève de Lavoisier* (Paris, 1954); Max Dorian, *The du Ponts: From Gunpowder to Nylon* (Boston, 1962); Darwin H. Stapleton, 'Élève des poudres: E. I. du Pont's Multiple Transfers of French Technology', in Brenda J. Buchanan (ed.), *Gunpowder, Explosives and the State: A Technological History* (Aldershot, 2006), 230–41; Van Gelder and Schlatter, *History of the Explosives Industry*, 117, 174–87.

52. Joseph LeConte, *Instructions for the Manufacture of Saltpetre* (Columbia, S.C., 1862).

53. James W. Frey, 'The Indian Saltpeter Trade, the Military Revolution, and the Rise of Britain as a Global Superpower', *The Historian*, 71 (2009), 552–3.

54. David Potter, *Renaissance France at War: Armies, Culture and Society, c.1480–1560* (Woodbridge, 2008), 155, gives figures in French *livres*, which weighed slightly more than an English pound, and *milliers* or thousands of *livres*. Geoffrey Parker (ed.), *The Cambridge Illustrated History of Warfare: The Triumph of the West* (Cambridge, 1995), 115, gives similar figures but equates *milliers* with tons. An English ton was equivalent to 2,042 *livres*.

55. John U. Nef, *Industry and Government in France and England, 1540–1640* (Philadelphia, 1940), 58–68, 97–8; André Guillerme. *The Age of Water: The Urban Environment in the North of France A.D. 300–1800* (College Station, Tex., 1988), 139, 255; Potter, *Renaissance France at War*, 153–7; Patrice Bret, 'The Organization of Gunpowder Production in France, 1775–1830', in Brenda J. Buchanan (ed.), *Gunpowder: The History of an International Technology* (Bath, 1996), 261–74; Jaime Wisniak, 'The History of Saltpeter Production with a Bit of Pyrotechnics and Lavoisier', *Chemical Educator*, 5 (2000), 205–9. Requisitions and quotas for *salpêtriers* under Francis I appear in *Collection des ordonnances des rois de France. Catalogue des actes de François Ier*, 10 vols. (Paris, 1887–1908). For comparison, see Bengt Åhslund, 'The Saltpetre Boilers of the Swedish Crown', in Brenda J. Buchanan (ed.), *Gunpowder: The History of an International Technology* (Bath, 1996), 163–81; Thomas Kaiserfeld, 'Saltpetre at the Intersection of Military and Agricultural Interrerests in Eighteenth-Century Sweden', in Brenda J. Buchanan (ed.), *Gunpowder, Explosives and the State* (Aldershot, 2006), 142–7.

56. Henry Stubbe, *Legends no Histories: Or, A Specimen of some Animadversions Upon the History of the Royal Society* (1670), 98; Nef, *Industry and Government*, 65; Bret, 'Organization of Gunpowder Production in France', 264; Surirey de Saint-Rémy, 'The Manufacture of Gunpowder in France (1702). Part 1: Saltpeter, Sulphur and Charcoal', ed. and trans David H. Roberts, *Journal of the Ordnance Society*, 5 (1993), 47.

57. Francis Malthus, *Pratique de la guerre* (Paris, 1681), chapter 1, 'Du salpêtre e poudre à canon', and chapter 2, 'Du nitre ou salpêtre et de son usage'. This edition also contains engravings on the manufacture of saltpeter, used in Chapter 5, Figure 13, above.

58. Pierre Surirey de Saint-Rémy, *Mémoires d'Artillerie* (Paris, 1697; Amsterdam, 1702), Surirey de Saint-Rémy, 'The Manufacture of Gunpowder in France', trans. Roberts, 47–55.

59. Frey, 'Indian Saltpeter Trade', 507, 526, 529, 531, 540.

60. Robert P. Multhauf, 'The French Crash Program for Saltpeter Production, 1776–94', *Technology and Culture*, 12 (1971), 163–81; Tony Travis, 'Revolutions and Gunpowder: Antoine Lavoisier', *Chemistry and Industry*, 9 (1994), 333–8; Jean-Pierre Poirier, *Lavoisier: Chemist, Biologist, Economist* (Philadelphia, 1996), 89–96; Arthur Donovan, *Antoine Lavoisier: Science, Administration, and Revolution* (Cambridge, 1996), 190–7; Charles Coulston Gillispie, *Science and Polity in France: The End of the Old Regime* (Princeton, 2004), 65.

61. *Journals of the Continental Congress*, vol. 15, 1152–4, 1164.

62. Antoine Laurent Lavoisier, *Œuvres*, 6 vols. (Paris, 1864–93), vol. 5.

63. Poirier, *Lavoisier*, 94, 117–19; Donovan, *Antoine Lavoisier*, 194–200; Multhauf, 'French Crash Program', 173; Bret, 'Organization of Gunpowder Production in France', 264–6.

64. TNA, BT 6/36. The British took comfort in the fact that French saltpeter cost 'rather more than the saltpeter that comes from the East Indies'.

65. Multhauf, 'French Crash Program', 173–5; William Scott, 'The Pursuit of "Interests" in the French Revolution: A Preliminary Survey', *French Historical Studies*, 19 (1996), 837–8; Bertrand Barère, 'La fabrication extraordinaire des armes et des poudres', in *Gazette Nationale, ou Le Moniteur Universel*, no. 135 (3 Février 1794), 542; 'William Jackson on Conditions in France, 1794', *American Historical Review*, 9 (1904), 527; Bret, 'Organization of Gunpowder Production in France', 266–9; Frey, 'Indian Saltpeter Trade', 548.

BIBLIOGRAPHY

Manuscript sources

Bodleian Library, Oxford
    Clarendon Ms. 14
    Tanner Ms. 63
British Library, London
    Add. Ms. 4458, Birch Papers
    Add. Ms. 11764, Star Chamber and Exchequer Cases
    Add. Ms. 21506, Original Letters
    Add. Ms. 22047, Anthony Roll
    Add. Ms. 29303, Parliamentary Papers
    Add. Ms. 38393, Liverpool Papers
    Add. Ms 41613, Tracts and Papers
    Add. Ms. 49093, Napier Papers
    Add. Ms. 72419, Trumbull Papers
    Add. Ms. 78278, Evelyn Papers
    Cotton Ms. Galba D XIII
    Cotton Ms. Ortho E VII
    Egerton Ms. 2716, Gawdy Papers
    Harley Ms. 1576, Law Papers
    Harley Ms. 4022, Star Chamber
    Harley Ms. 6070, Norwich Assize
    India Office Records E/3/102, F/4/126/2321–2, H/42, H/449, Ms. Eur. G112
    Lansdowne Mss. 5, 24, 25, 28, 30, 31, 57, 58, 61, 84, 80, 103, 113
    Royal Ms. 17 AXXXI
    Royal Ms. 18 DIII
    Sloane Ms. 1039, Resolutions of the Judges concerning Saltpeter
Dorset Record Office, Dorchester
    D/BOC/Box 22, Diary of Dennis Bond
Essex Record Office, Chelmsford
    Q/SR 267, Q/SR 269, Q/SR300, Q/SBa 2, Quarter Sessions
    T/A 418/107, Assize transcripts

Folger Shakespeare Library, Washington, D.C.
  Ms. Z.e.26, saltpeter receipts 1605
  Microfilm 164.70, Cecil Papers
Gloucestershire Archives, Gloucester
  D7115/1
Hatfield House, Hatfield
  Cecil Papers
Huntington Library, San Marino, California
  Ellesmere Mss.
  Hastings Mss.
Massachusetts Historical Society, Boston,
  Adams Family Papers (http://www.masshist.org/digitaladams/)
Massachusetts State Archives, Boston,
  Vol. 274, Certificates 1705–1781
The National Archives (TNA), Kew
  Board of Trade, BT 6/36, BT 6/184
  Chancery, C 1/108/61, C 1/308/71, C 1/1120/52, C 1/1159/30–32,
    C 1/1193/73–75.
  Cabinet Office, CAB 21/120.
  Exchequer, E 44/46, E 44/431, E 101/64, E 101/635, E 101/636, E 133/7,
    E 214/949, E 214/1124, E 219/437, E 315/255, E 351/2708
  Land Revenue, LR 9/130
  Privy Council, PC 2/46
  Star Chamber, STAC 2/15
  State Papers, SP 1, 12, 14, 15, 16, 29, 39, 46
  Ministry of Supply, SUPP 5/128, SUPP 5/762
  Treasury, T 64/276B/351
  War Office, WO 44–55
Oxfordshire Record Office, Oxford
  PAR 207/4/F1/1, St. Martin's accounts
Parliamentary Archives, London
  House of Lords Main Papers
Staffordshire Record Office, Stafford
  D 742/M, D 3074/J, D (W) 1778/V, Legge Papers
  Q/SR/245/1, Quarter Sessions
Suffolk Record Office, Ipswich
C/3/8/4/31, Ipswich Records
  FC 101/E2/19, Framlingham accounts
Surrey History Centre, Guildford
  More Molyneux Correspondence
University of Sheffield, Sheffield
  The Hartlib Papers (CD-ROM, 2nd edn., 2002)

Printed primary sources

Aber, Israel, *The Art of Manufacturing Saltpeter, by Cheap, Easy, and Expeditious Methods* (Newark, N.J., 1796).

An Abstract of the Cargo of the Ship HYDRA, from Bengal (Newport, R.I., 1788).

'An Account of the Quantities of Saltpetre Imported into, and Exported from, the United Kingdom in the years 1860–1863 inclusive, and 1864 to the present time, distinguishing the Countries from which the Saltpetre was Imported, 24 June 1864', *Parliamentary Papers* (1864).

Acts and Ordinances of the Interregnum, ed. C. H. Firth and R. S. Rait, 3 vols. (1911).

Acts of the Privy Council, ed. J. H. Dasent et al., 46 vols. (1890–1967).

Acts of the Privy Council, Colonial, ed. W. L. Grant et al., 6 vols. (1908–12).

(Adams) *Papers of John Adams*, ed. Robert J. Taylor, 15 vols. (Cambridge, Mass., 1977–2010).

Agricola, Georgius, *De re metallica* (Basel, 1556).

(Agricola) *Georgius Agricola, De re metallica. Translated from the First Latin Edition of 1556*, ed. Herbert Clark Hoover and Lou Henry Hoover (New York, 1950).

Analytical Index to the Series of Records known as the Remembrancia, ed. W. H. Overall and H. C. Overall (1878).

The Annual Register, or a View of the History, Politics, and Literature, for the Year 1763 (1764).

The Anthony Roll of Henry VIII's Navy, ed. C. S. Knighton and D. M. Loades, (Navy Records Society, vol. 2, 2000), 41–106.

(Bacon) *Letters from Redgrave Hall. The Bacon Family 1340–1744*, ed. Diarmaid MacCulloch (Suffolk Records Society, vol. 50, 2007).

Bacon, Francis, *Sylva sylvarum or A Naturall History in Ten Centuries* (1627).

Bacon, Francis, *The Historie of Life and Death* (1638).

Bacon, Francis, *The New Organon*, ed. Lisa Jardine and Michael Silverthorne (Cambridge, 2000).

Barère, Bertrand, 'La fabrication extraordinaire des armes et des poudres', in *Gazette Nationale, ou Le Moniteur Universel*, no. 135 (3 Février 1794).

Bate, John, *The Mysteryes of Nature and Art* (1634).

Binning, Thomas, *A Light to the Art of Gunnery* (1703).

Biringuccio, Vannoccio, *De la pirotechnia* (Venice, 1540).

(Biringuccio) *The Pirotechnia of Vannoccio Biringuccio*, ed. Cyril Stanley Smith and Martha Teach Gnudi (New York, 1942).

Boerhaave, Herman, *A New Method of Chemistry, Including the Theory and Practice of that Art* (1727).

Boillot, Joseph, *Artifices de feu, & divers instruments de guerre* (Strasburg, 1603).

Bourne, William, *The Arte of Shooting in Great Ordnaunce. Contayning very Necessary Matters for all sortes of Servitoures eyther by Sea or by Lande* (1587).

(Bowyer) *The Parliamentary Diary of Robert Bowyer 1606–1607*, ed. David Harris Willson (Minneapolis, 1931).

Boyle, Robert, 'A Physico-Chymical Essay, Containing an Experiment, with some Considerations Touching the Differing Parts and Redintegration of Salt-Petre', in Robert Boyle, *Certain Physiological Essays* (1661).

(Boyle) *The Correspondence of Robert Boyle. Vol. 1. 1636–61*, ed. Michael Hunter, Antonio Clericuzio, and Lawrence M. Principe (2001).

Boyle, Robert, *The Sceptical Chymist* (1661).

(Boyle) *The Works of the Honourable Robert Boyle*, 6 vols. (1772).

Brugis, Thomas, *The Discovery of a Projector: Shewing the Beginning, Progresse, and End of the Projector and his Projects* (1641).

Cabala, sive Scrinia sacra: Mysteries of State and Government...Second Part (1691).

A Calendar of the Court Minutes etc. of the East India Company, 1644–1649, ed. William Foster and Ethel Bruce Sainsbury (Oxford, 1912).

Calendar of Historical Manuscripts, Relating to the War of the Revolution, in the Office of the Secretary of State, Albany, 2 vols. (Albany, N.Y., 1868).

Calendar of the Patent Rolls, 1485–1582, ed. J. G. Black et al. (1914–48).

Calendar of State Papers, Colonial, ed. W. N. Sainsbury et al., 44 vols. (1860–1969).

Calendar of State Papers, Domestic, ed. Mary Anne Everett Green et al., 98 vols. (1856–1998).

Calendar of State Papers, Foreign, ed. William B. Turnball et al., 25 vols. (1861–1950).

Calendar of State Papers, Venetian, ed. Rawdon Brown et al., 38 vols. (1864–1951).

Calendar of Treasury Books, ed. W. A. Shaw et al., 32 vols. (1897–1934).

Calendar of Treasury Papers, ed. Joseph Redington et al., 6 vols. (1868–89).

Chaloner, Thomas, *A Shorte Discourse of the Most Rare and Excellent Vertue of Nitre* (1584).

Child, Josiah, *A Treatise Wherein is Demonstrated, I. That the East-India Trade is the most National of all Foreign Trades* (1681).

Clarke, William, *The Natural History of Nitre: or, a Philosophical Discourse of the Nature, Generation, Place, and Artificial Extraction of Nitre, with its Vertues and Uses* (1670).

Coke, Edward, *Quinta pars relationum...The Fift Part of the Reports* (1612).

Coke, Edward, *The Third Part of the Institutes of the Laws of England* (1644).

Coke, Edward, *The Twelfth Part of the Reports* (1656).

Collection des ordonnances des rois de France. Catalogue des actes de François Ier, 10 vols. (Paris, 1887–1908).

The Colonial Records of North Carolina, ed. William L. Saunders, 10 vols. (Raleigh, N.C., 1886–1907).

Commons Debates 1628, ed. Robert C. Johnson, Maija Jansson Cole, et al., 6 vols. (New Haven, 1977–1983).

The Compleat Gunner (1672).

D., W. C., *Considerations on the Importance of the Production of Saltpetre in England and its Dependencies* (1783).

Defoe, Daniel, *A General History of Discoveries and Improvements* (1726).

Duchesne, Joseph [as Iospehus Quersitanus], *The Practise of Chymicall, and Hermeticall Physicke, for the Preservation of Health*, trans. Thomas Timme (1605).

Eldred, William, *The Gunners Glasse* (1646).

The English Factories in India, ed. William Foster, 13 vols. (Oxford, 1906–27).

Ercker, Lazarus, *Beschreibung allerfürnemisten mineralischen Ertzt unnd Bergkwercks Arten* (Frankfurt, 1580).

(Ercker) *Lazarus Ercker's Treatise on Ores and Assaying translated from the German edition of 1580*, trans. Anneliese Grünhaldt Sisco and Cyril Stanley Smith (Chicago, 1951).

Essays upon the Making of Salt-Peter and Gun-Powder (New York, 1776).

Evelyn, John, *Sylva: or, A Discourse of Forest-Trees* (1664).

(Evelyn) *The Diary of John Evelyn*, ed. E. S. De Beer, 6 vols. (Oxford, 1955).

(Franklin) *The Papers of Benjamin Franklin*, ed. William B. Willcox, 39 vols. (New Haven, 1959–2008).

Fryer, John, *A New Account of East India and Persia. Being Nine Years' Travels, 1672-1681*, ed. William Crooke, Hakluyt Society, 2nd series, 19 (1909).

Glauber, John Rudolph, *The Works of the Highly Experienced and Famous Chymist John Rudolph Glauber* (1689).

(Greene) *The Papers of General Nathanael Greene. Vol. 1. December 1766–December 1776*, ed. Richard K. Showman (Chapel Hill, 1976).

Hakluyt, Richard, *Divers Voyages Touching the Discoverie of America, and the Ilands adjacent unto the Same* (1582).

Hakluyt, Richard, *The Principal Navigations Voyages Traffiques & Discoveries of the English Nation*, 12 vols. (Glasgow, 1903).

Hansard's Parliamentary Debates (1857, 1864).

Harrison, William, *The Description of England*, ed. Georges Edelen (Ithaca, N.Y., 1968).

Henshaw, Thomas, 'The History of Making Gun-Powder', in Thomas Sprat, *The History of the Royal-Society of London, For the Improving of Natural Knowledge* (1667).

Henshaw, Thomas, 'The History of the Making of Salt-Peter', in Thomas Sprat, *The History of the Royal-Society of London, For the Improving of Natural Knowledge* (1667).

Hill, Edmund, *Hints from the Manufacturers of the Raw Material of Saltpetre into Gunpowder, Oil of Vitriol, etc.* (1793).

Historical Manuscripts Commission, *Calendar of the Manuscripts of the Most Hon. The Marquis of Salisbury, Preserved at Hatfield House*, 23 vols. (1883–1973).

Historical Manuscripts Commission, *Report on the Manuscripts of Earl Cowper*, 3 vols. (1888–89).

Houghton, John (ed.), *A Collection for the Improvement of Husbandry and Trade* (nos. 224–7, 13 November–4 December, 1696).

The House of Commons, 1604–1610, ed. Wallace Notestein (New Haven and London, 1971).

(Jackson) 'William Jackson on Conditions in France, 1794', *American Historical Review*, 9 (1904), 525–32.

(Jefferson) *The Papers of Thomas Jefferson. Vol. 1. 1760–1776*, ed. Julian P. Boyd (Princeton, 1950).

Jorden, Edward, *A Discourse of Naturall Bathes, and Minerall Waters* (1632, 1673 edn.).

Journal of the House of Commons, 12 vols. (1802–3).

The Journals of Each Provincial Congress of Massachusetts in 1774 and 1775, ed. William Lincoln (Boston, 1838).

Journals of the Continental Congress 1774–1789, ed. Worthington Chauncey Ford et al., 37 vols. (Washington, D.C., 1904–37).

Kennedy, Archibald, *Observations on the Importance of the Northern Colonies* (New York, 1750).

(Laud) *The Works of the Most Reverend Father in God, William Laud*, ed. James Bliss, 7 vols. (Oxford, 1853).

Lavoisier, Antoine Laurent, *Œuvres*, 6 vols. (Paris, 1864–93).

LeConte, Joseph, *Instructions for the Manufacture of Saltpetre* (Columbia, S.C., 1862).

Lémery, Nicolas, *A Course of Chymistry: Containing the Easiest Manner of Performing those Operations* (1677).

Letters and Papers, Foreign and Domestic, of the Reign of Henry VIII, ed. J. S. Brewer et al., 21 vols. (1862–1920).

Letters of Delegates to Congress 1774–1789, ed. Paul H. Smith, 26 vols. (Washington, D.C., 1976–2000).

(Loder) *Robert Loder's Farm Accounts 1610–1620*, ed. G. E. Fussell (Camden Society, 3rd series, vol. 53, 1936).

Lovell, Robert, *Panoryktologia. Sive Pammineralogicon. Or An Universal History of Mineralls* (Oxford, 1661).

Lucar, Cyprian, *Colloquies Concerning the Arte of Shooting in Great and Small Peeces of Artillerie* (1588).

Macquer, Pierre-Joseph, *Elements of the Theory and Practice of Chymistry* (Edinburgh, 1777).

Malthus, Francis, *Pratique de la guerre: contenant l'usage de l'artillerie, bombes et mortiers, feux artificiels & petards, sappes & mines, ponts & pontons, tranchées & travaux* (Paris, 1681).

Malthus, Thomas (i.e. Francis), *A Treatise of Artificial Fire-Works* (1629).

(Mandelslo) 'The Voyages & Travels of J. Albert de Mandelslo', in Adam Olearius, *The Voyages & Travels of the Ambassadors Sent by Frederick Duke of Holstein, to the Great Duke of Muscovy, and the King of Persia*, trans. John Davies (1662).

The Mariage of Prince Fredericke, and the Kings Daughter, the Lady Elizabeth (1613).

Mayow, John, *Tractatus quinque medico-physici. Quorum primus agit de sal-nitro, et spiritu nitro-aereo* (Oxford, 1674).

Middleton, Thomas, *A Faire Quarrell* (1617).

Moore, Francis, *Cases Collect & Report* (1688).

Nichols, John (ed.), *The Progresses, Processions, and Magnificent Festivities of King James the First*, 4 vols. (1828).

Norton, Robert, *The Gunner: Shewing the Whole Practise of Artillerie* (1628).

Nye, Nathaniel, *The Art of Gunnery. Wherein is described the true way to make all sorts of gunpowder, gun-match, the art of shooting in great and small ordnance* (1647, 1670).

Pettus, John, *Fleta minor. The Laws of Art and Nature* (1683; reprinted 1685 and 1686).

Pettus, John, *Fodinae regales. Or the History, Laws and Places of the Chief Mines and Mineral Works in England, Wales, and the English Pale in Ireland* (1670).

Plat, Hugh, *The Jewell House of Art and Nature* (1594).

Portaleone, R. Abraham, *Shilte ha-Gibborim* [Shields of the Heroes] (Mantua, 1612; Jerusalem, 1970).

Proceedings in Parliament 1626, ed. William B. Bidwell and Maija Jansson, 4 vols. (New Haven, 1991–6).

Proceedings in the Opening Session of the Long Parliament, ed. Maija Jansson, 7 vols. (Rochester, N.Y., 2000–07).

Proceedings Principally in the County of Kent, in Connection with the Parliaments called in 1640, ed. Lambert B. Larking (Camden Society, 1852).

The Process for Extracting and Refining Salt-Petre, According to the Method practiced at the Provincial Works in Philadelphia (Philadelphia, 1776).

The Public Records of the State of Connecticut, from October, 1776, to February, 1778, Inclusive, ed. Charles L. Hoadly (Hartford, Conn., 1894).

Records of the Borough of Leicester…1603–1688, ed. Helen Stocks and W. H. Stevens (Cambridge, 1923).

Register of the Privy Council of Scotland, 37 vols. (Edinburgh, 1877–1970).

Remonstrance of the State of the Kingdom (1641).

Report of the Committee of Warehouses, on a Memorial from the Manufacturers of Gunpowder, and of other Commodities made from Saltpetre (1793).

Revolutionary Virginia. The Road to Independence. Vol. VII part 1. Independence and the Fifth Convention, 1776, ed. Brent Tarter (Charlottesville, Va., 1983).

Rolle, Henry, *Les reports de Henry Rolle* (1675).

The Royalist Ordnance Papers 1642–1646, ed. Ian Roy, Oxfordshire Record Society, vol. 43 (1964) and vol. 49 (1975).

Russell, Thomas, *To the Kings most Excellent Maiestie, the Lords Spirituall and Temporall, and the Commons in this Present Parliament* (1626).

Saint-Rémy, Pierre Surirey de, *Mémoires d'artillerie où, il est traité des mortiers, petards, arquebuses à croc, mousquets, fusils, &c* (Paris, 1697; Amsterdam, 1702).

Saint-Rémy, Surirey de, 'The Manufacture of Gunpowder in France (1702). Part 1: Saltpetre, Sulphur and Charcoal', ed. and trans. David H. Roberts, *Journal of the Ordnance Society,* 5 (1993), 47–55.

Salmon, William, *Seplasium. The Compleat English Physician: or, The Druggist's Shop Opened* (1693).

Saltpetre Wanting in England to a Great Degree (1695).

Seller, John, *The Sea Gunner: Shewing the Practical Part of Gunnery as it is used at Sea* (1691).

Several Methods of Making Salt-Petre, Recommended to the Inhabitants of the United Colonies, by the Honorable Continental Congress, and Re-published by Order of the General Assembly of the Colony of Massachusetts (Watertown, Mass., 1775).

Several Methods of Making Salt-Petre; Recommended to the Inhabitants of the United Colonies by their Representatives in Congress (Philadelphia, 1775).

Shaw, Peter, *Chemical Lectures* (1734).

Smith, Godfrey, *The Laboratory, or School of Arts* (1738).

Smith, John, *An Accidence for the Sea* (1636).

Sprat, Thomas, *The History of the Royal-Society of London, for the Improving of Natural Knowledge* (1667).

State Papers Relating to Musters, Beacons, Shipmoney, etc. in Norfolk, ed. Walter Rye (Norwich, 1907).

Statutes of the Realm, 11 vols. (1810–28).

Stephenson, John, *Treatise on the Manufacture of Saltpetre* (Calcutta, 1835).

Stuart Royal Proclamations, ed. James F. Larkin and Paul Hughes, 2 vols. (Oxford, 1973–83).

Stubbe, Henry, *Legends no Histories: Or, A Specimen of Some Animadversions Upon the History of the Royal Society* (1670).

Tartaglia, Niccolò, *Quesiti et inventioni diverse* (Venice, 1546).

[Tavernier], *Travels in India by Jean-Baptiste Tavernier,* ed. William Crooke, 2 vols. (Oxford, 1925).

Thraster, William, *The Marrow of Chymical Physic; or, The Practice of Making Chymical Medicines* (1669; 1679).

Thybourel, François, *Recueil de plusieurs machines militaires, et feux artificiels pour la guerre, & recreation* (Pont-à-Mousson, 1620).

Watson, Richard, *Chemical Essays* (1781).

(Webb) *Correspondence and Journals of Samuel Blachley Webb. Vol. 1. 1772–1777*, ed. Worthington Chauncey Ford (New York, 1983).

Whitehorne Peter, *Certain Waies for the orderyng of Souldiers in battelray…And moreover, howe to make Saltpeter, Gunpoulder, and divers sortes of Fireworkes,* (appended to his translation of Niccolò Machiavelli's *Arte of Warr*, 1562; reprinted 1574 and 1588).

Wilson, George, *A Compleat Course of Chemistry* (1699).

Wilson, George, *A Course of Practical Chemistry* (1746).

Winthrop Papers. Volume VI. 1650–1654, ed. Malcolm Freiberg (Boston, 1992).

Newspapers

Boston Evening Post, 1775.

Boston Gazette or Country Journal, 1775.

Connecticut Courant, 1775.

Connecticut Gazette, 1775.

Dunlap's Pennsylvania Packet or, the General Advertiser, 1774.

The Economist, 1854–1910.

Evening Post, 1745.

Gazette Nationale, ou Le Moniteur Universel (Paris) 1794.

General Evening Post, 1740.

London Magazine, or Gentleman's Monthly Intelligencer, 1767.

London Evening Post, 1747.

Massachusetts Spy: or, American Oracle of Liberty, 1776.

Mercurius Politicus, 1655.

New London Gazette, 1775.

Newport Mercury, 1775.

Pennsylvania Gazette, 1775.

Pennsylvania Magazine: Or, American Monthly Museum, 1775.

Pennsylvania Mercury, 1775.

Pennsylvania Mercury and Universal Advertiser, 1775.

Royal American Magazine (Boston), 1774–75.

St. James's Evening Post, 1745.

Virginia Gazette, 1775.

Proclamations

By the Queene. A Proclamation for the calling in and frustrating all commissions for the making of salt-peeter, 13 January 1590.

By the Queene. A Proclamation for the reformation of many abuses and misdemeanours committed by Patentees, 28 November 1601.

By the King. A Proclamation for prevention of future abuses in Purveyance, 23 April 1606.

By the King. A Proclamation for prevention of abuses touching Gunpowder and Salt-peeter, 16 January 1623.

By the King. A Proclamation for the preservation of Grounds for making of Salt-Peeter, and to restore such Grounds which now are destroyed, 26 December 1624.

By the King. A Proclamation for the maintenance and encrease of the Mines of Salt-peter, and the true making of Gunpowder, and reforming abuses concerning the same, 13 April 1625.

By the King. A Proclamation for the better making of Saltpeter within this Kingdome, 2 January 1627.

By the King. A Proclamation for the maintaining and increase of the Mines of Salt-peter, and the true making and working of Saltpeter and Gunpowder, and reform-ing of all abuses concerning the same, 23 July 1627.

By the King. A Proclamation for preservation of Grounds for making of Saltpeter, and to restore such grounds as are now destroyed, and to command Assistance to be given to His Majesties Saltpeter-Makers, 14 March 1635.

By the King. A Proclamation Prohibiting the Exportation of Saltpeter, 17 March 1664.

By the King. A Proclamation For the effectual prosecution of His Majesties Commis-sion for the Providing and Making of Salt-peter and Gun-powder, 16 July 1666.

A Proclamation to Prohibit the Exportation of Salt Petre, 25 July 1689.

Secondary Sources

Ágoston, Gábor, *Guns for the Sultan: Military Power and the Weapons Industry in the Ottoman Empire* (Cambridge, 2005).

Åhslund, Bengt, 'The Saltpetre Boilers of the Swedish Crown', in Brenda J. Buchanan (ed.), *Gunpowder: The History of an International Technology* (Bath, 1996), 163–81.

Andrews, Kenneth R., *Ships, Money and Politics: Seafaring and Naval Enterprise in the Reign of Charles I* (Cambridge, 1991).

Aylmer, Gerald, *The King's Servants: The Civil Service of Charles I, 1625–1642* (New York, 1961).

Balasubramiam, R., 'Saltpetre Manufacturing and Marketing in Medieval India,' *Indian Journal of History of Science*, 40 (2005), 663–72.

Bovill, E. W., 'Queen Elizabeth's Gunpowder', *Mariner's Mirror*, 33 (1947), 179–86.

Bown, Stephen R., *A Most Damnable Invention: Dynamite, Nitrates, and the Making of the Modern World* (Toronto and London, 2005).

Bret, Patrice, 'The Organization of Gunpowder Production in France, 1775–1830', in Brenda J. Buchanan (ed.), *Gunpowder: The History of an International Technology* (Bath, 1996), 261–74.

Buchanan, Brenda J. (ed.), *Gunpowder: The History of an International Technology* (Bath, 1996).

Buchanan, Brenda J., '"The Art and Mystery of Making Gunpowder": The English Experience in the Seventeenth and Eighteenth Centuries', in Brett D. Steele and Tamera Dorland (eds.), *The Heirs of Archimedes: Science and the Art of War through the Age of Enlightenment* (Cambridge, Mass., 2005), 233–74.

Buchanan, Brenda J. (ed.), *Gunpowder, Explosives and the State: A Technological History* (Aldershot, 2006).

Bull, Stephen, 'Pearls from the Dungheap: English Saltpetre Production 1590–1640', *Journal of the Ordnance Society*, 2 (1990), 5–10.

Bull, Stephen, *The Furie of the Ordnance: Artillery in the English Civil War* (Woodbridge, 2008).

Burgen, Arnold, 'An Explosive Story', *European Review*, 12 (2004), 209–15.

Burgon, John William, *The Life and Times of Sir Thomas Gresham*, 2 vols. (1839).

Carlton, Charles, *Going to the Wars: The Experience of the British Civil Wars 1638–1651* (1992).

Carp, E. Wayne, *To Starve the Army at Pleasure: Continental Army Administration and American Political Culture 1775–1783* (Chapel Hill, 1984).

Chase, Kenneth, *Firearms: A Global History to 1700* (Cambridge, 2003).

Chaudhuri, K. N., *The English East India Company: The Study of an Early Joint-Stock Company 1600–1640* (New York and London, 1965).

Chaudhuri, K. N., *The Trading World of Asia and the English East India Company 1660–1760* (Cambridge, 1978).

Conway, Stephen, *War, State, and Society in Mid-Eighteenth-Century Britain and Ireland* (Oxford, 2006).

Cook, Chris, and Brendan Keith, *British Historical Facts 1830–1900* (1975).

Cook, Chris, and John Stevenson, *British Historical Facts 1760–1830* (1980).

Cook, Weston F. Jr, *The Hundred Years War for Morocco: Gunpowder and the Military Revolution in the Early Modern Muslim World* (Boulder, San Francisco, and Oxford, 1994).

Cressy, David, *Bonfires and Bells: National Memory and the Protestant Calendar in Elizabethan and Stuart England* (1989).

Cressy, David, *England on Edge: Crisis and Revolution 1640–1642* (Oxford, 2006).

Crocker, Glenys, *The Gunpowder Industry* (2nd edn., Princes Risborough, 1999).

Cruickshank, C. G., *Army Royal: Henry VIII's Invasion of France 1513* (Oxford, 1969).

Cust, Richard, *Charles I: A Political Life* (Harlow, 2005).

Dale, Stephen F., *The Muslim Empires of the Ottomans, Safavids, and Mughals* (Cambridge, 2010).

Davis, Robert, *Christian Slaves, Muslim Masters: White Slavery in the Mediterranean, the Barbary Coast and Italy, 1500–1800* (Basingstoke and New York, 2003).

Debus, Allen G., 'The Paraceslsian Aerial Niter', *Isis*, 55 (1964), 43–61.

Debus, Allen G., *The Chemical Philosophy: Paracelsian Science and Medicine in the Sixteenth and Seventeenth Centuries* (New York, 1977).

DeVries, Kelly, 'Gunpowder Weaponry and the Rise of the Early Modern State', *War in History*, 5 (1998), 127–45.

DeVries, Kelly, 'Sites of Military Science and Technology', in Katherine Park and Lorraine Daston (eds.), *The Cambridge History of Science. Vol. 3. Early Modern Science* (Cambridge, 2006), 308–11.

Donovan, Arthur, *Antoine Lavoisier: Science, Administration, and Revolution* (Cambridge, 1996).

Dorian, Max, *The du Ponts: From Gunpowder to Nylon* (Boston, 1962).

Eamon, William, *Science and the Secrets of Nature: Books of Secrets in Medieval and Early Modern Culture* (Princeton, 1994).

Edwards, Peter, 'Gunpowder and the English Civil War', *Journal of the Arms & Armour Society*, 15 (1995), 114–17.

Edwards, Peter, 'Logistics and Supply', in John Kenyon and Jane Ohlmeyer (eds.), *The Civil Wars: A Military History of England, Scotland and Ireland 1638–1660* (Oxford, 1998), 242–55.

Edwards, Peter, *Dealing in Death: The Arms Trade and the British Civil Wars, 1638–52* (Stroud, 2000).

Emsley, John, *The Shocking History of Phosphorus: A Biography of the Devil's Element* (2000).

Evans, R. J. W., *Rudolf II and his World: A Study in Intellectual History 1576–1612* (1997).

Ferling, John, *Almost a Miracle: The American Victory in the War of Independence* (Oxford, 2007).

Ferris, J. P., 'The Salpetremen in Dorset, 1635', *Proceedings of the Dorset Natural History and Archaeological Society*, 85 (1963), 158–63.

Fischer, David Hackett, *Washington's Crossing* (Oxford, 2004).

Fissel, Mark Charles (ed.), *War and Government in Britain, 1598–1650* (Manchester and New York, 1991).

Fissel, Mark Charles, *English Warfare 1511–1642* (2001).

Frey, James W., 'The Indian Saltpeter Trade, the Military Revolution, and the Rise of Britain as a Global Superpower', *The Historian*, 71 (2009), 507–54.

Friedel, Robert, *A Culture of Improvement: Technology and the Western Millennium* (Cambridge, Mass., 2007).

Gillispie, Charles Coulston, *Science and Polity in France: The End of the Old Regime* (Princeton, 2004).

Glete, Jan, *Warfare at Sea 1500–1650: Maritime Conflicts and the Transformation of Europe* (1999).

Golinski, Jan, *Science as Public Culture: Chemistry and Enlightenment in Britain, 1760–1820* (Cambridge, 1992).

Grassl, Gary C., 'Joachim Gans of Prague: The First Jew in English America', *American Jewish History*, 86 (1998), 195–217.

Gray, E., H. Marsh, and M. McLaren, 'A Short History of Gunpowder and the Role of Charcoal in its Manufacture', *Journal of Materials Science*, 17 (1982), 3385–400.

Greengrass, Mark, Michael Leslie, and Timothy Raylor (eds.), *Samuel Hartlib and Universal Reformation: Studies in Intellectual Communication* (Cambridge, 1994).

Guillerme, André, *The Age of Water: The Urban Environment in the North of France A.D. 300–1800* (College Station, Tex., 1988).

Guilmartin, John F., 'The Earliest Shipboard Gunpowder Ordnance: An Analysis of its Technicalities, Parameters and Tactical Capabilities', *Journal of Military History*, 71 (2007), 649–69.

Gunn, Steven, 'Archery Practice in Early Tudor England', *Past and Present*, no. 209 (November 2010), 53–81.

Hale, J. R., *Renaissance War Studies* (1983).

Hall, Bert S., 'The Corning of Gunpowder and the Development of Firearms in the Renaissance', in Brenda J. Buchanan (ed.), *Gunpowder: The History of an International Technology* (Bath, 1996), 87–120.

Hall, Bert S., *Weapons and Warfare in Renaissance Europe: Gunpowder, Technology, and Tactics* (Baltimore, Md., 1997).

Hall, Bert S., 'Introduction' to J. R. Partington, *A History of Greek Fire and Gunpowder* (2nd edn., Baltimore, Md., 1998).

Hammer, Paul E. J., *Elizabeth's Wars: War, Government and Society in Tudor England, 1544–1604* (Basingstoke and New York, 2003).

Harris, L. E., *The Two Netherlanders: Humphrey Bradley and Cornelius Drebbel* (Leiden, 1961).

Haythornthwaite, Philip J., *The Armies of Wellington* (1998).

History of the Ministry of Munitions. Vol. 7. The Control of Materials (Crown Copyright 1922, reprinted 2008).

Hodgetts, E. A. Brayley (ed.), *The Rise and Progress of the British Explosives Industry* (1909).

Howard, Robert A., 'Realities and Perceptions in the Evolution of Black Powder Making', in Brenda J. Buchanan (ed.), *Gunpowder, Explosives and the State: A Technological History* (Aldershot, 2006).

Hunter, Michael, *Boyle between God and Science* (New Haven and London, 2009).

Huston, James A., *The Sinews of War: Army Logistics 1775–1953* (Washington, D.C., 1966).

Kaiserfeld, Thomas, 'Saltpetre at the Intersection of Military and Agricultural Interests in Eighteenth-Century Sweden', in Brenda Buchanan (ed.), *Gunpowder, Explosives and the State: A Technological History* (Aldershot, 2006), 142–7.

Kenyon, John, and Jane Ohlmeyer (eds.), *The Civil Wars: A Military History of England, Scotland and Ireland 1638–1660* (Oxford, 1998).

Kerridge, Eric, *The Agricultural Revolution* (1967).

Khan, Yas Muhammad, 'Bārūd', *Encyclopedia of Islam*, (2nd edn., Leiden, Brill Online, http://www.paulyonline.brill.nl, accessed May 2009).

Krishna, Bal, *Commercial Relations between India and England (1601 to 1757)* (1924).

Leather, J. W., and Jatindra Nath Mukerji, *The Indian Saltpetre Industry* (Calcutta, 1911).

Lee, H., and J. H. Quastel, 'Biochemistry of Nitrification in Soil', *Biochemical Journal*, 40 (1946), 803–28.

Leng, Thomas, *Benjamin Worsley (1618–1677): Trade, Interest and the Spirit in Revolutionary England* (Woodbridge, 2008).

Levine, Joseph M., *Between the Ancients and the Moderns: Baroque Culture in Restoration England* (New Haven and London, 1999).

L'hirondel, Jean, and Jean-Louis L'hirondel, *Nitrate and Man: Toxic, Harmless or Beneficial?* (Wallingford and New York, 2002).

McCann, John, 'Dovecotes and Pigeons in English Law', *Transactions of the Ancient Monuments Society*, 44 (2000), 25–50.

McNeill, William H., *The Pursuit of Power: Technology, Armed Force, and Society since A.D. 1000* (Chicago, 1982).

Martin, Colin, and Geoffrey Parker, *The Spanish Armada* (1988).

Matar, N. I., *Britain and Barbary, 1589–1689* (Gainesville, Fla., 2005).

Mauskopf, Seymour H., 'Gunpowder and the Chemical Revolution', *Osiris*, 2nd series, 4 (1988), 92–118.

Mauskopf, Seymour H., ' "From an Instrument of War to an Instrument of the Laboratory: the Affinities do not Change": Chemists and the Development of Munitions, 1785–1885', *Bulletin of the History of Chemistry*, 24 (1999), 1–15.

Mauskopf, Seymour H., 'Bridging Chemistry and Physics in the Experimental Study of Gunpowder', in Frederick L. Holmes and Trevor H. Levere (eds.), *Instruments and Experimentation in the History of Chemistry* (Cambridge, Mass., 2000), 335–65.

Mostert, Tristan, *Chain of Command: The Military System of the Dutch East India Company 1655–1663* (M.A. thesis, University of Leiden, 2007; http:vocwarfare. net).

Multhauf, Robert P., 'The French Crash Program for Saltpeter Production, 1776–94', *Technology and Culture*, 12 (1971), 163–81.

Needham, Joseph, *Science and Civilisation in China. Vol. 5. Chemistry and Chemical Technology, Part 7: Military Technology: The Gunpowder Epic* (Cambridge, 1986).

Nef, John U., *Industry and Government in France and England, 1540–1640* (Philadelphia, 1940).

Newman, William R., 'From Alchemy to "Chymystry",' in Katherine Park and Lorraine Daston (eds.), *The Cambridge History of Science. Vol. 3. Early Modern Science* (Cambridge, 2006), 497–517.

Newman, William R., and Lawrence M. Principe, *Alchemy Tried in the Fire: Starkey, Boyle, and the Fate of Helmontian Chymistry* (Chicago, 2002).

Nummedal, Tara, *Alchemy and Authority in the Holy Roman Empire* (Chicago and London, 2007).

O'Neil, B. H. St. J., 'Stefan von Haschenperg, an Engineer to King Henry VIII, and his Work', *Archaeologia*, 91 (1945), 137–55.

Oxford Dictionary of National Biography (Oxford, 2004–11, http://www.oxforddnb.com/)

Pacey, Arnold, *Technology in World Civilization: A Thousand-Year History* (Oxford, 1990).

Panciera, Walter, 'Saltpetre Production in the Republic of Venice from the Sixteenth to the Eighteenth Century', *Icon: Journal of the International Committee for the History of Technology*, 3 (1977), 155–66.

Parker, Geoffrey (ed.), *The Cambridge Illustrated History of Warfare: The Triumph of the West* (Cambridge, 1995).

Parker, Geoffrey, 'The *Dreadnought* Revolution of Tudor England', *Mariner's Mirror*, 82 (1996), 269–300.

Parker, Geoffrey, *The Military Revolution: Military Innovation and the Rise of the West, 1500–1800* (2nd edn., Cambridge, 1996).

Partington, J. R., *A History of Greek Fire and Gunpowder* (Cambridge, 1960; 2nd edn., Baltimore, Md., 1998).

Poirier, Jean-Pierre, *Lavoisier: Chemist, Biologist, Economist* (Philadelphia, 1996).

Potter, David, *Renaissance France at War: Armies, Culture and Society, c.1480–1560* (Woodbridge, 2008).

Powell, J. R., *The Navy in the English Civil War* (1962).

Prestwich, Michael, *Armies and Warfare in the Middle Ages: The English Experience* (New Haven and London, 1996).

Quastel, J. H., and P. G. Scholefield, 'Biochemistry of Nitrification in Soil', *Bacteriological Reviews*, 15 (1951), 1–53.

Quintrell, Brian, 'Charles I and his Navy in the 1630s', *Seventeenth Century*, 3 (1988), 159–79.

Raymond, James, *Henry VIII's Military Revolution: The Armies of Sixteenth-Century Britain and Europe* (London and New York, 2007).

Reynolds, Donald E., 'Ammunition Supply in Revolutionary Virginia', *Virginia Magazine of History and Biography*, 73 (1965), 56–77.

Rich, George W., and David F. Jacobs, 'Saltpeter: A Folkloric Adjustment to Acculturation Stress', *Western Folklore*, 32 (1973), 164–79.

Rivière, René Dujarric de la, *E. I. du Pont, élève de Lavoisier* (Paris, 1954).

Rodger, N. A. M., *The Safeguard of the Sea: A Naval History of Britain 660–1649* (1997).

Rodger, N. A. M., *The Command of the Ocean: A Naval History of Britain 1649–1815* (New York and London, 2005).

Rogers, Clifford J. (ed.), *The Military Revolution Debate: Readings on the Military Transformation of Early Modern Europe* (Boulder, 1995).

Roos, Anna Marie, *The Salt of the Earth: Natural Philosophy, Medicine, and Chymistry in England, 1650–1750* (Leiden and Boston, 2007).

Russell, Conrad, *Parliaments and English Politics 1621–1629* (Oxford, 1979).

Russell, Conrad S. R., 'Monarchies, Wars, and Estates in England, France, and Spain, c.1580–c.1640', *Legislative Studies Quarterly*, 7 (1982), 205–20.

Salay, David L., 'The Production of Gunpowder in Pennsylvania during the American Revolution', *Pennsylvania Magazine of History and Biography*, 99 (1975), 422–5.

Sarkar, Jagdish Narayan, 'Saltpetre Industry of India in the Seventeenth Century', *Indian Historical Quarterly*, 14 (1938), 680–91.

Schogol, Jeff, 'Are New Recruits Secretly Given Saltpeter?' *Stars and Stripes* (http:www.stripes.com/blogs/the-rumor-doctor, accessed June 2010).

Scott, William, 'The Pursuit of "Interests" in the French Revolution: A Preliminary Survey,' *French Historical Studies*, 19 (1996), 811–51.

Sharpe, Kevin, *The Personal Rule of Charles I* (New Haven and London, 1992).

Stapleton, Darwin H., '*Élève des poudres*: E. I. du Pont's Multiple Transfers of French Technology', in Brenda J. Buchanan (ed.), *Gunpowder, Explosives and the State: A Technological History* (Aldershot, 2006), 230–41.

Steele, Brett D., and Tamera Dorland (eds.), *The Heirs of Archimedes: Science and the Art of War through the Age of Enlightenment* (Cambridge, Mass., 2005).

Steers, William D., 'Viagra—After One Year', *Urology*, 54 (1999), 12–17.

Stephenson, Orlando W., 'The Supply of Gunpowder in 1776', *American Historical Review*, 30 (1925), 271–81.

Stewart, Richard W., 'Arms and Expeditions: The Ordnance Office and the Assaults on Cadiz (1625) and the Isle of Rhé (1627)' in Mark Charles Fissel (ed.), *War and Government in Britain, 1598–1650* (Manchester and New York, 1991), 112–32.

Stewart, Richard Winship, *The English Ordnance Office 1585–1625: A Case Study in Bureaucracy* (Woodbridge, 1996).

Strachan, Hew, *From Waterloo to Balaclava: Tactics, Technology, and the British Army, 1815–1854* (Cambridge, 1985).

Tedder, Arthur W., *The Navy of the Restoration from the Death of Cromwell to the Treaty of Breda: Its Work, Growth and Influence* (Cambridge, 1916).

Thick, Malcolm, *Sir Hugh Plat: The Search for Useful Knowledge in Early Modern London* (Totnes, 2010).

Thrush, Andrew, 'The Ordnance Office and the Navy, 1625–40', *Mariner's Mirror*, 77 (1991), 339–54.

Tierie, Gerrit, *Cornelius Drebbel (1572–1633)* (Amsterdam, 1932).

Tomlinson, H. C., *Guns and Government: The Ordnance Office under the Later Stuarts* (1979).

Travis, Tony, 'Revolutions and Gunpowder: Antoine Lavoisier,' *Chemistry and Industry*, 9 (1994), 333–8.

Urbanski, Tadeusz, *Chemistry and Technology of Explosives*, 3 vols. (New York, 1964–7).

Ure, Andrew, *A Dictionary of Arts, Manufactures, and Mines: Containing a Clear Exposition of their Principles and Practice*, 2 vols. (4th edn., Boston, 1853).

Van Gelder, Arthur Pine, and Hugo Schlatter, *History of the Explosives Industry in America* (New York, 1927).

Wanklyn, Malcolm, and Frank Jones, *A Military History of the English Civil War, 1642–1646* (Harlow, 2005).

Webster, Charles, *The Great Instauration: Science, Medicine and Reform 1626–1660* (New York, 1976).

Webster, Charles, 'Benjamin Worsley: Engineering for Universal Reform from the Invisible College to the Navigation Act', in Mark Greengrass, Michael Leslie, and Timothy Raylor (eds.), *Samuel Hartlib and Universal Reformation: Studies in Intellectual Communication* (Cambridge, 1994), 213–35.

West, Jenny, *Gunpowder, Government and War in the Mid-Eighteenth Century* (Woodbridge, 1991).

Wheeler, James Scott, 'Logistics and Supply in Cromwell's Conquest of Ireland', in Mark Charles Fissel (ed.), *War and Government in Britain, 1598–1650* (Manchester and New York, 1991), 38–56.

Wheeler, James Scott, *The Making of a World Power: War and the Military Revolution in Seventeenth-Century England* (Stroud, 1999).

Wilkinson-Latham, Robert, *British Artillery on Land and Sea 1790–1820* (Newton Abbot, 1973).

Williams, A. R., 'The Production of Saltpetre in the Middle Ages', *Ambix: The Journal of the Society for the History of Alchemy and Chemistry*, 22 (1975), 125–33.

Wisniak, Jaime, 'The History of Saltpeter Production with a Bit of Pyrotechnics and Lavoisier', *Chemical Educator*, 5 (2000), 205–9.

Wrey, E. C., 'Saltpetre House, Ashurst Wood, Colbury', *Papers and Proceedings of the Hampshire Field Club and Archaeological Society*, 18 (1954), 335–6.

York, Neil L., 'Clandestine Aid and the American Revolutionary War Effort: A Re-Examination', *Military Affairs*, 43 (1979), 26–30.

Zupko, Ronald Edward, *A Dictionary of English Weights and Measures from Anglo-Saxon Times to the Nineteenth Century* (Madison, Wis., and London, 1968).

Zupko, Ronald Edward, *British Weights and Measures: A History from Antiquity to the Seventeenth Century* (Madison, Wis., 1977).

Zupko, Ronald Edward, *A Dictionary of Weights and Measures for the British Isles: The Middle Ages to the Twentieth Century* (Philadelphia, 1985).

INDEX

41